THE SHADY LADY'S
GUIDE TO NORTHEAST
SHADE GARDENING

AMY ZIFFER

the SHADY LADY'S GUIDE *to* NORTHEAST SHADE GARDENING

University Press of New England

Hanover and London

University Press of New England
www.upne.com
© 2014 University Press of New England
All rights reserved
Manufactured in the United States of America
Designed by Mindy Basinger Hill
Typeset in Calluna

The photograph of *Erythronium* 'Pagoda' is used courtesy
of Christopher Lindsey/www.hort.net. The photograph of
Ajuga reptans is used courtesy of Missouri Botanical Garden.
The photograph of the deer on page 53 is © Bill Lupton |
Dreamstime.com. The photograph of *Cornus canadensis* on
page 200 is © Stephan Pietzko | Dreamstime.com. All other
photographs included here are the author's.

Library of Congress Cataloging-in-Publication Data

Ziffer, Amy.
  The Shady Lady's guide to Northeast shade gardening /
Amy Ziffer.
        pages   cm
Includes index.
ISBN 978-1-61168-525-1 (pbk.: alk. paper)
1. Gardening in the shade—Northeastern States.
2. Shade-tolerant plants—Northeastern States. I. Title.
SB434.7.Z54 2014
635.9'543—dc23   2013041213
5   4   3   2   1

CONTENTS

PREFACE

Why Buy This Book?

First things first. Why should you buy this book? Thousands of garden books have been published throughout the years. Many of them are probably on your shelf; certainly, many are on mine. Some of the garden books I've read are useful, some are just pretty, and some have a bright future as kindling. Given that there are lots of candidates for inclusion in all three of those categories, what possible need could there be for one more garden book?

I've worked in horticulture for more than fifteen years, and I've been gardening for almost four decades. I've seen the gardening world from the standpoint of homeowner, professional gardener, master gardener, garden author, garden photographer, garden editor, and garden educator. I've asked gardening questions, and I've had other people come to me for answers.

I've found that the goal of most home gardeners, in a nutshell, is to have a landscape that is attractive, sustainable for many seasons, not too labor intensive, and not too expensive. Simply put, most people are willing to make an effort, but they don't want to spend all their time or money gardening. A successful garden is one that performs reliably and doesn't drive its owner crazy with demands.

Garden books don't always help gardeners attain the seemingly simple, undeniably widespread goal of creating successful gardens as I've defined them. Publishers often repackage English garden books for an American audience, overlooking the fact that most of the United States is utterly unlike the British Isles in many of the critical factors that influence gardening. Garden book consumers, for their part, often buy these books simply because they contain mouthwatering photographs, despite the fact that the landscapes they picture cannot be duplicated in many other locales.

Each region of the world presents to gardeners a unique combination of climate, soils, topography, rainfall, native vegetation, wildlife, and dozens of other things that, taken together, comprise the palette of tools with which a gardener works and the set of challenges a gardener must face. Understanding and respecting those region-to-region differences is critical to creating successful gardens, and that's why only a regional gardening book can show you the way.

When you garden by acknowledging the conditions that surround you, deciding to work with them instead of fighting or ignoring them, you make an important and wise choice. Your reward, in the long term, will be a more successful garden with lower cost and less effort, because you'll get the greatest value out of what you invest in your landscape by avoiding common mistakes and the waste that results.

A quick word about what I hope this book will accomplish. It was my intention to write a book that can stand alone and provide all the essential information for building a satisfying perennial landscape in a shady situation in the part of North America where my experience is most relevant. Although you might *want* to further explore shade gardening (or just gardening in general) by reading about it in more depth and trying a wider range of plants, it's my hope that every bit of advice you truly *need* to create a rewarding shade garden is contained in these pages.

Who Is This Book Written For?

Some years ago, I attended a luncheon function and found myself seated opposite a friendly, chatty woman. When she found out that I gardened for a living, her eyes brightened. "Maybe you can give me some advice," she said optimistically. "I have a privacy fence," she began, "but it's such a big, austere thing. I want to grow something on it to hide it and soften it. What would you recommend?"

"How big is the fence?" I inquired.

"It's a stockade," she answered, "eight feet tall."

I asked if her side of the fence was shady or sunny. "Oh, very shady," she said, describing a positively penumbral yard under a dense canopy of trees. "And of course, deer are a problem," she added. The fence didn't go around the whole yard—it just ran down one side, so deer could get in from every other direction.

As we talked a little more, she kept adding to the list of desirable features the wished-for plant required, until she'd eliminated nearly everything that grows in this part of the world. Finally, I suggested a nice leafy vine that, with a little help, would have turned the penitentiary enclosure she possessed into a wall of vegetation. At least, I told her, the wall would blend into the background.

"And what kind of flowers does it have?" she asked.

"It's a foliage plant," I told her. "You grow it for the leaves." No readily available plant, native or otherwise, I assured her, would do what she wanted: survive our unpredictable, sometimes bitter winters; grow quickly to cover a tall fence; fail to interest deer; require no maintenance; *and* flower profusely and spectacularly in deep shade.

A look of disappointment came over her face, and she sighed, "Well, there has to be *something*."

At that point, the raspberry bleat of a game-show buzzer sounded in my head, but I refrained from regaling her with my rendition of it. Unfortunately, her belief—that there had to be some plant to fulfill her wish list—was simply false. Just because we want a plant to exist doesn't mean that it has to.

Of course, the woman I met at that luncheon wasn't trying to be unreasonable. She didn't realize that her demands were excessive. I have wondered many times what, if anything, she ever tried growing on her fence. I wish her the best, but I'm afraid that if she's still insisting on the existence of imaginary plants, that fence is probably still bare.

And that brings me to the answer to the question posed in the title of this section: who is this book written for? I wrote it for gardeners firmly grounded (pun intended) in reality. I wrote it for gardeners who value sustainable landscapes that will work over contrived ones that require too much time, energy, and money to maintain, or are prone to repeated failure because of poor choices or inadequate preparation. I wrote it for gardeners who are willing to adapt their tastes to what's possible rather than search fruitlessly for plants that don't exist. In short, this book is written for practical gardeners who are willing to accept good advice based on long experience and—I'm not ashamed to admit—lessons learned from an abundance of my own failures as well as those of other gardeners.

This book is also written for gardeners in a certain region. It is expressly *not* a book for a national audience. In fact, the first piece of good advice I'll offer readers is this: there is no such thing as advice applicable to every gardener in our enormous, environmentally varied country, which contains every ecosystem from desert to temperate rain forest.

So, what is the region in question? Broadly, this book is written for gardeners in that somewhat nebulous area known as "the Northeast." It comprises an area from above the Canadian border south through New England and New York, tapering off into the mid-Atlantic states along the coast, and extending inland beyond Pennsylvania. Even gardeners in the arc of states from Michigan to Tennessee will find much of use here.

This beautiful part of the world is characterized by mountains and valleys inland, generally rising in elevation with latitude or proximity to the spine of the Appalachian Mountains; a narrow tidal shelf along the coast; extensive woodland of striking diversity; mostly (but not exclusively) acidic soils, often sandier near the shore; plentiful wildlife, including many animals that damage common garden plants; lots of precipitation distributed evenly throughout the year; sultry, sometimes punishingly humid summers with daytime temperatures that can push three digits one day and make you dig into the sweater drawer the next; and extremely variable but basically cold winters, in which water can fall from the sky in any conceivable form—or even *all* conceivable forms simultaneously in what we euphemistically call a "wintry mix"!

> Oh, what a blamed uncertain thing
> This pesky weather is;
> It blew and snew and then it thew,
> And now, by jing, it's friz!
> —*Philander Johnson*

Small twisters are common enough for a strip of central New England to be known as a "tornado alley." Hurricanes fly up the eastern seaboard and morph into our famous (and sometimes infamous) "nor'easters," such as the devastating storm Sandy, which washed away coastal neighborhoods in several states in late 2012. And then there are the occurrences that go by only the cryptically understated name "wind events." I live in New England, and I can attest to the truth of the saying, "If you don't like the weather in New England, just wait a minute." Wait long enough, and something will drown you, broil you, freeze you, wring you out, or sweep you away by force of air or water.

Even in this geographically compressed area, there are major differences from microregion to microregion—Cape Cod, for instance, is a world unto itself: the climate verges on Zone 7, and the ground underfoot can be pure sand—yet there is a common denominator. The non-meteorological attribute that distinguishes this region more than any other—you could say *defines* it—is forest. A spectacular temperate forest of mixed hardwoods and conifers once blanketed almost the entire Eastern Seaboard. Although virtually no old-growth forest is left in the Northeast, luckily there is still a great deal of forest; and where there is forest, there is shade.

If those of us who live in this arboreal wonderland are to make ornamental gardens, we must learn how to cope with shade. I believe that the average home gardener has the greatest chance of creating a successful shade garden by following the approach I outline in this book. That approach specifies not only what to do, but also what *not* to do, so you can avoid making costly, frustrating mistakes. It presents limited rather than limitless options, focusing only on those most likely to succeed. Because it uses knowledge of local conditions and relies on years of local experience, this book can help gardeners in my area and similar areas create successful gardens that will thrive and delight season after season.

At the risk of sounding like a broken record, I'll reiterate why I stress so strongly the importance of relying on *local* advice and designing for *local* conditions when making a garden: because a garden made in such a way maximizes your chances of success.

I'm not saying that you *can't* have a garden that ignores local conditions—for example, a garden that relies heavily on tender plants that must be dug and overwintered in a greenhouse or under other protection. Nor am I saying that having a garden of tender exotics is somehow bad. I'm only saying that if you create such a garden, it will require a significant expenditure of time, energy, and/or money to maintain. The more a garden diverges from a landscape adapted to local conditions, the greater that expenditure will be. Gardeners who are fortunate enough to possess enormous financial and other resources can absorb regular landscape losses and expenses, but this book is for the rest of us.

How Is This Book Organized?

This book is based on a class (or, in its shortened form, a lecture) I've given regionally for about the last fifteen years. As part of the class, I have always provided a large handout with notes on plants, cultural tips, and other information I think participants will want to have as a reference.

Even when giving the presentation as a full-length class, I have always wanted to go into more detail than time has allowed. So eventually, I decided to expand on all parts of the class, and this book is the result. Readers who have seen me give the class on which this book is based will recognize the same basic flow of information.

First, I present short introductory sections on facts you should know about shade plants, cultural tips, deer control, plant selection, soil preparation, mulching, fertilization, design, and more. I follow these with a gallery of recommended plants, each entry accompanied by a photo or photos, containing the sort of practical information you need to select and grow each one successfully. At the end of the book, you'll find some resources for additional information, lists to help you identify the best plants for very specific growing conditions, and an index including plants by common and Latin name.

I welcome your feedback on the organization and content of this book. If you have a constructive suggestion for improving future editions, please contact me through the publisher.

ACKNOWLEDGMENTS

If we know anything, it's because others have taught and supported us. My first gardening teachers were my grandmother Julia (I'm thankful that the gardening turned out better than the knitting) and, in a modest way, my mother Helen, who grew exactly one plant (*Mirabilis jalapa*) but grew it well.

I am very grateful for the valuable master gardener training I received in the Common Ground Garden Program two decades ago, and I want to say a special thank you to volunteer master gardeners everywhere for their dedication to horticultural knowledge and public outreach.

Throughout the years, many others have helped me learn to better communicate about gardening, including my patient clients; the spirited audiences who have come to hear me speak about all manner of gardening topics; and those who have generously allowed me to share photographs of their shade gardens, especially Robin Zitter and Stan and Kathy Scherer. I would also like to thank the entire team at University Press of New England for helping me communicate with readers about gardening through this book, and Associate Extension Educator Dawn Pettinelli, MS, CANR, University of Connecticut, for graciously reviewing selected portions of this book for accuracy.

Finally, I pay tribute to the best and most tireless teacher of all, nature itself.

THE SHADY LADY'S GUIDE TO NORTHEAST SHADE GARDENING

SHADE AND SHADE PLANTS

Getting Specific about Shade

Shade would be easier for gardeners to handle if there were only one *kind* of shade. The real world isn't that cooperative, unfortunately. Shade is something that exists on a continuum, like the wavelengths of light. Determining how much shade you really have is essential to getting good results in your shade garden, so it's important to give this subject some thought.

In recent years, I've seen several products on the market designed to help gardeners pin down how much shade they've got. Sun Stick and SunCalc are two examples, although I have not used either product and don't have an opinion about them. Short of going into your garden with some sort of light meter and literally measuring the strength of the sunlight, there's no way to pinpoint *exactly* how shady your yard is. We have to rely on imprecise descriptions and estimates, and do our best.

The deepest kind of shade, aptly called *deep shade*, is found under mature evergreen trees. Deep shade is almost never appropriate for gardening. The conditions are simply too inhospitable: little light, dry soil, and stiff competition from tree roots. Even in the wild, little can be found growing underneath, say, a dense grove of hemlocks on a north slope. Nature is always an excellent guide to what's possible in gardening. If nature can't fill the space under mature evergreens with a dense undergrowth of plants, we gardeners won't be able to, either.

Where mature evergreens are planted not in a grove, but singly or in a row, it may be possible to garden nearby if you maintain a suitable distance (beyond the tree's root zone). Even if an evergreen's lower branches are limbed up to let in more light, you probably should not try to garden right underneath it because of root competition and dryness.

Full shade is the customary term for the shade under a canopy of deciduous trees. In a full-shade situation, the ground does not receive any significant direct light when the trees are in leaf, but may receive a fair amount of indirect light if an open area is on one side. The more indirect light that reaches the area, the better. Full shade is a challenging but not impossible situation for gardeners.

The suitability of a full-shade area for gardening depends on many factors, including the types of trees comprising the canopy and the closeness of their spacing. Maples, for instance, are notorious for having roots that cluster near the surface. Gardening under maples is difficult even in the short term and usually near impossible in the long term. Obviously, the denser the forest, the greater the shade cast, and the more difficult it is to garden underneath regardless of which trees compose the woods.

Moderate shade is a far better environment for gardening. When shade is moderate, that's usually because the trees casting the shade are small or spaced far apart. This also translates to less competition in the soil for moisture and rooting space, so plants growing underneath benefit in a number of ways when shade is lighter. Moderate shade is a broad term that includes *half shade* (meaning exactly what it sounds like—direct light reaches the ground for about half the time the sun is up) and *filtered shade* or *dappled shade* (the shade cast by high branches in a relatively small number of trees, creating a dappled pattern of light on the ground).

Finally, *light shade* is what you find under one specimen deciduous tree, where indirect and direct light can reach the area underneath from all sides if not from directly above; or at a large enough distance from a line of trees that bright indirect light reaches the ground all day long, even if direct light does not strike it at all. Light shade is, of course, the best for gardening.

You should evaluate the heaviness of the shade in your garden as honestly as you can. If you have any doubts about how dense the shade is, assume it's heavier than you imagine it to be. You can't make a mistake that way, whereas if you assume lighter shade than you have, you will probably select some inappropriate plants that will just languish or die in your garden from lack of light.

The exact amount of light available for plant growth in a given location can be affected by all sorts of factors exterior to the garden, including the materials and surfaces in surrounding areas. Sand and water at the seashore can reflect light into shady areas more effectively than most natural surfaces found inland;

this results in higher overall light levels than might be assumed from direct sun exposure alone. Similarly, artificial surfaces such as light-colored walls, concrete, and asphalt can either reflect or soak up light to have a noticeable effect on light levels in adjacent areas. For these and other reasons, one of the best ways to assess light levels in your garden is to observe what, if anything, is growing there already.

I'll also mention that the old saying "A picture is worth a thousand words" is very true. If you go to a nursery to seek advice on what might work well in your garden, take along some photographs showing clearly not just the garden itself, but also its context: what's casting the shade, how the space to be gardened relates to the house, and views of the garden from multiple angles. Photos can only help.

One last thing before we leave this topic: people frequently ask me why they had no luck growing a plant that is supposed to do well in "part shade to shade" (based on the information on the tag in the plant's container when purchased) when they felt it should have had enough light. In most cases, this is the result of a simple misunderstanding. Information on plant tags and in most garden books (but not this one) is generalized to be applicable to gardeners over a wide geographic range. Many plants that require shade in the deep South require full sun in the North. Here in the Northeast, assume that plants will need the sunniest conditions for which they are said to be suitable.

About the Plants Recommended in This Book

The second half of this book is a gallery of recommended perennials, ferns, and bulbs for shade garden situations. This suggests an obvious question: what qualities did a plant need to make the cut?

My criteria were these: (1) the plant must thrive, not just survive, when grown without direct exposure to sun; (2) it must be well behaved, that is, not too invasive, unless it is a native plant useful for naturalizing or a groundcover that spreads in an easily controllable fashion; (3) it must have enough "presence" to make an impact when used appropriately; (4) it must be visually appealing on some level; and (5) it should have few or no common pest or disease problems. Ideally, the plant should also be readily available, although I acknowledge that some of the plants profiled here can be procured only with special effort, and I note when that's the case. A surprising number of plants commonly available to gardeners do not meet all these criteria, which is why it's helpful for gardeners to have a guide to only those plants that do.

Within this group of recommended plants, I make vital distinctions based on a plant's usefulness for various garden roles, and that is one of the core differences between this book and others. It's important to understand how I arrived at these distinctions and how they can guide plant use for the best ornamental effect; so even if you skim the rest of this book, please read those sections completely before trying to use the Plant Gallery, or you won't get as much out of this book as you might.

Because this book is for gardeners at northern latitudes, the bulk of the plants covered in the Plant Gallery are cold hardy to at least US Department of Agriculture (USDA) Zone 4. Many within that group can withstand Zone 3 or even Zone 2. For those unfamiliar with USDA zones, here's a brief explanation. Any two places in the same USDA zone share the same average minimum winter temperature. In the USDA zone system, Zone 1 is tundra, and Zone 10 is the southern tip of Florida and Southern California, with everything in between occupying Zones 2 through 9. The lower the zone number, the colder the climate to which it corresponds, so gardeners in the North need perennial plants rated for low USDA zones. This is often referred to as the *cold hardiness* of a plant, and is often expressed in this way: "Plant X is cold hardy to Zone 5." The descriptive tags that are tucked into potted plants in the nursery usually indicate the cold hardiness of the plant in terms of the coldest zone it can be expected to survive.

However, just because two regions share the same average minimum winter temperature, this doesn't necessarily mean that they share other qualities. It's important to realize that a USDA zone rating tells you the coldest winter temperatures a plant can probably survive, *but it tells you nothing else*. Often, other factors—such as the amount and type of winter precipitation common in a particular region—dictate a plant's survival as much as do winter temperatures.

Most plants also have a southern limit to their range, but that is not of concern to gardeners in the region this book covers, so I won't waste space addressing it.

Note that this is not a book specifically written to advocate native plant use. I do, in fact, recommend the use of native plants whenever and wherever appropriate. But I recognize that not everyone is committed to using native plants exclusively or even primarily. I also acknowledge the reality that the average homeowner-gardener might be dissatisfied with a shade garden made up exclusively of natives because to many people, part of what makes a garden pleasing is its very difference from the natural surroundings.

I've tried to be more subtle in encouraging the use of native plants. First, I've indicated which of the plants discussed in this book are native to eastern North America (not necessarily the Northeast) to the best of my knowledge. Second, I've tried to present them realistically, so that gardeners who try these plants aren't disappointed and don't give up on natives in general as a consequence. It's my hope that by having a few small successes with native plants, people will be inclined to experiment more and discover the wealth of wonderful plants right under our noses.

Lastly, here and elsewhere in this book, I ask readers to consider leaving large portions of their property in a natural state, removing exotic plants if possible, but otherwise leaving the land undisturbed as refuges where both plants and animals can avoid mower blades, foot traffic, and soil disturbance. In several sections I discuss *naturalizing*—the process of encouraging appropriate native plants to spread and fill previously disturbed "wild" areas for both aesthetic and practical reasons—and I suggest suitable plants for that purpose.

If you aren't sure what the whole native plant–exotic plant debate is all about, or aren't sure why you should care, I strongly recommend reading the excellent book *Bringing Nature Home* by Douglas Tallamy. The author explains very simply the positive ecological impact of native plant use, and why ordinary homeowner-gardeners have a big role to play in restoring ecosystem health.

Readers who educate themselves on this topic and decide to take personal action by reducing or eliminating the exotic plants they find on the undeveloped parts of their property will find that local Cooperative Extension offices and arboreta can often assist in identifying plants and developing a plan for managing property in an environmentally sensitive way.

Now, a word on what this book is *not*. This book does not provide a comprehensive list of every *herbaceous* (non-woody) plant that will grow in the shade in the Northeast, and it's that way by design.

A complete list of all perennials, ferns, and bulbs that grow in the shade would be nearly impossible to compile and not very useful to gardeners even if it existed. Why? If you've ever gone for a walk in the woods, you've surely noticed that the understory is sometimes quite thick with plants—carpeted, even. Yet relatively few of them would make good *garden* plants. Many are not particularly ornamental. Many are just too small to make an impact in a cultivated setting. Yet others (even if they are native) are highly invasive—what experienced gardeners refer to as "thugs" when they explain to other gardeners why they'll never plant *that* thing again!

The last point is particularly important. I eliminated from consideration several ornamental and highly shade-adapted plants because of their rampant invasiveness. Dedicated gardeners with a wealth of time on their hands might be able to control these plants, but ordinary gardeners simply can't, and I want this book to be valuable to ordinary gardeners.

This advice is not limited to shade gardens. If you've ever thought to yourself, "Gee, I *want* something that spreads," think again. Spreading plants do not stop when and where you want. If you truly want to minimize garden maintenance, avoid invasive plants. You will do yourself and the environment a favor. Invasive plants are suitable only for naturalized areas, not cultivated gardens, and then only if they are native.

Henry Beston, noted naturalist and author of *The Outermost House*, wrote, "As well expect Nature to answer to your human values as to come into your house and sit in a chair." The act of gardening could be described as persuading plants to follow your agenda, not their own—in other words, to answer to your values. That job is much easier if you invite into your garden *only* plants that are attractive and adaptable but, at heart, somewhat restrained in their behavior.

Some Plant Terms You Need to Know

Descriptive terms. This book promises information on selecting and using perennials, ferns, and bulbs for shade. The term *perennial* is often confusing to novice gardeners, so let's define it right now. Perennials are plants that live for many years (or at least longer than two growing seasons); are herbaceous (that is, they are non-woody—their stems and leaves die back to the ground each winter); and don't grow from a bulb, corm, or tuber. Because of the herbaceous requirement, all shrubs and trees are excluded from the category called perennials, although obviously shrubs and trees live for many years.

An actual definition of the term *fern* would sound rather clinical, so although it may be cheating to do this, I'll fall back on the fuzzy-logic method of saying that most of us know a fern when we see one. Despite the enormous number of fern species on Earth, ferns as a group show a remarkable consistency of appearance in the mature, spore-bearing phase of their life cycle (it's this sort of language that makes me not want to attempt a definition!). This makes it possible for most people to distinguish ferns from non-ferns in the garden most of the time. And although ferns are technically perennials, in practice the term perennial is usually used to describe flowering plants; because ferns don't flower, customarily we put them in their own category.

Bulb is one of those catchall words used to describe a disparate group of things, in this case *true bulbs*, *corms*, and *tubers*. What are these things? Certain plants, as they evolved, devised ways to store energy (starch, basically) in various organs below ground through the very dry or very cold months when they are dormant. True bulb, corm, and tuber are the terms we use for three different forms taken by plants with this ability. Don't get too hung up trying to understand the differences between true bulbs, corms, and tubers; from the average gardener's standpoint, it's just not important. In practice, the three are lumped together under the single term *bulb*. Common plants such as daffodils (true bulbs), dahlias (tubers), and gladioli (corms) are all, in this inexact sense, bulbs. The bulbs that bloom in spring (daffodils, tulips, and so on) are, for obvious reasons, called *spring bulbs*.

Let's return to perennials briefly. Many plants are genetically programmed to have shorter lives than perennials. Those that germinate, grow, flower, set seed, and die in less than a year are called *true annuals*. The common sunflower (*Helianthus annuus*) is a true annual that is incapable of living longer than one growing season.

To complicate matters, lots of plants start flowering in their first year of life, and would be perennial in a warm climate, but they are unable to survive northern winters. In the North, these plants are still called annuals (although technically they are not) because they can be used for gardening purposes in the same way as true annuals. Impatiens (*Impatiens walleriana*), a plant that for decades was sold by the flat in enormous quantities at every nursery in the Northeast every spring (until a recent outbreak of a pernicious disease), is actually a perennial that we treat as an annual simply because it cannot survive freezing temperatures.

In this book, I'll use the word *annual* to mean any plant that is a true annual or has to be treated as an annual in the North. Actually, very few annuals grow well in considerable shade at our latitudes, so my discussion of them is minimal.

There's one last group of plants to cover. *Biennials* are those plants that germinate and grow in one year, then go dormant over winter and complete their life cycle the next year. The herb parsley is an example of a biennial. The reason you replant parsley in your herb garden every year is that in its second year, the plant produces few of the nice green leaves we harvest to season our food. Instead, as soon as the weather warms, a year-old parsley plant will flower, set seed, and die. There's nothing you, as a gardener, can do to alter that process. Few biennials with strong ornamental qualities grow in shade, so this book includes no discussion of biennials.

Latin and common names. Garden plants are usually identified in one of two ways: by Latin name (also called a binomial name) and by common name. The advantage of the Latin name is that each Latin name identifies exactly one kind of plant, so when you purchase a plant and specify it by Latin name, you can be reasonably certain you're getting the plant you want. (I say "reasonably" because the system is good, but not perfect.) A common name, in contrast, can refer to many different plants, so common names are of little practical use, even though they are almost always more charming and endearing.

The reason Latin names are so specific, but common names are not, is that

Latin names were assigned to plants systematically for the purpose of identifying them uniquely, whereas common names have their origins in folklore and vernacular language. The same plant growing in two different areas might be known to the local people by two completely different names; or two different populations might historically have used the name "blue-flowered thingie" to refer to two completely different plants. You can see the problem: which name do you use when you want to buy a particular plant? The answer is to use the Latin name, not the common one.

Don't be intimidated by Latin names! You don't have to know how to say them, and you don't have to memorize them, but using Latin names when you shop at the nursery will help you get the plant you want. It's advantageous to keep track of the Latin names of the plants you put in your garden so that if and when you want to buy more of a favorite one, you can be confident of getting what you intended.

A Latin name always consists of at least two parts—the *genus* and *species* names—along with a *cultivar* name if one applies. The genus and species names will always sound like Latin, but the cultivar name might not. The standard way of writing out a Latin name is to capitalize the first letter of the genus name, lowercase the species name completely, and use single quotes for the cultivar name (if there is one) with an initial capital letter. In addition, genus and species names are italicized in print, but cultivar names are not. So, for example, *Alchemilla mollis* is made up of genus (*Alchemilla*) and species (*mollis*) names, but no cultivar name. *Anemone vitifolia* 'Robustissima,' on the other hand, has all three.

In a context where the genus of a plant is known, its genus name is frequently abbreviated to just its first letter. For example, in the entry for *Aquilegia* (columbine) in the Plant Gallery section of this book, *Aquilegia alpina* is abbreviated to *A. alpina* because the entry concerns only members of the genus *Aquilegia*, so there can be no ambiguity about what the *A.* references.

The word *cultivar*, by the way, is a contraction of *culti*vated *var*iety. A cultivar is a plant of a particular genus and species, with a desirable and reproducible trait—a flower color, for instance—that differs from that of other members of the same genus and species. So, *Phlox paniculata* 'Starfire' has flowers of a particular bright red, while *Phlox paniculata* 'Orange Perfection' has flowers of an eye-popping orange. It's the cultivar names that help distinguish the two.

Although Latin names can get a little more complicated than this, what I've just explained is all you'll need to know 95 percent of the time, so don't worry about the rest.

Lastly, a few common abbreviations you'll see used in this book and elsewhere are sp. for species (singular), spp. for species (plural), subsp. for subspecies, syn. for synonym, var. for variety, and cv. for cultivar (plural cvs.). An "x" between the genus and species names for a plant, as in *Ilex* x *meserveae*, signifies a hybrid species.

Surprising Shade Plant Facts

Plants adapted to shady conditions often have a lot in common. When you stop to think about this, it makes sense that plants that have evolved under a particular set of conditions should have similarities. In fact, you can often determine the likely sun and shade needs of an unfamiliar plant just by looking at it.

I need to stress that the points I make in this section *are not hard-and-fast rules, but generalizations with numerous exceptions.* Exceptions aside, if a plant has the characteristics of a sun-adapted plant, it probably will not grow well in shade. On the other hand, many plants well adapted to shade also grow well in moderate or even full sun at our northern latitudes; you can use this trait to your advantage, as you'll see in the Shade Garden Design chapter that follows.

So, what are these alleged traits of shade plants and sun plants? First, let's look at flowering time.

Flowering time. Remember that in a largely deciduous forest in the North, leaves are on the trees for only about six months of every year. The other six months, deciduous trees are dormant and leafless. Of course, during most of that dormant period it is winter, and the weather conditions don't permit the growth of any kind of tender shoots or leaves. However, from early spring until the trees leaf out (sometime in late April or May, depending on your exact location), conditions are very good for growth and, notably, *the forest floor is flooded with sunlight.* For that month or so, spots that will be in shade for the next six months are, briefly, warm, bright, and extremely conducive to plant growth.

Now, the plants that evolved in these forested environments are no fools. They don't poke around waiting until June to stick their heads up out of the soil. The second it's warm enough and light enough to grow, they do. And they don't just grow—they try to do every energy-intensive task they can while they have lots of energy (sunlight) at their disposal. Significantly, one of the most energy-intensive tasks a plant has to perform every year is . . . flowering.

The upshot of all this is that a sizeable majority of shade-adapted plants flower in spring, specifically in April and May. *Not* June, when you want to have a garden wedding. *Not* July and August, when the shade garden might seem particularly inviting as welcome relief from the scorching heat of summer. And *not* September, when you'll be having your annual Labor Day barbeque. They bloom in April and May, finishing up right about the time we think of as the *start* of the gardening season.

Now, don't stop reading—or reach for the chainsaw! There's more to the story.

Gardeners who are lucky enough to have suitable garden areas in both shade and sun have the luxury of allowing shady areas to be spring gardens and sunny areas to be summer gardens. That way, they can enjoy the widest spectrum of plant choices in all areas. But not every property affords its owner that luxury.

If you're a reader whose shade garden needs to look its best during the height of summer, you'll want to use three techniques to attain your goal.

1. *Use more of the small number of summer-flowering shade plants in preference to the spring bloomers* when designing your garden. This actually makes design simpler because the plant choices are limited.

2. *Take advantage of the wide variety of fine perennial foliage plants that thrive in shade* to add interest to your composition. Understandably, gardeners tend to be biased in favor of flowers over foliage, but consider that perennials flower for only two to three weeks on average, whereas ornamental foliage enlivens a garden all season long. Don't give foliage plants short shrift—the more you use them, the more you'll come to appreciate their value.

3. *Scatter groups of flowering annuals and brightly colored tender foliage plants throughout your shade garden*, especially along walkways and near patios or other areas where you stroll or sit regularly.

Sad to say, recently this third technique got harder to do. For decades, *Impatiens walleriana* was the queen of shade annuals. Its shade tolerance was unsurpassed by any other flowering plant, and it offered flower colors ranging from bluish-violet through pink, red, orange, salmon, and white. Then, disaster struck in the form of an epidemic disease called impatiens downy mildew. As I write this, growers and gardeners are struggling with what to use as a replacement, because it will probably be five or more years before we can grow this impatiens in our gardens again. We still have at our disposal the old-fashioned wax begonia, which is nearly as good a performer as *Impatiens walleriana* but doesn't offer the same broad range of flower colors.

Happily, in recent years, new types of impatiens and begonia have been introduced that expand the versatility of these two shade standbys. The SunPatiens impatiens is a hybrid, reportedly not susceptible to impatiens downy mildew and also reportedly for both shade and sun. I don't have enough experience with these plants to say how well they perform. So far, I've seen them offered only in 4-inch pots, which makes them an expensive option for bedding but affordable in containers or as an accent here and there in the garden. New Zealand impatiens, which is also being touted in some quarters as a replacement for *Impatiens walleriana*, has been around for a long time. However, these plants do well only in very light shade, so I can't really consider them a substitute for *Impatiens walleriana*.

In the begonia camp, I rely heavily on the Dragon Wing series, available with pink or red flowers. They have the size (up to 24 inches tall), elongated leaves, and big flower sprays of angel wing begonias combined with the glossy foliage and smooth leaf edges of wax begonias. They're simply gorgeous, but again, they aren't available in six-packs. At about $8 for a 6-inch pot, they're pricey, but even one plant can fill a pretty big space, and they are incredibly floriferous. Many other kinds of begonias can be bought at better nurseries for $5 to $10 per plant in 4-inch pots. Remember that begonias are actually tender perennials that can be overwintered inside if you have the skill and the right conditions. I've also been extremely impressed by the beauty of *Begonia boliviensis*, which looks more like a pendant fuchsia than a begonia.

A small number of other tender perennials can also take a fair amount of shade, especially the foliage plants *Caladium*, *Syngonium*, and *Solenostemon* (coleus), which all grow about 18 to 24 inches tall. The former two can be expensive, but one "houseplant" that looks great in the garden and *is* available in economical six-packs is polka dot plant (*Hypoestes phyllostachya*).

If you have a spot that can accommodate trailing plants, pendant forms of wishbone flower (*Torenia*), such as 'Summer Wave Blue,' bloom quite well in light shade. They combine beautifully with golden creeping jenny (*Lysimachia nummularia* 'Aurea'), a fast-growing trailer with gold-green leaves that's actually a hardy perennial plant most often sold for use as an annual. Variegated forms of tender heartleaf philodendron (*Philodendron scandens*) and trailing vinca (*Vinca major*) can be used in much the same way. All these trailing plants (as well as *Begonia boliviensis*, mentioned earlier) are also excellent in containers, where they can drape elegantly.

Follow all three of the techniques I've just outlined to maximize flowering and bright foliage color after the spring "rush," and you might be surprised at how vibrant your summer shade garden turns out.

Appearance. Now, let's look at differences in the appearance of shade-adapted and sun-adapted plants. Shade plants either have to make do with the meager light that reaches them, or have to develop a way of capturing more. One of the ways a plant can capture more light energy is by having broad, plate-like leaves such as those found on many hostas.

In contrast, plants adapted to sunny, arid climates frequently have thin, needlelike leaves that clasp their stems in an upright posture instead of spreading out to intercept as much light as possible. Often they are silvery to reflect excess light, or fuzzy to inhibit the evaporation of moisture from the leaf surface. Shade plants virtually never exhibit these qualities.

Plants not only need to grow well; they also must be able to reproduce. Many plants rely on insects to pollinate their flowers so they can set seed, and many insect pollinators find flowers visually. It's advantageous to these plants if their flowers stand out from their natural environment. Now think about how various colors look in low light. White, yellow, pink, and pastel shades pop out of the shadows, but blues, reds, and dark colors blend in or disappear. (It's actually a bit more complicated than this, but again, we don't need to explore this subject in depth.)

It will come as no surprise, then, that a large number of shade plants have white or light-colored flowers. Even shade plants that start blooming in early spring when sunlight is abundant usually find themselves in shade before they've finished flowering, so this rule of thumb applies to them, too. These plants are in a race with time, but they don't need to cross the finish line before the trees leaf out—they just need a good head start.

Summer dormancy. The last of the traits exhibited by a small number of shade-adapted plants is a tendency to go dormant at some point during summer instead of autumn, when frost forces the issue. You're probably thinking that this isn't a very desirable quality for a garden plant! Actually, sometimes it is, or at least it *can* be.

Within this group of plants, there is some variability. Many go dormant so soon after flowering that they are collectively called *spring ephemerals*. The word *spring* in the name refers to the season when the plants are actively growing and flowering. *Ephemeral* reflects the fact that long ago in their evolutionary history, these plants decided that once they'd flowered and set seed in late spring, there wasn't much point in sticking around for the rest of the year. For two months or so they move at a frenetic pace, but once they've accomplished what they came to do—reproduce—they really—*yawn!*—must—*yawn!*—get back to—*yawn!*—sleep . . . !

Spring ephemerals are, effectively, one-season plants. They come up in early spring, bloom shortly after emerging from the soil, set seed quickly, and then go dormant in late May or early June. In other words, they behave in exactly the same way spring bulbs do, but they aren't bulbs, so we had to give them a different name. Our showy native Virginia bluebell (*Mertensia virginica*) is a classic example of a spring ephemeral.

The key to using spring ephemerals effectively is to treat them much the same way you would bulbs. I've found that there are two good ways to place spring ephemerals in the garden. The first option is to position them behind plants that will emerge later, such as hostas, counting on the surrounding perennials to mask the sight of the dying spring ephemeral foliage once it's done its stuff.

The second option is to position spring ephemerals—many of which are rather small and not easily seen if planted too far back in a deep garden bed—toward the front of the garden in spots around which annuals can be planted in early June. There may be a brief awkward period during which the annuals are far too small to conceal the aging spring ephemerals, but this will pass quickly. As long as you plant the annuals before the spring ephemerals have gone to ground again, you won't have to worry about damaging the crowns of the ephemerals and possibly killing them. Just make sure to remove those annuals from the ground carefully in late autumn without digging aggressively, or your dormant spring ephemerals will almost certainly suffer some casualties.

Remember: once a spring ephemeral has gone dormant, there's no aboveground indicator of its position; this is also true with bulbs such as crocuses or snowdrops. Plan carefully when planting these transitory but delightful shade plants.

One last note about spring ephemerals: some reference books refer to any small woodland plant that begins flowering very early in the year as a spring ephemeral even though the plant might have a leafy presence right up until frost. I do not use the term in this way. In this book, a spring ephemeral is a plant that goes entirely dormant well before the end of the normal growing season.

One other group of plants bridges the gap between spring ephemerals and what, for lack of a better term, I'll call "normal" plants. Instead of going dormant immediately after flowering and conveniently clearing the deck for annuals or late-emerging perennials, they dawdle and stick around until July or August. There is no commonly used term for these plants, or at least I've never encountered one. They are, simply, plants with a tendency to go dormant at some point in summer rather than fall.

This makes them challenging to use in the garden, and as a consequence, I've eliminated most of them from consideration for this book. Gardeners who simply want a rewarding landscape and are not interested in collecting plants for the sake of collecting plants will probably find them too frustrating to cope with. Because the purpose of this book is to focus on the most rewarding and foolproof plants for shade gardens, most of those "in-between" plants didn't make the cut.

Of course, if *most* of them didn't make the cut, that means one or two did! One example is old-fashioned bleeding heart (*Dicentra spectabilis*). This longtime favorite of gardeners grows into spectacular, large specimens with strikingly showy and beautiful flowers in May, followed by excellent blue-green foliage. Its sole shortcoming is its tendency to go dormant around mid-August. This would not be such a problem if the plant weren't so large. A mature bleeding heart can be three or four feet in diameter! When it goes dormant, it leaves behind a rather large gap in the garden at a fairly inconvenient time.

In the Plant Gallery where I profile bleeding heart, I suggest some ways to position the plant to minimize the effect of its premature departure from your garden. I didn't want to leave it out entirely, though, because it is so common, so beloved, and so gorgeous when in flower and leaf.

These plants all illustrate the difficulty of lumping living things into easy categories. Plants are no exception. They have their own agenda—flowering, going dormant, and in fact, doing everything when it suits *them*, not *us.* We gardeners often forget that plants do not exist to please us. We are just lucky that by following their own course, they can also give us so very much pleasure.

SHADE GARDEN DESIGN

Types of Shade Gardens

Garden design is a big, complicated topic that could (and does) fill entire books. Because this book isn't dedicated to landscape design as a general subject, I won't give broad design advice but rather specific hints and tips on working with different kinds of shady spaces and the plants that grow well in them.

In this book I frequently distinguish between (1) the *shady border*, (2) *naturalized areas*, (3) the *woodland garden*, and (4) *shady rock gardens*. Precisely defining all four is difficult because outdoor spaces aren't uniform from property to property. Like plants themselves, landscapes are hard to categorize. Nature certainly doesn't slap convenient labels on them, and we humans are bound to run into difficulties and inconsistencies when we try to pigeonhole them. Nonetheless, it's important to convey as accurately as possible what I mean when I use these labels.

By shady border, I mean a garden that is highly intentional—organized and regularly cultivated, with an overall effect ranging from "kept up" to "manicured." It's a garden that *looks* like a garden. Because maintenance in a shady border will be fairly intensive, only areas highly suitable for gardening should be developed as shady borders. Steep slopes and rocky areas are *not* suitable for shady borders.

By naturalized area, I mean an expanse in which some or all plants are left to fend for themselves, seeking out their own order and receiving little or no maintenance. A naturalized area, even if it was designed and planted intentionally, might look no different from the wild. In fact, replicating the wild might be the goal in a naturalized area. Naturalizing is often the best approach to dealing with areas where the slope of the land, the soil quality, or other factors fall far short of what's needed for a shady border.

By woodland garden, I mean a planting that bridges the divide between a shady border and a naturalized area, where plants are guided by the hand of the gardener but where maintenance is minimal and structure less distinct than in a border. Quite literally, a woodland garden might taper off into the wild or into a naturalized area without a hard and fast dividing line.

Lastly, by shady rock garden, I mean a lightly shaded area, often but not always on a slope, where naturally occurring boulders and ledge outcroppings cradle shallow, fast-draining soil pockets. Terracing of such areas, if possible at all, can be a waste of time and money because the underlying rock is simply not friendly to intensive planting at soil level. These areas hold little potential for substantial improvement of the growing conditions and present a significant landscaping challenge. The most practical and economical approach to beautifying them is to find ways to actually showcase attractive rocky features and complement them with plants suitable for shady rock garden conditions. Only rock garden plants should be planted in rock gardens, which cannot support anything else.

In practical terms, the first three of these plantings types are easier to categorize subjectively, on the basis of their appearance. Looking at a well-maintained shady border, a viewer would definitely say, "Yes, that's clearly a garden." Looking at a woodland garden, a viewer might say, "It blends with the natural surroundings, yet it's different—it looks more cared for than the wild." Looking at a naturalized area, a viewer might not recognize it as a "garden" at all, but just an area filled with plants, preferably attractive, pretty much indistinguishable from the wild, whatever "the wild" might be in that part of the world.

There can be a lot of overlap between shady borders, woodland gardens, and naturalized areas. (Rock gardens are somewhat a breed apart.) One way to look at them is as three points on a continuous spectrum. However, drawing distinctions between them is still useful, especially because *some plants are suited to one of these garden types but not to the others.*

When you begin thinking about making a shade garden on your property, you should first decide which of these types of shade garden it will be. Many people prefer a highly cultivated, ordered look for spaces along the approach to their front door, but are open to more informal gardens on parts of their property that aren't so "public." So, part of the decision involves your tastes and preferences. But even more important are the factors discussed in the

Situating Your Garden section that follows. The best general advice I can give is to respect the natural topography and features of your property, trying to work with them instead of against them. Fighting the layout of your land can lead to major expense and big, painful headaches. Be flexible enough to recognize the difference between what you want and what you need, and always give preference to the latter.

One assumption I've made with this book is that you're reading it because you already have shady conditions. In other words, you're not looking for advice on which trees to plant. You may need some advice on how to manage the trees you've already got, and you'll find that in the chapter Managing Shady Areas.

Also, you might have trees but no real shrub layer. Depending on the size and nature of your property, you might want to add shrubs to your garden. Advice on that subject appears in the section Shrubs in this chapter.

That leaves the herbaceous plants, which are covered in this chapter under the section Selecting Plants and, of course, in the Plant Gallery.

Situating Your Garden

Make every effort to situate gardens on your property where *all* conditions (not just light levels) are most suitable for gardening, even if those areas aren't what you would consider ideal for other reasons, such as providing views of the area from a window of the house or from the approach to the house. Again, this returns to the idea of minimizing cost, effort, maintenance, frustration, and failure by choosing to work with nature, not against it. When you elect to put a garden in a marginally suitable area, you may still succeed, but it will require much more work.

What qualities make one area more suitable for gardening than others? Here are some:

Good soil, or the ability to create good soil through amendment or by bringing in high-quality topsoil

Availability of water for irrigation

Enough light for the plants you want to grow, or a willingness to alter your list of prospective garden plants to match the existing light levels

A grade no steeper than you can walk up and across very comfortably with no sensation of being off-balance or making an exertion

An absence of junk in the soil from, for example, the construction of your house, driveway, patio or walkway

An absence of significant roots from major trees

Easy accessibility, both for you and for the largest piece of maintenance equipment you expect to use in the garden (this can be as small as a cart or wheelbarrow, or as large as a garden tractor)

Ideally, proximity to areas where bulk materials such as compost or mulch will be delivered, made or stored

Of course, few spots have all these qualities, but you're looking for the areas that have most of them. Also, you should prioritize the items on that list according to your own needs and preferences. Gardeners with physical limitations, for instance, might make easy accessibility the first priority.

One of the more problematic items on that list of qualities is the one about grade. Because much of the region this book covers is hilly or mountainous, many readers will have sloping areas on their property in spots where some sort of garden would normally be desirable. If the slope is anything more than gentle, there are really only three options: (1) terracing the sloped area to create flat garden beds that can accommodate the foot traffic and soil disturbance that are just a normal part of perennial garden maintenance; (2) massing one groundcover throughout the area; or (3) naturalizing the area with suitable spreading plants.

Terracing—the practice of retaining a slope with a series of walls—is the most expensive but also the most desirable of these possibilities because it provides instant, long-lasting control over a problem area and permits the greatest flexibility in planting. Terracing should be done so that each wall holds back a volume of dirt that is as close as possible to flat on top. I often see badly done terracing in which each section is sloped nearly as steeply as if it hadn't been terraced at all! This is the result of installing fewer, shorter, and more widely spaced sections of wall than the job really requires in an effort either to keep costs down or to avoid getting permits, which are often required for walls of a certain height. To my mind, this is little better than not terracing at all.

If terracing is not affordable, then you must either mass a groundcover or naturalize the area; both options rely on plants rather than structures to maintain the integrity of the slope over time. Bear in mind that there are limits to what plants can do. To paraphrase the old saying, "Don't send a boy to do a man's job," plants should never be used as a substitute for a retaining wall or another structure.

Selecting Plants

When it comes time to pick out the plants you'll put in your shade garden, how do you do it? Most people would start out by picking plants they like—and that's where they'd make their first, and worst, mistake.

Huh? What? Surely I can't be advising you to pick out plants you *don't* like! No, of course not. But think about this for a second. When you go shopping for a new car, do you just pick the one you like the best? No—at least not if you're like most of us. If that's all it took, we'd all be driving around in snazzy BMWs and Lamborghinis with lots of numbers and letters in their names because people like sports cars and that's what they'd choose. However, most sports cars won't do what most people need a car to do: get up a snowy hill on a winter day and deliver you to your job in one piece, or get enough miles to the gallon to not break the fuel budget.

Instead of just picking out a car we like, most of us have to consider questions like these: How much will the monthly payment be? How much will it cost to insure? Does it have a good reliability rating? Is it expensive to repair if I'm in an accident? Can it accommodate everything and everyone I need to cart around? What kind of gas mileage does it get?

In other words, we consider *practical* things. As weird an idea as this will seem to many people, you should do the same thing when you pick out plants—*if* you want your garden to look good with minimal effort and expense for the longest possible season. Not all plants are equally good at doing that. In fact, for any given type of garden in any given region, only a small number of plants will give that kind of superior performance, in the same way that, in all likelihood, only a small number of cars will satisfy your criteria for budget and functionality.

So, what are the practical questions you should ask when picking out plants? Well, this author has already asked them for you, and this book contains the answers, but you should still know what the key questions are because at some point, you may have to evaluate plants for yourself.

First, the obvious questions:

Is the plant cold hardy where I live?

Does the plant prefer the conditions I can offer it, or does it just *tolerate* them?

Because this is a book for gardeners living in the Northeast, virtually all the plants covered here are cold hardy to at least USDA Zone 5, which prevails throughout most of central New England, with the bulk of them hardy to colder zones. Cold hardiness is noted in each plant's individual entry in the Plant Gallery as well as in the list of plants by USDA zone in the Resources section of this book.

Likewise, all the plants covered here are suitable for shade at northern latitudes. Because "shade" doesn't mean just one thing, as we've already discussed, plants in the Plant Gallery are divided up broadly into two categories: those that will do well in deeper shade, and those that require light shade to perform well. This is a way for readers with considerably shady gardens to weed out the marginal performers right off the bat.

It's also important to understand something about shade plant terminology. Again and again, at nurseries and in books and other resources, you'll encounter the term *shade tolerant*. That word choice isn't accidental, and you'll notice that it's *not* "shade loving"! There's a really critical difference between a shade-*tolerant* plant and a shade-*loving* plant, and it's self explanatory: shade-tolerant plants *tolerate* shade, performing reasonably well even though shady conditions might not bring out their best. Shade-loving plants, on the other hand, perform as well or better in lots of shade as compared to sun. You should devote as much space as possible to shade-loving plants, not just shade-tolerant plants.

You'll often see these two terms used interchangeably, which is unfortunate because they aren't the same at all. To make things more complicated, a plant's love of or tolerance for shade *isn't a fixed thing*. It depends on where the plant is grown. A plant that needs shade to grow well in Georgia might accurately be called a shade lover there, but might only be shade tolerant in Vermont, where the sun's rays at midday in summer aren't nearly as strong. That's why gardeners need regional gardening books to help guide their choices; you can't generalize about plants across wildly different geographic areas.

You can assume that any plant in this book rated for deeper shade is a shade *lover* in our Northeast region. Anything that requires lighter shade is merely a shade-*tolerant* plant in our region.

So, what else do you need to ask yourself in order to pick the best plants for shade? Here are a few more questions:

Is the plant disease resistant?

Is the plant prone to insect infestation?

Is the plant unpalatable to deer and other potential browsers?

Does the plant spread or seed aggressively?

Does the plant typically go dormant before first frost?

Does the plant have foliage that looks good all season long?

(Notice that we still haven't even allowed ourselves to ask about flowers, the thing most gardeners consider first, sometimes to the exclusion of all other things!)

The benefits of disease and pest resistance are obvious. Hostas are superb plants for the shade garden, but wouldn't they be even better if they weren't attractive to slugs? Of course! And many lungworts have unique speckled foliage that can brighten shady nooks and crannies, but most of them are prone to a disfiguring fungal disease called powdery mildew that leaves them coated with an unattractive whitish film. (Some lungworts are resistant, and in the Plant Gallery, I tell you which ones.)

In the Northeast, gardeners are all too familiar with the problem of deer browsing. No one can guarantee that deer won't eat a particular plant, but some plants are almost sure to be eaten while others usually won't be. Unless you want to create a completely predictable problem situation in your garden, you'll use only a small number of plants (if any) that deer tend to browse, and you'll take measures to protect them.

Earlier, I explained the downside of aggressively spreading plants. Aggressive spreaders = problem, plain and simple. If you have any doubts, Google the plant name *Houttuynia cordata* 'Chameleon' and see what comes up in gardener forums online. This groundcover, commonly known as chameleon plant, grows well in a wide range of shady conditions and looks lovely and colorful at first, but eventually invades every square inch of ground available to it and is so ineradicable that most people rue the day they ever put it in their garden. Many other shade gardening books recommend it simply because it does grow in shade, ignoring the disaster it will create in most environments; you will not find it recommended here.

Next, we come to the question of whether a plant will perform well over a long season. Obviously, we'd all prefer a garden that looks full and good from April through November to one that looks good only from April through June, July, or August. But many shade plants that are beautiful in spring and early summer fade before summer's heat departs. Their foliage declines in quality, and they don't produce new, fresh foliage to replace it, or they go completely dormant long before first frost. With a lot of these plants in your garden, you can't hope to have a long-season landscape. I will tell you which plants you can rely on to look admirable well past Labor Day so you can get the longest possible display in your garden.

Okay, we've covered a lot of ground. Are there other questions that should be on our list? You bet there are!

Does the plant have attractive, prominent flowers? (Finally!)

Do the flowers have a scent that is nice, objectionable, or simply absent?

Do the flowers last a long time?

And there you have it: questions about flowers are in last place. Now, I want to clarify something. Everyone, including me, and even the chronically allergic, enjoys looking at flowers. So I understand perfectly why so many home gardeners give in to the temptation to fill their properties with plants that have beautiful flowers. The problem is that we don't live in an ideal world. Flowers fade, and most perennials produce flowers for only two to three weeks every year under the best of circumstances. That's not very long, so if you pick plants based on how well you like their flowers, you won't get much bang for your buck.

I'm not saying that you should ignore a plant's flowers when making choices. I'm just saying that most of the time, you should be considering the flowers of only those plants that have passed muster in a lot of other ways first. Flowers should be your last consideration, not your first.

When you do get around to considering flowers, you don't need my advice, because this is where personal taste takes over. As one example of how variable *that* can be, I've always found it strange that some people cut off the flowers of hostas. I think they're very showy, and sometimes they have a wonderful perfume, but you know the saying: "There's no accounting for taste."

On the subject of flower fragrance, a quick word: many flowers don't have any scent to speak of, but some do, and this is another one of those areas where personal taste varies widely. I can't tell you how many times I've seen the plant *Cimicifuga racemosa*, commonly known as bugbane, referred to as "fragrant" in reference books, with no further elaboration. Indeed, bugbane is fragrant . . . but it's not the kind of fragrance *I* want wafting in my bedroom window at night! I would describe it as heavy and cloying, though unobjectionable from a distance. But not everyone would agree with me. A client of mine who may have a more finely tuned sense of smell once cut some bugbane stalks for an all-white flower arrangement, but hastily removed them when she detected an odor she described as "something that had died!"

In a similar vein, I love the perfume of *Geranium macrorrhizum* leaves. They exude the same kind of aroma you get from what are called *scented geraniums* (actually members of the genus *Pelargonium*, not true geraniums at all). But I have known people who can't stand the very same smell that I go out into the garden expressly to enjoy!

It's all a matter of taste, so when a plant's leaves or flowers are described as "fragrant," don't assume you'll like the perfume. Check it out before you buy.

As for that final question on our list—how long a plant's flowers will last—it's of minimal importance. Why? Well, most perennials bloom for only two to three weeks a year anyway. That's a result of genetic programming, and there's nothing you can do to change it. But it's also not true for all plants. Several spring-blooming and fall-blooming plants flower longer simply because cooler air temperatures permit flowers to stay fresh longer. A few shade plants will rebloom if deadheaded, but they're a distinct minority. Most annuals, of course, will keep blooming until frost once they've started—but there are very few annuals that will bloom in moderate and deeper shade in our region.

The upshot is that it's not realistic to expect a primarily perennial shade garden in the North to have flowers, flowers everywhere all season long, and this has nothing to do with plant choices. That's why knowledgeable garden designers constantly advise people to use lots of good foliage plants in their shade garden. Flowers are fleeting, but you'll look at foliage for months.

Backbone Plants . . . and Everything Else

A finite number of plants will grow in any given set of conditions. The longer your list of demands, the fewer plants will be available to you. It *is* possible to hone the list down to zero, as the woman at that luncheon did in the anecdote I shared in the preface of this book. There's no such thing as an ideal plant, and you should no more expect perfection from a plant than from a person, so you may have to give a little when it comes to your preferences.

Looking back at all the questions I've recommended you ask yourself about a plant when considering it for your garden, I want to be clear that I'm not telling you there's *any* plant for which the answer to all those questions is what you want it to be. I'm just saying that for some plants, a lot more of those questions have good answers, and those are the plants you should use to fill most of the space in your shade garden.

In fact, I have a name for these superior garden candidates: *backbone plants*. These are ornamentals whose exceptional qualities make them the best choices for filling the majority of the space in your garden. If you use them in abundance, they'll hold your garden together and keep it solid, like a spine supports a body. Everything else, to one degree or another, is "filler."

To use another analogy, consider how most of us compose a meal: usually, we have large portions of staple foods and just a little bit of side dishes and delicacies. The backbone plants are like beans and rice or meat and potatoes, not onion dip or caviar! Yet, life is richer with onion dip and caviar, so it's always nice to have some.

Strive to use backbone plants for *at least* 75 to 80 percent of your garden. Actually, you could build your garden from nothing but backbone plants, but for the sake of variety, you may allocate 15 to 20 percent of the space to secondary, filler plants that I refer to as *accent plants*. Finally, you can devote perhaps 5 percent of the space to a few annuals or tender perennials. Don't include either bulbs or spring ephemerals in any of these categories. Bulbs and spring ephemerals have such a short season that they function more like appetizers: they precede the main course entirely. When designing your garden, fit spring ephemerals and bulbs in between the long-season perennials so that when they go dormant, they do not leave noticeable gaps. Alternatively, put them in areas where annuals will be planted when the weather warms.

In the Plant Gallery, backbone plants are grouped separately to make them easy to identify, as are accent plants, ferns, and bulbs.

I know that my "practical" approach to plant selection will seem backward to many readers. Gardeners are inundated with the message that gardening is all about personalizing your space and expressing your taste. While that is true, it also glosses over some inconvenient facts. Successful gardening means finding a manageable way to get good results, and for most homeowners, that means putting functionality first.

I hope I've persuaded you of the value of using my approach to selecting plants for your shade garden. If you need a little more convincing, consider this. In the early years of my ornamental shade gardening experimentation, I bought a lot of plants I liked a lot and proceeded to . . . kill them. Mostly—because I was trying to determine the limits of their shade tolerance (or love!)—I subjected them to inadequate light, and of course, a lot of them expired. I feel kind of guilty about it now, but all that "horticide" did have a point—I was trying to figure out what you won't have to, because you now have this book to tell you what performs well in shade in this neck of the woods.

Interestingly, over the years, the list of plants I consider my "favorites" has totally changed. Before, it consisted of lots of plants with blue flowers and wonderful perfumes (is there any human being who isn't born loving lavender?), yet now it also includes lots of plants that have earned my respect for their ability to survive tough conditions—whether a dry woodland, a waterlogged lowland, or the exposed, wind-buffeted cap of a bald mountain. I've come to view plants from an ecological perspective, as residents of more or less challenging niches in the environment. When I see a plant surviving in a difficult situation, I get the same feeling one might from seeing a person persevere and overcome obstacles.

So, my list of favorite plants didn't shrink—it *grew*. Along with the fragrant blue beauties that have always knocked my socks off, I now have high esteem for hellebores, woodland asters, and epimediums—plants I wouldn't have thought twice about if I'd bought a house on a sunny lot. It's not that I don't still love delphiniums. I just know that I can't grow them in the shade, and fortunately I discovered lots of wonderful plants that *will* work. I hope you will come to appreciate them as much as I have.

Plants for Both Shade and Sun

As I mentioned earlier, a number of plants that grow well in shade also grow well in some degree of sun. This is advantageous to gardeners with properties having both shady and sunny garden areas. A property as a whole will look more cohesive if at least a few of the garden plants used are distributed throughout all the gardens. This would be impossible if all plants tolerated *only* sun or *only* shade.

The extra adaptability of plants that can grow across a range of light conditions makes them especially useful. Gardeners who enjoy a best-of-all-possible-worlds circumstance, with both sunny and shady gardens, should take special care to incorporate into their garden designs at least a few plants with broad light tolerance. A list of these plants can be found in the Resources section of this book.

Using Colorful Foliage in the Shade

When you think of plants with colorful foliage, hostas probably come to mind first. Many hostas have bright white or yellow variegation that makes them jump out of the shadows. It's easy to forget, however, that the opposite is also true: plants with dark leaves tend to disappear in low light. For example, burgundy-leaved cultivars of *Cimicifuga* get swallowed up in shade. What's more, their rich color doesn't develop well without some direct light, and what does develop isn't retained long, because these plants tend to fade to green as the season progresses, a phenomenon commonly called "greening out."

My advice is to put plants with burgundy leaves in the sun, placing them next to plants with golden leaves, such as *Spiraea* 'Gold Mound,' for extra impact. In the shade, use lots of plants with variegated leaves, especially gold, which counters the blue cast of light in shaded areas even more effectively than white.

Arranging Plants

Let's assume that, using the Plant Gallery in this book as your primary resource, you've compiled a list of possible plants for your garden, whatever type of shade garden it will be. If it's a shady border or woodland garden, you might have twenty plants on your list. If it's a naturalized area or a bed to be filled with a groundcover, you might have four possibilities from which to choose.

Where groundcovers are concerned, arranging plants is a simple matter. The only rule is this: never mix groundcovers. In other words, select one groundcover to fill an area, and do not plant another groundcover with it. At first, a mix of groundcovers can look charming. Over time, however, such plantings tend to look more messy than anything else, and once two groundcovers mix, there's no separating them. (To be strictly accurate, there are occasions when mixing groundcovers can work, but achieving a satisfying mix is so difficult, in my opinion, that for the average gardener it's just not worth trying.)

The standard spacing to use when planting a groundcover is 6 inches. In other words, keep each plant about 6 inches distant from its neighbors. Planted at this density, most groundcovers will fill an area in about three growing seasons. During the three years when a groundcover is getting established and spreading, it is essential to mulch the area, especially if the bed is on any significant slope. After the groundcover fills in, you probably won't need to mulch, but you might elect do that in late winter if the groundcover is deciduous.

The method for arranging plants isn't much different for naturalized areas. The plants are going to spread and move over time, anyway, so initial placement isn't too critical. Assuming uniform conditions over the expanse of the area to be naturalized, simply strive for a roughly uniform distribution of plants.

Shady borders and woodland gardens are where plant placement has a real impact on the effect the garden produces. They're also an opportunity to have some fun and express creativity.

You'll probably want to work out your ideas on paper before purchasing plants; otherwise, you may find that you've spent money on plants you don't end up using. Plus, if you're trying to work out a design in winter or early spring, you don't have the option of working with real plants because nurseries aren't selling them yet.

I know that lots of people think they "can't draw." Don't worry about it. Just put your inhibitions and reservations aside. Your drawing doesn't have to be exact, and it doesn't have to be a work of art. You don't even have to show it to anyone else. You just want something rough to work with.

Measure your garden's dimensions, and sketch a quick *plan view* of it on a pad of paper, using graph paper if you think that will help you make it more accurate. Plan view means that you draw it as if you were looking down on it from above. (You can also just take a photograph of the space and work from that, in which case you'll be drawing more of what's called an *elevation* than a plan view.)

Put a piece of tracing paper over your drawing or photo—taping it in place is a good idea—and you're ready to continue. From this point forward, draw only on tracing paper, never on your original sketch or photo. That way, you can try out many ideas and compare them without having to erase anything or redo your original drawing.

The next step is to select a small palette of backbone plants with contrasting forms. Six might be enough for a small garden scaled for just a portion of a typical residential lot, with commensurately more for a large garden (although a small selection can work for a large garden, too). Why so few?

I'll answer by relating a conversation I had with an artist who once asked my advice about starting a new garden. I began by saying, "Well, the first thing is to pick a core group of six or eight plants . . ." She interrupted to ask why I'd restrict the variety so severely. I asked her to consider how she would start work on a painting. "Don't you choose your color palette first?" I asked. "You wouldn't consider using every tube of paint you've got in your paint box, would you?"

"You're right," she agreed. She knows that simplicity is often more visually satisfying than complexity, that infinite variety isn't infinitely pleasing; it's directionless. A painting employing every color would simply look poorly conceived, as if the artist had no particular vision in mind. The same is true in the garden. It's the particular limited combination of paints or plants, or whatever you use when creating something, that gives rise to a mood or a style. A garden composed of repeated groupings of just a half dozen fundamentally different *but very good* plants will outshine a garden composed of twenty different mediocre plants any day.

So, choose a fairly small plant palette, make sure *all* the plants are backbone plants, and stick to it. Make sure all your choices can take the conditions your garden offers. There's no point in including a plant that can tolerate only bright indirect light, such as lady's mantle, if the garden is densely shaded. You'll almost certainly want to include one kind of fern, perhaps two or more.

This core group of backbone plants will comprise 75 to 80 percent of your garden. On your tracing paper, start laying out groups of your chosen plants throughout the garden using commonsense rules:

Put taller, bushier plants at the rear.

Use groups whose size seems in proportion to the overall dimensions of the garden, erring on the side of larger groups if you're not sure.

Repeat some patterns in your arrangement.

Do not make the layout too formulaic or symmetrical unless you're aiming for that kind of look.

Fill all prominent spots with backbone plants.

As you place plants, think about form, size, color, leaf shape, and flowering sequence. You can even use highlighters to color groupings, perhaps making all the spring bloomers blue, all the summer bloomers pink, all the fall bloomers yellow, and all the foliage plants green. That way, you'll get a better sense of how you've distributed everything.

I'll add that symmetry is often expected, and especially pleasing, at the start and end of a path as well as anywhere plants flank a doorway or something with an obvious center.

If, as you try various layouts, you find that some of the spots in the garden seem hard to fill with any of the plants you selected, go back and adjust your list of core plants.

The next step is to fill the remaining space. Select a few accent plants or even a different group of backbone plants, or a mix of the two. Now distribute these plants in what seem like pleasing groups throughout the remaining space. Very small plants that can only be enjoyed close up, such as trilliums, generally need to be near the front.

As you work with plants more and more, you'll probably develop favorite plant combinations, as I have. I like to grow Solomon's seal behind and even interspersed with epimedium because the epimediums provide a nice "skirt" in front of or around the bare Solomon's seal stems. Any plant without much foliage near ground level may need a little help from a leafier but low-growing companion.

Finally, you may choose to devote some space to annuals or tender perennials. These can be planted in the ground or in decorative containers suitable for bringing inside with the plant in winter.

At this point, you should be able to generate a shopping list of plants for your project. Assuming the garden is already thoroughly prepped for planting, I suggest you head to the nursery with your list, get your plants, install the garden, and live with it for a year or preferably two. If its elements don't work, then rearrange or replace plants accordingly. Only then, after you're sure you have a basic layout that is attractive and workable, and if you feel the need to add bulbs, spring ephemerals, or other accent plants, should you make additions.

Where calculating quantities of plants is concerned, remember that different plants increase in size at different rates. Hellebores and many hostas, for instance, need several years to bulk up, but many epimediums grow thickly almost from day one, so compensate for that when planting. Buy larger sizes of slow-growing plants if they're available and if you can afford them. Overall, allow everything enough room for a few years' growth, or you'll find yourself having to divide many of the plants in your garden sooner than you might want to.

Using Bulbs and Spring Ephemerals

I am not an advocate of using bulbs extensively in perennial gardens. There—I said it. It's not that I don't find them beautiful. Who could fail to be cheered at the sight of sunny yellow crocuses in the full flush of growth while the rest of the plant world is just waking? Or amazed at the almost miraculous toughness and tenacity of snowdrops that emerge already in bloom from under massive snow drifts?

I advise using caution with bulbs in the perennial garden for strictly practical reasons: they complicate maintenance enormously. As one-season plants, their exact location is a mystery for three-quarters of the year. If you divide and rearrange your perennials in autumn, you'll need a photographic memory of where your bulbs are or risk the garden equivalent of a traffic accident the following spring because you put an astilbe smack on top of a clump of Siberian squill. That's in addition to the danger of accidentally spearing and destroying your bulbs with a garden fork when you dig adjacent plants.

And bulbs are not necessarily benign neighbors. I have seen gardens (albeit, sun gardens) so overplanted with bulbs that the perennials—which are, after all, the main attraction—were literally being choked to death by thick swaths of rotting bulb foliage. Even in the shade, bulbs that seed around a lot can become real pests, popping up in the midst of perennial clumps and creating an untidy look.

Despite all this, bulbs have an undeniable allure. They can be a powerful tonic for the winter blahs because the vast majority of them bloom in early spring when gardeners are desperately hungry for any sign of plant life. Early in the year, when the weather is often bone-chillingly raw and it can be hard to find the motivation to do what needs to be done outside, bulbs are morale boosters, reminding us of the rewards for getting our hands dirty.

The best approach for most gardeners is to use bulbs judiciously. Planting bulbs somewhat sparingly and always grouping them in clumps—never spreading them throughout the perennial garden—is a workable compromise. I also advise holding off on planting bulbs until your new garden is at least a year old. You really need to see all your perennials come up and coexist for a full growing season to determine how well your overall garden design works. After the first year, if everything seems generally pleasing and no major changes are required, *then* plant your bulbs. But if you'll be doing substantial rearranging, you'll sure be glad you don't have to worry about where a few hundred bulbs are.

Spring ephemerals are problematic to incorporate into a new garden for exactly the same reason, and I suggest waiting a season or two before planting them, as well. I recommend this despite the fact that a couple of spring ephemerals are among my favorite plants, and I personally have a hard time resisting them.

The only exception is when you are naturalizing an area with native plants. Because it's unlikely you'll ever lift and divide the plants in a naturalized garden, there's no compelling reason not to put in native bulbs and spring ephemerals at the start. In fact, it will be easier then, as opposed to after the principal perennials have begun to spread.

All that said, I'm not suggesting you should altogether forgo spring ephemerals and bulbs in shady cultivated gardens. The key to satisfying results is to pay careful attention to their placement.

After spring ephemerals and bulbs finish flowering, they go through an awkward stage in which their foliage looks less and less attractive but can't be removed without harming the health of the plants. Here's a tip for placing them to minimize that awkwardness: position them near a perennial with similar foliage or flowers. That way, as the spring ephemeral or bulb fades, something that looks nearly the same is growing close by to take its place, and the transition is smoother. Examples of these pairs include Virginia bluebells (*Mertensia virginica*) with woodland phlox (*Phlox divaricata*); Dutchman's breeches (*Dicentra cucullaria*) with native bleeding heart (*Dicentra eximia*); and windflower (*Anemone blanda*) with spotted geranium (*Geranium maculatum*).

One last note about bulbs. The ones that will do truly well in shade are the so-called minor bulbs. Minor bulbs are, for the most part, physically smaller (both the bulbs themselves and the plants they produce) than the heavily hybridized tulips, daffodils, and hyacinths that dominate the flower-bulb market. Because they aren't considered as "showy" as the major bulbs, they are often ignored.

But it's precisely the small stature and similarly modest needs of such bulbs as windflower, crocus, and squill that allow them to thrive in shade. They don't need as much light to store enough energy to flower year after year.

In order to make an impact, minor bulbs need to be planted in quantity. Whereas you might group eight or ten daffodils together when you plant them, you'll want to put twenty crocuses in one planting hole. Luckily, minor bulbs are frequently very inexpensive, making it affordable to purchase large quantities. And although larger bulbs have to be planted deeply, minor bulbs do not. The depth at which they get planted is in proportion to the size of the bulb. So, you can turn one spadeful of soil over to make a deep enough planting hole for minor bulbs. All in all, you might be able to plant two or three times as many minor bulbs as major bulbs for the same money and less work.

Shrubs

The subject of shrubs for shade is tricky, and even though this book focuses on perennials, ferns, and bulbs, shrubs require at least passing attention. Most gardeners will want something in their landscape that bridges the gap between trees and the relatively ground-hugging herbaceous layer, as well as some options for a foundation planting.

Many books present long lists of shrubs ostensibly for shade. A few hours before I sat down to write this section, I perused one list in a standard reference book. It was more honest than many: next to a large percentage of entries was a note to the effect that the shrub could tolerate only partial shade, or could be grown only in shade in the South.

What's more, nothing better illustrates the sometimes stark difference between coastal and inland Northeast gardening than the subject of shrubs. Numerous mouthwateringly beautiful woody plants reach the northern limit of their useful range (and the operative word here is *useful*) just a few miles from the coast throughout the Northeast.

Southern Fairfield County, Connecticut, is a mere thirty miles south of me as the crow flies, but worlds away in terms of the shrub options. There, *Hydrangea macrophylla* flowers annually. Where I live, this plant is a constant disappointment to gardeners because it is root hardy but not bud hardy (meaning it will grow and leaf out well, but usually not flower). In fact, the single most common question I get from gardeners is why their *Hydrangea macrophylla* doesn't flower.

What this all boils down to is that the number of garden-worthy shrubs that will thrive in substantial shade throughout the Northeast is small, and of those that will, many are deer chow. What's more, my experience working with the gardening public through the years has taught me that most people have a strong preference for evergreen shrubs, and not just for foundation plantings. That list is smaller still.

Gardeners would benefit from using more deciduous shrubs—their options would expand and maintenance would be easier. As a general rule, deciduous shrubs are more amenable to having their size controlled with pruning, and they spring back from damage better than most evergreens.

With all this in mind, here are some thoughts on shrubs that at least have potential for use in the shade in our challenging climate. Visit my website at www.amyziffer.com to see photographs of most of the shrubs mentioned here.

SHRUBS FOR MODERATE SHADE

The *ericaceous* shrubs always top the list of shade contenders. Named for the plant family to which they belong (the Ericaceae), they are also frequently called the *acid-loving* shrubs. This group includes rhododendrons (*Rhododendron*), azaleas (also *Rhododendron*), andromedas (*Pieris*), mountain laurels (*Kalmia*), and leucothoe (*Leucothoe*, pronounced loo-COE-thoe-ee, with a "th" as in "thing"). Don't be confused by the fact that rhododendrons and azaleas belong to the same genus. Although there are technical distinctions between the two, home gardeners really don't need to know what they are. In this book, I use the terms as you would find them used at most garden centers.

Usually, the term *rhododendron* refers to broad-leaved shrubs, many of which can get quite large (8 feet tall and 12 feet wide) over time. (In this context, broad-leaved simply means not needle-leaved, like many conifers, and doesn't actually connote much about the size of the leaves.) Native rosebay rhododendron (*Rhododendron maximum*, Zone 3b), as well as the ubiquitous hybrids *R.* 'Nova Zembla,' *R.* 'English Roseum,' *R.* 'Roseum Elegans' (all Zone 4b), *R.* 'Chionoides' (Zone 5), and other large rhododendrons, are all common elements of foundation plantings and evergreen screens throughout the Northeast. They are fast growing, tolerant of significant shade as well as clay soils, and showy when in flower. They are evergreen, but their leaves curl in a less than attractive way when temperatures drop below freezing, so they can look a little sorry in the depths of winter.

Evergreen azaleas look much like miniature versions of rhododendrons as just described. They are often planted in front of rhododendrons to form a shorter skirt around their bigger cousins. They usually attain a mature size of up to 3 feet tall and wide, which can make them more suitable than rhododendrons for gardens where space is at a premium, but often they grow slowly and demand patience. Hardiness varies widely by cultivar.

Deciduous azaleas are a personal favorite of mine. These can have the height of rhododendrons, but not the "weight," because their underlying woody structure is more delicate and twiggy, their leaves are generally smaller with a brighter color, and their natural shape is more slender and upright. As their name states, they are deciduous, not evergreen, so they will lose their leaves in autumn and replace them, generally just after flowering, in spring.

Several species of deciduous azalea are native to the Northeast, and they all make excellent garden plants if attention is paid to their specific needs. (Some prefer moist soil, for instance, and hardiness varies by species.) Several more species native to the mid-Atlantic region also make good choices. Homeowners frequently pass up these shrubs in favor of evergreen rhododendrons for foundation plantings, but I encourage their use anywhere their needs can be met and a homeowner will tolerate leafless shrubs through the winter. Note, however, that some deciduous azaleas, such as the Exbury and Exbury-type hybrids, are really sun plants in the North.

As an aside, I often use this analogy to help clients understand the aesthetic difference between different woody plants: broadly, I characterize some trees and shrubs as Audrey Hepburn types and others as Mae West types. When my clients imagine the figures and personae of those two women, they get it instantly! Our native flowering dogwood, *Cornus florida*, is a willowy Audrey Hepburn tree whose very delicacy is its strong point, while the Asian kousa dogwood, *Cornus kousa*, is a Mae West tree, buxom and bold (and decidedly not for shade).

Likewise, the broad-leaved rhododendrons are Mae West shrubs. They tend to stand out in a crowd all the time. Deciduous azaleas, however, can come out of nowhere to take your breath away with their grace and then step aside in a stately way to allow other plants their time in the spotlight. One isn't better than the other; they're just different, and there's no reason you can't plant and enjoy both.

One similarity all members of the genus *Rhododendron* share, however, is tastiness to deer. Whatever kind of rhododendron or azalea you plant, you may have to take steps to deter deer browsing.

It's precisely because deer like rhodies and azaleas that homeowners often use andromeda (*Pieris japonica*, Zone 5) as a substitute. (There is also a native andromeda, *Pieris floribunda*, but it is so rare in the trade that the average homeowner is unlikely to encounter it.) Andromedas are considered broad-leaved evergreens, although their leaves are much smaller than those of the typical rhododendron. Their flowers are also very different, opening into a cascade of little lily-of-the-valley-like bells very early in spring well before rhodies bloom.

The downside of andromedas is that they are somewhat finicky. They can be spectacular successes, but they can also be a real headache. They're very particular about the exact amount of light they receive. Too much, and they are very prone to infestations of lace bug, a troublesome insect pest. Too little, and they languish, never increasing much in size or flowering (and they can still be bothered by lace bug). Not infrequently, they expire for mysterious reasons. In summary, although they are almost certain not to get browsed by deer, andromedas are hardly without problems.

Mountain laurels (*Kalmia latifolia*, Zone 5) are so much a part of the natural Northeast landscape that they are the state flower of Connecticut and Pennsylvania. They are broad-leaved evergreens that look very similar to andromedas when not in flower. They bloom in mid- to late June in the Northeast, covering themselves with oddly geometric flowers in shades of white and pink.

Deer often browse mountain laurels, which are just part of their diet in the wild. That's why native stands of mountain laurel are often limbed up to a height just above a deer's reach. Laurels actually look quite good arborized (made "tree-like") in this way, but they will probably need protection in garden settings when they're young, and most homeowners will want something planted in front of them to conceal any bare trunks that develop.

Leucothoe (also called fetterbush or doghobble) is another native broad-leaved evergreen shrub widely available but not as widely used as rhodies, azaleas, and laurels because its flowers aren't as showy and its growth habit is different. The two species available in the trade are *L. axillaris* and *L. fontenesiana*, along with a number of cultivars.

L. fontenisiana is said to be hardy to Zone 4, although I rarely see it grown far inland, perhaps because it can look quite ragged in spring if grown in spots exposed to substantial winter winds or subject to heavy snow. I highly recommend it both for coastal areas and in sheltered spots inland. *L. axillaris* is hardy only to Zone 5b.

Leucothoes are slowly suckering shrubs that form a mound of arching branches, typically growing just 2 to 3 feet tall and 3 feet wide, but in milder areas they can grow substantially larger. Because of their mounding shape, leucothoes can be severely damaged by very heavy snow loads, so gardeners should take precautions against snow damage by erecting snow barriers over or around their leucothoes if needed. However, if they are damaged by snow and ice, leucothoes can be cut back hard, and they'll spring back in just two to three years, faster than most shrubs.

Leucothoes may occasionally be browsed by deer but are unlikely to get hit very hard. They are also somewhat prone to fungal diseases that mar the leaves with brown spots, but these rarely develop into anything too unattractive. They produce new shoots and leaves in late May or early June, a little later than most woody plants. Flowers are reminiscent of those of andromeda.

By far the most shade-tolerant shrubs hardy in the North are the yews, members of the genus *Taxus* (Zone 2 to 6 depending on the species). These fine, soft, needle-leaved evergreens used to be common as dirt throughout the Northeast, but their high palatability to deer has led to a steep drop-off in their use. For fullness, deep-green color year-round, and amenability to shaping, nothing beats a yew. In fact, nothing comes close. If you'll be implementing a program to control deer browsing, by all means plant yews. Otherwise, avoid them. Note that yew berries are highly toxic if ingested, but it is possible to purchase male clones that will not produce berries.

Another plant grown more for its evergreen foliage and berries than for its flowers is holly (Zone 5 and sometimes colder). The name *holly* can be confusing because different people use it in different ways. Using that term can open up a can of worms, but it's unavoidable. For the purpose of this book, I'll use holly the way most homeowners do—to refer to the evergreen shrubs with the glossy, serrated leaves and bright red berries we associate with Christmas. The ones available here that match that description generally belong to the hybrid species *Ilex* x *meserveae* and are sometimes called the "blue hollies." Many of the cultivars in that group have the word *blue* in the name ('Blue Girl,' 'Blue Boy,' 'Blue Prince,' 'Blue Princess,' and so on).

These hollies are superb landscape shrubs, second only to the yews in their overall adaptability. If grown well and pruned regularly and sensitively, they will be gorgeous, dense, healthy looking shrubs that can be maintained at reasonable sizes almost indefinitely. If not pruned regularly, most hollies will quickly grow too large for most suburban landscapes, and reducing their size after the fact is an act of butchery that rarely gives satisfactory results. On the whole, though, they are among the easiest evergreen shrubs for homeowners without special gardening skills to keep attractive.

These hollies can also produce big crops of ornamental red or orange berries. Gardeners need to understand that only female hollies produce berries, and a suitable male holly must be in the vicinity (usually within 50 feet) for pollination to take place and berries to result. If you elect to grow hollies, go to a reputable nursery with a knowledgeable woody-plant person on staff who can recommend a good female holly and its "mate." Only one male holly is needed to pollinate many females.

At the risk of confusing some readers, I'll mention that some hollies are naturally smaller than the ones just described, and not all of them have serrated leaves. Rather than try to cover all bases here, I suggest that readers discuss hollies in depth with the staff at a trusted nursery, asking them to recommend the best ones for the growing conditions and space available. Deer will usually browse the blue hollies, so some sort of winter protection is a good idea.

Hydrangeas have caused more distress among Northeast gardeners than any other shrubs in existence. In fact, *H. macrophylla* could better have been named *H. heartbreakeri*. This is the principal species among the hydrangeas that sport the giant blue or pink "mophead" or "lacecap" flowers that nearly all gardeners find irresistible. Gardeners snap up the shrubs and plant them, only to be stood up by the flowers year after year after year after . . . I wouldn't be surprised one day to discover a support group called Hydrangea Lovers Anonymous, founded to help gardeners cope with the disappointment!

If you aren't sure what I'm talking about, here's the deal. The flowers of bigleaf hydrangea (*H. macrophylla*) are to die for. The shrub itself is hardy to Zone 4; the problem is that its flower buds are not. In other words, even after a very cold winter in the Northeast, virtually all bigleaf hydrangeas will leaf out and grow. Unfortunately, most of them won't bloom. Their flower buds, formed the previous year on what's called *old wood*, failed to survive the winter even though the leaf buds (from which the leaves grow) did just fine.

Gardeners within a few miles of the coast or along major lakes and waterways might not even be aware of this problem because the shrub generally blooms reliably for them. For example, the coast of New England is just mild enough (Zone 6 or even warmer) for bigleaf hydrangea's flower buds to survive winter in most years. But those of us more than a few miles inland aren't as lucky.

To make the whole hydrangea hullabaloo even more agonizing, there are exceptions to the "You can't grow bigleaf hydrangea inland" rule. Not a five-minute walk from my house, I know of a blue specimen that blooms faithfully year after year. It's a few feet from the shoreline of a small lake in a protected valley. The microclimate there permits it to flower. How many inland gardeners have such a site? This might be a tad facetious, but I'd guess something like .1 percent. I know *I* don't.

Plus, as one last complication, there are now bigleaf hydrangeas on the market that supposedly bloom on both old wood *and* new wood, which would mean they should bloom for everyone, whether on the coast or in a more frigid area. They belong to a series with a name just pregnant with promise: Endless Summer. I have not grown any of them myself (I joke that I've been hurt too many times, but in reality I just haven't had a good opportunity), but I've asked several people who've grown them about their experiences with the plants. I'd have to say that the verdict is still out. People do report flowering and good color, but they also report that plants don't get very large, and flowers may not appear until August. It's also worth noting that since the Endless Summer hydrangeas became readily available at retail, my part of New England has experienced a series of mild winters. In my opinion, it will take longer to determine conclusively how well the Endless Summer hydrangeas perform throughout the Northeast.

The upshot is that gardeners on the coast have several hydrangeas from which to choose for shady spots. Inland gardeners must control their jealousy and either roll the dice with Endless Summer or limit themselves to smooth hydrangea (*H. arborescens*, Zone 3b). The species itself is almost never offered for sale, but the more ornamental (read: it has bigger flowers) cultivar 'Annabelle' is a nursery staple. Its blossoms are gigantic white snowballs. An attractive, dusky-pink cultivar called 'Invincibelle Spirit' was introduced recently, and I think it's quite nice.

Smooth hydrangea is a suckering shrub that will slowly spread to form a thicket over time, although the pink form does not seem to spread as readily. The shrub is unfortunately susceptible to rust (a fungal disease) but otherwise has few problems. The biggest issue for 'Annabelle' is that its flowers are *too* large. Its stems become so top-heavy that they can flop unattractively or even break under their own weight. Heavy rain or high winds during peak flowering time will make a mess of the plant. Several cultivars are available that purportedly have stronger stems, including 'Incrediball' (said to have even larger flowers than 'Annabelle') and 'Ryan Gainey' (said to have smaller flowers), and other selections are available to gardeners willing to search out the uncommon.

One other hydrangea that can be grown in some shade in the Northeast is *H. quercifolia*, the oakleaf hydrangea. It produces flowers not in mopheads but in cone-shaped panicles, and its leaves resemble those of red oaks. It is subject to the same limitations as bigleaf hydrangea, that is, flower-bud tenderness; but in milder areas, it's an excellent choice.

The great thing about all hydrangeas is that their flowers look good for a long time. After opening (*H. arborescens* generally starts in early to mid-July) and putting on a really good show for several weeks, the flowers slowly bleach to a buff or tawny brown color that can be attractive right through autumn.

On the downside, hydrangeas are palatable to deer. Gardeners may or may not have to apply a deer repellent to their hydrangeas, depending on the preferences and habits of their local deer herd.

The viburnums are a large group of shrubs including a few that will grow in one degree of shade or another. The most shade tolerant by far is our under-appreciated native maple-leaf viburnum (*Viburnum acerifolium*, Zone 4). It is one of the most adaptable shrubs anywhere, tolerating shade, sun, dry feet, wet conditions, and a wide range of soils, making it as close as anything can get to a foolproof plant and perfect for naturalizing. It doesn't even get browsed by deer.

Maple-leaf viburnum is ubiquitous in our woodlands. Its name comes from the resemblance of its leaves to those of maples, with three pointed lobes. In passing resemblance to its namesake, its foliage can take on some decent fall hues—usually a deep wine, sometimes touched with a bit of scarlet.

Maple-leaf viburnum grows anywhere from two to four feet high and wide, depending on light levels. It produces small, flat-topped clusters of white flowers in late spring and early summer. These develop into sprays of small, deep-blue berries later in the year.

When grown in lots of shade, which is how it's found most frequently in the wild, maple-leaf viburnum is a sparse, airy plant without a lot of substance, sweet but barely even shrub-like. Give it bright indirect light, though, and it gets considerably bushier. It can be effective massed as part of a backdrop to a woodland garden. I think the key to its use is quantity in combination with other shrubs; maple-leaf viburnum isn't a shrub to plant singly.

SHRUBS FOR LIGHT SHADE

We'll pick up where we left off in the previous section, with the viburnums. Of the more common, nonnative viburnums, doublefile viburnum (*V. plicatum* var. *tomentosum*, Zone 5) does the best in light shade. Although it will neither flower nor fruit as profusely in shade as in sun, it is still the most ornamental of the viburnums that do not require full sun. Its large white flowers and red fruits present themselves with an elegance matched by few other shrubs, which is the reason for its great popularity. It's also one of the largest shrubs that can be grown in shady conditions.

The most common mistake gardeners make when planting doublefile vibur-num is failing to give it adequate space. This shrub ultimately grows to a height of about 10 feet and a width of 15 feet or more. It's enormous when mature, and to look its best, it should never be pruned to control its size. The beauty of the plant revolves around its strongly horizontal branching habit. If you start lopping away at it, you ruin that.

Another shrub in this genus that is tolerant of bright indirect light is leather-leaf viburnum (*V. rhytidophyllum*, Zone 5). It's so named because its leaves have the texture and thickness of coarse leather. It has a slightly stiff branching habit, and if left unpruned, it will grow to about 10 feet tall and 8 feet wide, becoming more open as it ages. It bears large, creamy-white clusters of flowers followed by dangling groups of red berries that turn to black.

Whether you will prune leatherleaf viburnum is something you should decide before planting. If pruned, it can be quite dense, and it takes pruning so well I've actually seen it used for a hedge. However, pruning will diminish flowering and/ or fruiting, depending on the time of year it's done, so there's always a trade-off.

Next on the list is fothergilla (*Fothergilla major* and *F. gardenii* and their cultivars, Zone 5). These southeastern US natives bear distinctive white, bottle-brush flowers that open before their leaves appear. They have an open, rounded branching structure and broad, somewhat coarse leaves with prominent veining. Out of flower, they could be mistaken for young witch hazels, although with a little training it's not hard to tell them apart.

F. major grows 5 to 6 feet tall and wide, while *F. gardenii* has a mature size of 2 to 3 feet tall and wide. The latter species, especially its cultivar 'Blue Mist,' has foliage with a bluish cast. All fothergillas are renowned for their excellent red and orange fall color, but to attain this in the North, they must be grown in substantial sun, so don't be disappointed if your fothergillas in light shade don't become a blaze of fiery hues in autumn.

Two evergreen possibilities in light shade are inkberry (*Ilex glabra*, Zone 5) and boxwood (genus *Buxus*; hardiness varies by cultivar to as cold as Zone 5). Inkberries are relatives of, and somewhat similar to, hollies, but their leaves are small and aren't glossy. They don't grow as fast, which makes them a bit less likely to get out of hand, and females produce small blue berries late in the year. If grown in anything but the lightest shade, their lower branches will die out, leaving "bare ankles" that can be somewhat unattractive, so they're best used as a backdrop for smaller shrubs. In a foundation planting, use the species, which can grow to 6 feet tall and wide, and prune it to size. When a smaller form (3 feet tall and wide) is needed, try the cultivar 'Shamrock.'

Boxwoods have small, dark-green leaves, grow densely, respond well to shearing, and are unpalatable to deer. But don't try to push their shade tolerance far, hoping to build a deer-proof garden. Browsing by deer isn't any more disappointing than a shrub that just won't grow because of lack of light. In bright indirect light, however, boxwoods can do reasonably well, and they are less likely than inkberries to thin out at the bottom. Boxwoods need regular light prunings to keep them neat.

Virginia sweetspire (*Itea virginica*, at least Zone 5b) is native to the mid-Atlantic area, where it is apparently quite shade tolerant. In the North, it really does best and is most ornamental in sun, but it's still a possibility for lightly shaded areas. It produces racemes (long strands) of creamy-white flowers like those of chokecherry, and with enough sun, it develops great red and burgundy fall color. It suckers aggressively, especially in sandy soils, which limits its use, but some gardeners might wish to try it in selected spots. The cultivar 'Henry's Garnet' is the best choice, growing 3 to 4 feet tall with an indefinite spread over time.

Cutleaf stephanandra (*Stephanandra incisa* 'Crispa,' Zone 4) starts out as a small, ground-hugging shrub that sends out long stems in all directions, quickly spreading into a mound surrounded by a wide, thick skirt covered with small, deeply cut leaves. Eventually it reaches a height of 3 feet and a spread of 5 feet and takes on the somewhat rangy shape of a cotoneaster. It looks best tumbling around and over boulders and stone walls, so it's a good choice for lightly shaded rock gardens. It can also be used elsewhere, but the plant is hard to position because it changes shape so radically over time and is offered for sale only as a young plant.

I highly recommend serviceberries (*Amelanchier* spp., also called shadbush, shadblow, and Juneberry, Zone 4) but with a warning: in the nursery trade, there is a great deal of inconsistency in labeling of these plants, and even taxonomists seem unclear about just what is what. Most serviceberries are actually small trees very common in Northeast woods, where they produce an airy cloud of white flowers very early, at the same time when the red maples bloom. Birds eat the fruit of serviceberries, so the plants are desirable for wildlife gardens. Occasionally bush forms of serviceberry are available, growing about 8 feet tall and probably derived from West Coast species; these are suitable for plantings at the woodland edge.

OTHER POSSIBILITIES

To round out this section, I'd like to mention several deciduous shrubs that are not currently in common use for landscaping, but in many cases ought to be. They are not flamboyant shrubs likely to knock your socks off at first, but their quiet presence and undemanding nature suit those of us who want gardening to be a pleasure rather than a battle. All will do best in light shade, although you can push that a bit with the first two on the list. All of these shrubs may be difficult to find at nurseries, but mail-order sources exist for them all.

At the top of the list is our native spicebush (*Lindera benzoin*, Zone 4). Spicebush is one of the most common residents of our Northeast woodlands. It would be hard to take a walk in my neighborhood without seeing dozens of them. Spicebush grows only 6 to 8 feet tall and about as wide, and often has multiple stems. In April, its slender branch tips are covered with tiny, sulfur-yellow flowers that I anticipate for many weeks. Next spring, look carefully into the woods for delicate clouds of yellow just around the time when the red maples bloom. Those will be the spicebushes, and I can almost guarantee you'll never fail to notice them again.

Spicebush is a *dioecious* shrub, which means that individual plants are either male or female, like the hollies described earlier. Both males and females flower, but only females develop small, scarlet, oblong berries late in the year. These, too, are subtle but undeniably ornamental.

Another great quality of spicebush is its amenability to pruning. Anyone with moderately good pruning skills will be able to maintain spicebush indefinitely at a desired shape and size (as long as it's not *very* small). Spicebush can seed around quite a bit, but because it's a native plant, this isn't a cause for concern, and it's unlikely to become a problem in the garden.

One of the largest of our native shrubs, witch hazel (*Hamamelis virginiana*, at least Zone 4) can become a very interesting specimen plant. It tends to grow wider than tall (8 feet tall by 12 to 15 feet wide at maturity is typical, and over time its branches can arch over and take on strongly architectural shapes. In terms of overall form, it is very similar to the Asian witch hazels that are more commonly sold in nurseries, but our native version blooms in only one color—yellow—with smaller flowers, and these appear in November rather than late winter and early spring.

Witch hazel doesn't *need* moist soil, but it loves water and can often be found growing streamside in the wild. If you try it in your garden, give it plenty of room and as much light as possible to encourage denser growth. It, too, takes pruning with aplomb when it's young.

Many people are familiar with the Northeast's beautiful native flowering dogwood tree but don't realize that numerous shrubby dogwoods are also native to this part of the world. Silky dogwood (*Cornus amomum*, Zone 4), a mounding shrub about 8 feet tall and wide in light shade and considerably less in deeper shade, is a common denizen of lowlands, where it thrives in soil that's moist all summer long. Silky dogwood is an obvious choice for naturalizing wet areas, but it also tolerates drier soils. With a bit of light, it can grow fairly dense, and it makes a good component of a mixed-shrub backdrop to a perennial garden, but it's a bit rangy for use in more prominent spots. Cymes (flat-topped clusters) of white flowers in very late spring become blue berries that provide food for birds.

Gray dogwood (*C. racemosa*, Zone 4), shares silky dogwood's general appearance except that it can grow half again as tall and wide, and suckers to form thickets. Its leaves have a distinctly gray or olive-green cast, and its fruits are white. Both of these shrubby dogwoods are ideal low-care plants for naturalizing—they are hardy to Zone 4, extremely adaptable, regenerate rapidly after pruning, and provide food and cover for birds and other animals.

One decidedly uncommon but very interesting native shrub is *Sambucus pubens* (Zone 3), the early-flowering and early-fruiting scarlet elderberry. It's fairly large (6 to 8 feet tall and up to 12 feet wide) but sparse, with a distinct, flared vase shape. More shade tolerant than its cousin, the more common American elderberry (*S. canadensis*), it blooms in the blink of an eye quite early, and the fruits come and go just as fast. Don't see that as a drawback, however. The fruits disappear quickly because they are an important food source for many birds. If you have a particular interest in supporting native bird populations, this is definitely a shrub to place on your property, but note that the raw berries are mildly poisonous to people. Of the native shrubs mentioned here, this one will be the most difficult to find for sale.

Some other shrubs to try in lightly shaded areas are winterberry (*Ilex verticillata*, Zone 3b) and its cultivars; summersweet (*Clethra alnifolia*, Zone 4); New Jersey tea (*Ceanothus americanus*, Zone 4); and sweetshrub or Carolina allspice (*Calycanthus floridus*, Zone 5). All of these would actually prefer to be given at least a few hours of direct sun daily, which is why I'm not going to cover them in detail, but I will give a little information about each. All are deciduous and have an informal look.

Winterberry is usually grown for its fall display of scarlet berries that supply food for birds. A dioecious, Northeast native shrub, at least one male is required within 50 feet of females for pollination. It's a strongly vertical shrub, growing up to 8 feet tall and 4 feet wide.

Summersweet is named for its pleasantly aromatic, late-summer flowers held erect in slender bottlebrushes. A lover of moist soils, it does surprisingly well in very dry locations, too. A suckering shrub, it can form a small thicket over time but isn't obnoxious this way. It leafs out later than most shrubs, so you must be tolerant of that to put it in a prominent spot. It grows up to 6 feet tall and 3 feet wide, and is native to the Northeast. Named cultivars, such as 'Hummingbird,' may be only half as tall.

New Jersey tea is a low-growing, Northeast native shrub that sprawls to a mature size of 2 to 3 feet tall by 4 feet wide. It has small clusters of white flowers in late spring and early summer. Its tenacious roots make it a good choice for naturalizing slopes in half sun.

Carolina allspice is an old-fashioned shrub, at one time a favorite for planting near house foundations because of the heady pineapple scent of its peculiar, inconspicuous summer flowers. It grows 6 to 8 feet tall and wide, and is native to the Southeast.

Vines

This will be a short section because only a small number of climbing plants grow well in northern shade. Basically, your choice boils down to Virginia creeper (*Parthenocissus quinquefolia*), Boston ivy (*Parthenocissus tricuspidata*), English ivy (*Hedera helix*), and climbing hydrangea (*Hydrangea petiolaris*, also sometimes identified as *H. anomala* subsp. *petiolaris*).

Virginia creeper and Boston ivy do not have significant flowers, and although they are often advertised as having great red fall color, usually they develop that color only if grown in some sun. However, Virginia creeper is a native vine and so cold hardy that it can be grown well up into Canada, so it can be an easy problem solver. It grows at an astonishing pace, and you can cut it back again and again all season long (*if* you can reach it!) to contain it within a designated space. On the downside, it can spread via seed in quantities great enough to become annoying. All in all, I'm a big fan of Virginia creeper, even if a lot of people regard it with the contempt of overfamiliarity.

Boston ivy is said to be hardy to Zone 4, but I don't believe it! Zone 6, yes, but I think even Zone 5 is pushing it. Along the coast, however, it's a common and lovely plant. Its three-lobed leaves combine elegant simplicity with lush fullness. Unfortunately, it's not native and has a reputation for invasiveness.

English ivy, like the previous pair, is grown for its foliage rather than its flowers or fruit. Technically evergreen, it will be deciduous at the limit of its northern range, which is only Zone 5, and then only for the hardiest cultivars. Many varieties will not survive north of Zone 6, so choose your ivy carefully, consulting reliable local authorities. It, too, can become invasive and must be pruned for containment.

Climbing hydrangea (Zone 4) does have ornamental flowers, but these diminish in both quantity and quality with light levels. If not grown in a fair amount of direct sun, climbing hydrangea will not become the "wall of flowers" you see in photographs. It will just be a fairly decent bloomer providing fairly decent coverage of whatever it's grown on. It's also a classic example of a "sleep, creep, leap" plant, meaning that after planting, it will establish itself at a leisurely pace but will eventually become a vigorous grower. For as many as three years after planting, it may leaf out but decline to show much other activity—such as elongation of its stems! Just about the time you start to wonder if someone forgot to tell it it's a climbing plant, it will get around to growing. After seven or eight years, it should be putting on several feet of new growth every season. This is just the way the plant is, and you have to humor it.

Other vines often recommended for shade, from the perennial variegated porcelain vine (*Amelopsis brevipedunculata* 'Elegans') to clematis (*Clematis*) and akebia (*Akebia*), need light levels so high I would not call them "shade." At that point, what you really have is part sun. If you try to grow these and other plants in that shadowland just at the limit of their real light needs, what you often find is that they grow and leaf out, but flower poorly or not at all. If this happens to you when you try a flowering vine, it's probably because of too much shade.

All climbing plants are capable of damaging the surfaces on which they grow, so think carefully about what you're doing before you attempt to establish a plant on, say, the side of a house with cedar siding. The plant will trap moisture against the siding, encouraging rot; in addition, stained or painted cedar siding must be *re*stained or *re*painted regularly, and the plant will have to be removed from the side of the house in order to do that.

It is possible to install detachable trellises as plant supports to make it easier to perform routine maintenance on siding and other exterior surfaces, but then you're moving toward a less pragmatic approach to gardening than is workable for most homeowners. When it comes to climbers, ask yourself if the trouble of maintaining them is worth the aesthetic benefit you'll reap.

Moss

When I was a child, I dreamt what it would be like to sleep on a bed of moss. On walks in the woods, I'd kneel to brush the back of my hand over tight, pincushion-like mounds of *Leucobryum* or sink my fingers into deep, springy mats of *Polytrichum* (whose unprepossessing common name—hairy cap moss—always seemed wildly off the mark to me). Mosses impart a mood as serene and meditative as the woodland environments in which they're commonly found, and they are often an integral element of Japanese gardens.

Despite the beauty and nearly universal appeal of mosses, not every gardener will have a place where they make sense from a landscaping perspective. Mosses are not terribly compatible with shady borders or other well-filled gardens built around perennial plants that must be lifted and divided regularly. But they can be beautiful and practical in less intensively planted areas with or without suitable companions. They can also make an inviting pathway surface for very light foot traffic.

If you want to actively encourage the growth of moss on your property, look for a shady spot where disturbance will be minimal. Damp rocks and high humidity are desirable, but not absolutely essential. In general, mosses prefer a soil pH on the acidic side, but I've seen plenty of moss growing on neutral to mildly alkaline soil.

Moss is really not that hard to establish, but finding a commercial source of specific mosses to transplant or propagate has never been easy. You may have to do some legwork to identify one local to you. I don't advocate removing moss from the wild for use in the garden, but if you already have moss on your property, and it's growing in conditions similar to those in the area where you want to transplant it, then using some of your existing moss patch is an economical approach that's also pretty likely to succeed. If you attempt to move moss in this way, the consensus among moss experts is that *matching the growing conditions where you found it* is key. Pay attention to soil pH and moisture as well as the amount and type of shade.

You can transplant patches of moss just as you would move most any perennial plant. But instead of digging a planting hole, all you need to do is rake the soil in the new location lightly and dampen it with water. You might wish to rake in a little bit of compost or leaf mold or peat moss. (If you add peat moss, be extra sure to dampen the area thoroughly.) Press the moss patch firmly into the soil so it makes good contact, and then water it. You may wish to use an earth staple to secure it. Water lightly, as often as necessary (perhaps three times a week) for a couple of months or until the moss appears well established.

There's an alternative method you might prefer if you're trying to establish moss on rocks or over a fairly large area. This method has many variations, but basically it involves tossing some source moss and water, in about equal volumes, into a blender. (Doesn't everyone have a garden blender? I bought a used one at a garage sale years ago for just this purpose.) Mix them for a couple of seconds until they form a slurry. Be sure to remove any pebbles clinging to the underside of the moss first, or you might ruin the blender blades! You can also add half as much buttermilk as you did water to the mix, and that will help things along.

Pour the slurry into a watering can whose rose has large-diameter holes, and "water" the prepared area with the slurry. Or, if you're trying to establish moss on rocks and boulders, pour the slurry into a shallow container such as a roller tray (the kind normally used for painting), and then apply it to the rock surface using a paintbrush or roller. Mist these areas with water several times a week until the moss is well established, but avoid wetting down the area with a sprinkler or spray nozzle because the force of the water might wash away the dried slurry.

To encourage an existing mossy area to grow more thickly, try the buttermilk trick. Mix one part buttermilk to seven or eight parts water, and apply it to your moss garden using a watering can as just described. Or, strain the blend through four layers of cheesecloth and use a backpack sprayer for the job. Do this every spring and fall. You can also try using a hose-end sprayer, following the label directions to get the right proportions of buttermilk to water. Be sure to thoroughly rinse your sprayer afterward to prevent any buttermilk solids from drying inside and clogging it.

Garden companions that will grow through or with mosses without smothering them include partridgeberry (*Mitchella repens*); small patches of trillium (*Trillium* spp.) and merrybells (*Uvularia* spp.); native columbine (*Aquilegia canadensis*); polypody ferns (*Polypodium* spp.); native saxifrages (not covered in this book, but a very sweet group of plants for tiny garden compositions); and small spring ephemerals, such as trout lily (*Erythronium americanum*) and Dutchman's breeches (*Dicentra cucullaria*). Generally speaking, you'll want to plant these first and then try to establish moss around them. Plants that grow from seed readily, such as the columbine, are exceptions: just sprinkle their seed over a mossy area, and you can expect pretty good germination.

For more information, there are two authoritative books on moss gardening in the United States. Despite having a title appropriate for a scholarly monograph, George Schenk's *Moss Gardening: Including Lichens, Liverworts, and Other Miniatures* is lyrical and decidedly idiosyncratic, with lots of literary and cultural references and some interesting digressions. William Cullina's much newer *Native Ferns, Moss and Grasses* is more overtly practical in its approach and language, yet remains a good read. They are both worthwhile additions to any shade gardener's library.

MAINTENANCE: THE IMPORTANCE OF BEING DILIGENT

A garden is a highly artificial thing. It may be composed of natural elements—plants, soil, stone, and living creatures from earthworms to resident birds—but nothing like a garden exists or ever will exist in nature. The fundamentals that distinguish a garden from the wild are a sense of order and continuity over time. Nature also exhibits order, but not the same kind we impose on the landscape when we garden. In nature, for instance, there is no such thing as a "weed." Who would be making such a value judgment? And as for continuity, nature never stands still. But most gardens are intended to arrest time to one degree or another, maintaining a particular arrangement of plants and other elements in a sort of perpetual prime of life. That's why we weed, divide, and perform all manner of gardening tasks.

When we fail to maintain the artificial order of our gardens, they revert to the wild quickly and are lost. I have seen many gardens so neglected and overgrown that the only advice I could offer their owners was to rent a backhoe, dig it all up, and start over. Gardens are, in fact, fragile things that are destroyed rather easily.

There's a saying attributed to Thomas Edison (and many other people): "Success is 10 percent inspiration and 90 percent perspiration." He could have been thinking of gardening when he made that quip. In the equation for gardening success, three things contribute to the total in roughly equal amounts: (1) planning and site preparation, (2) good layout and appropriate plant selection, and (3) ongoing maintenance.

Of course, it's easy to understand why maintenance is often overlooked: it's not as fun as, say, buying plants. Plus, people are busy, and when differing demands compete for their time, the home landscape can get pushed to the bottom of the priority list—or off it altogether.

Another problem is that people consistently and substantially underestimate the care gardens require. I am frequently asked about "low-maintenance" gardening. *Everyone* wants a low-maintenance garden. Few people, however, understand what low maintenance means.

Maintenance is always relative. Some gardens do have lower maintenance needs than others, but it's important to realize that *all gardens are inherently maintenance intensive*. A low-maintenance garden simply needs less maintenance than a higher-maintenance garden.

There are few, if any, true shortcuts to reducing maintenance. As a general rule, gadgets, gizmos, and products do not take the place of elbow grease. Gardens are much the same as children in this respect: nothing can replace quality time.

In fact, I equate gardens with children on many levels. No one who decides to have children believes that kids are going to be "low maintenance." Or, if they do, eventually they receive a big shock! Thinking about your garden as another child might keep you from overextending yourself.

As a consequence of all this, I'll offer a few suggestions to help keep your garden a source of pleasure rather than an endless list of chores.

First, start small—very small. Reginald Farrer, a noted twentieth-century English plantsman, reportedly said that "a little garden, the littler the better, is your richest chance for happiness and success." I couldn't agree more.

A small garden, impeccably maintained, will be more attractive and satisfying than an estate's worth of neglected plants. If you are inexperienced and don't have a clear picture of how much maintenance a garden of a given size will require, talk to people who have more experience, make your best guess … and then double or triple your maintenance estimate to give yourself plenty of wiggle room. Better to have extra time on your hands and expand later than make an investment in too large a garden, only to lose a portion of it or have it underperform. In gardening, quality always trumps quantity.

Second, put garden tasks in your calendar just as you would any other obligation. It takes almost no time to jot down a few reminders of what needs to be done when, and you'll be amazed at how this will help you keep track of things otherwise easily forgotten. I garden for a living, and I keep a calendar for each and every client as well as for myself. The habit is invaluable.

Third, perform needed maintenance regularly, in small bites, instead of trying to do a lot infrequently. This reduces maintenance overall for a whole host of reasons. For instance, if you inspect your garden regularly, you're far more likely to notice problems while they're still small and manageable. Nip problems in the bud, and they will take less effort to rectify than if they'd gotten out of hand. Similarly, by weeding for fifteen minutes a day instead of three hours every other Saturday, you'll prevent enough weeds from going to seed to make a real difference in how many weeds germinate. That means less work down the line.

This idea is boiled down to its essence in yet another saying—attributed variously to everyone from Lyndon Johnson to some anonymous gardener—that I like to share with people: "The best thing for a garden is the shadow of the gardener." This means that your regular presence in the garden is what will keep it in good shape.

And doing a little bit of garden work every day instead of being a weekend warrior will mean fewer sore muscles, too, which you'll appreciate tremendously some day, if you don't already!

Remember: you can't eliminate garden maintenance, but you can manage and even minimize it by being organized and committed, and by not biting off more than you can chew. Keep in mind also that the approach to shade gardening outlined in this book is intended to help you create a lower-maintenance garden by emphasizing what works best rather than by presenting every possible option.

So, exactly what kind of maintenance should be performed in the typical shade garden, at a minimum? Beginning in spring, all these jobs must be done:

Pruning woody plants

Raking stray leaves from garden beds

Mulching (every year to every third year, depending on the mulch used)

Dividing any perennial plants that have grown too large for their allotted space just before they begin active growth (every third year for many plants, but practically never for others)

Cutting back any groundcovers that are starting to creep over their edging, to prevent them from escaping their beds (every one to three years, depending on the groundcover)

Planting annuals, if used

Weeding as often as once a week from May through October

Watering whenever adequate rain hasn't fallen

Applying deer repellent, if necessary, as often as every two weeks from April through October

Applying products or using other methods to control any severe pest or disease problems that occur

Possibly fertilizing occasionally

Grooming plants to your standard of attractiveness by cutting off spent flowers and fading leaves

Raking newly fallen leaves in autumn and shredding them for mulch or composting them

Cutting back all herbaceous plants in late autumn or early spring

Putting up deer fencing or applying long-lasting deer repellent to woody plants, if necessary, in preparation for winter

That's quite a list, and it really represents the bare minimum. It's easy to see why so many people find it hard to keep up with "yard work." It should also reinforce why starting small is a wise approach.

Fertilization and mulching are two subjects so misunderstood that they will get their own sections, but I'll say a few words about watering here. Even in an area such as the Northeast, where droughts occur infrequently, gardeners should be prepared to irrigate their gardens at any time from April through October. Surprisingly, chilly late April can be one of the driest times of the year in shade gardens because the leaves of deciduous trees shading our gardens have not yet appeared, and the sun is getting quite intense at our latitudes. Be on the lookout for sun-stressed plants in your shade garden during that transitional period!

Most people try to get by with a hose and sprinkler for watering, but only *very* small gardens can be irrigated with a hose and sprinkler on a regular basis because the headache of running hoses and changing sprinkler positions can be considerable. An underground irrigation system with a programmable timer should be installed for large gardens. If you make the job quick and easy by installing an automated or semi-automated system, it's much more likely to get done. A third alternative is a network of soaker hoses, but this option comes with several caveats. First, setting up a functional soaker-hose system is harder than most people anticipate. Second, these systems are also unattractive if exposed, and keeping them covered by mulch is more difficult than it sounds. Finally, they're not necessarily well suited to every kind of garden or soil type.

If you do water with a hose and sprinkler, my advice is to invest in at least one very high-quality sprinkler with adjustable patterns (I'm a big fan of the Gardena

Aquazoom series, and I buy them for my clients) as well as a hose shutoff valve to control water volume so you can get water just where you need it. As with all gardening chores, the easier it is to perform the job, the more likely it is to get done.

As for the remaining maintenance tasks on that list, if jobs such as pruning, deadheading, and division seem mysterious, I recommend that you take a class through a local continuing education provider or arboretum. Gardening methods are generally best taught in a face-to-face environment where you can ask specific questions and see demonstrations. It pays to get expert instruction, because some methods vary from plant to plant, and although you don't need to become an expert in maintaining every plant, you should at least know how to maintain the ones you have.

DEER

To many gardeners, *deer* is a four-letter word in every sense of that expression! Personally, I consider myself lucky to live in an area where I can regularly see such an exquisite animal. Nonetheless, I understand the desire of gardeners to keep deer from eating their gardens, and I will offer my best advice.

The rule where deer are concerned is . . . there are no rules. But there are trends. If deer are known to prefer a plant profiled in this book's Plant Gallery section, and can be expected to browse that plant, I note it prominently. The good news is that most of the plants profiled here are considered deer resistant.

However, saying that a plant is deer resistant is not a guarantee that deer won't eat it. It only means that past experience has shown that *most* deer won't eat it *most* of the time in *most* places . . . but the deer in your neighborhood might!

I have seen deer eat almost anything in the right circumstances, but interestingly, I have also seen certain populations of deer in certain areas completely ignore plants that are considered "deer candy." You just never know; and that's why I strongly encourage you to ask your neighbors what has and has not been browsed by deer in their gardens. Even then, your experience might differ, so whatever happens, don't be surprised.

There are many ways to control deer browsing. Not all of them are options for everyone. Ultimately, you will have to choose what makes the most sense for you based on efficacy and the time commitment required to apply the product you select.

Products Applied to Plants and Gardens

There are too many individual products used as deer repellents to name here, but they all fall into two broad categories: things with odors that deer don't like, and things with tastes that deer don't like. Some products may work both ways. There's also a distinction between products used during the growing season and products used for winter protection of shrubs. Many of the latter products must be applied by a licensed pesticide applicator; homeowners cannot legally buy or apply them, which is just as well because their application involves equipment in which most homeowners won't want to invest. Because this book is devoted to perennials, ferns, and bulbs that will be dormant during the winter months, I won't discuss products for keeping deer off woody plants in winter.

Note that I am not recommending any of the products in the following discussion; I am simply sharing what I know about several types of products commonly used as deer repellents.

The majority of deer repellents are sprays. They may come in a ready-to-use formulation or in a concentrate that you must dilute according to label instructions before use. Some come in a sprayer; others require you to buy a separate sprayer. If convenience is important to you, buy a ready-to-use (and of course more costly) formulation packaged in a sprayer.

Most spray repellents are made from ingredients such as rotten eggs and garlic—the source of their powerful smell. When applying any of them, you'll want to make sure you're wearing gloves and old clothes, because if you get any of the repellent on your clothes or skin, you won't be able to stand the smell until you've changed your clothes and washed. You apply the product to the plants you want to protect, and then reapply every two weeks or so. Once these products dry on plants, their odor isn't usually noticeable to people.

An interesting alternative to the rotten-egg recipe uses ingredients such as clove, cinnamon, and other botanical oils. One such product is Country Fare Super Repellent Multi-Mix Blend (known as Deer Solution in a previous incarnation). It has a very nice, spicy smell, but you still won't want to get it on your clothes or skin just because it's very strong. For obvious reasons, you may wish to use this kind of product for spraying gardens and container plantings near outdoor seating areas or underneath windows left open in summer.

A very different kind of product to help control deer browsing during the growing season is Milorganite. Milorganite is actually a granular fertilizer made from sewage sludge. (Yes, really: the "Mil" refers to Milwaukee, Wisconsin. I've heard that a number of other municipalities offer similar products for sale, available locally or regionally.) When dry, Milorganite has an odor that is strong but not too unpleasant. Although the product wasn't developed as a deer repellent, it was observed that deer appear to avoid areas in which Milorganite has been applied. If you broadcast it lightly in your garden (that is, take a handful and swing your arm while letting the product slip through your fingers, spraying it thinly), you probably won't notice the smell when you walk through your garden, but the product will usually repel deer for about two to three weeks. Rain or irrigation washes it into the soil, so you have to reapply it fairly often in rainy areas.

Applying Milorganite to an ordinary residential landscape should take no more than fifteen minutes, so it's a very fast, easy, and inexpensive method of keeping deer away, and you are providing your plants with a small amount of fertilizer each time you do it.

Because Milorganite does have a moderate smell, store it in a shed rather than your garage if possible, fold the bag over to "seal" it after you've opened it, and keep the unused portion of the product absolutely dry. If a large volume of Milorganite gets wet, well, you'll be avoiding that area for a while!

Some people are uncomfortable using Milorganite because of its heavy-metal content and perhaps just because of distaste about what it is. If you have questions about Milorganite, I suggest you visit the company's website and also explore online gardener forums, searching specifically for comments about Milorganite (or your local alternative).

Some product names you might encounter in your search for a suitable deer repellent include Bobbex, Ropel, Deer Away, Deer Off, Deer Scram, Deer Chaser, Not Tonight Deer, Plantskydd, and Hinder. Some of these are also supposed to discourage browsing by rabbits and by rodents such as groundhogs, or they come in special formulations (Bobbex-R is an example) intended to repel rodents as well as deer.

Other things commonly said to repel deer include human hair, bar-soap sachets, dried blood (aka bloodmeal), and human urine and the urine of various predators such as coyotes. I've read about people getting bags of hair clippings from beauty salons to spread in their gardens, but I've never tried it. I have used soap sachets to good effect. To do this yourself, just buy any inexpensive soap, cut it into chunks, and place each chunk in a small drawstring muslin bag of the sort you can purchase at natural food stores, craft stores, or tea shops. (An online search for "muslin bag" will give you some mail-order options if you can't find them locally.) Close the bags and hang them from stakes or from the branches of any woody plants in your perennial garden.

My understanding is that it's the animal fat (otherwise known as tallow) in bar soap that repels deer. If that's the case, then obviously only soaps that contain animal fat will work. The vast majority of cheap soaps on store shelves do contain tallow, so don't buy expensive soaps (which may *not* contain tallow) for this purpose. Also, the fragrance of the soap doesn't appear to matter, despite legends about the efficacy of Irish Spring. Just buy the cheapest soap you can find.

I use soap sachets only in winter to discourage deer from getting into the habit of crossing garden areas I don't want them to browse during the growing season, and this seems to work. Although soap sachets apparently are effective at halting deer browsing of bark on woody plants year-round, I doubt that soap alone would prevent browsing of tender, succulent growth on herbaceous plants in spring and summer when the temptation is enormous.

Dried blood is a by-product of the meat processing industry. It's applied the same way as Milorganite and is also a nitrogen fertilizer. In my experience, one gets the same results as the other. Many people find the idea of using dried blood kind of creepy, but if they knew what went into most fertilizers, they wouldn't single out dried blood to shudder at!

Finally, there's the topic of . . . urine. The jokes are endless in the gardening community about wives sending their husbands out into the garden to empty their bladders at night around the perimeter of the garden. I have no personal experience with this method of deer deterrence, but many people swear by it. You'll have to find out for yourself, because my husband doesn't follow my orders and I'm not about to pee in my garden! As for the use of animal urines, my understanding is that the urine is collected from captive animals, and I cannot condone that practice or the use of products obtained in that manner.

The key to using a product (as opposed to, say, a fence—more on that to come) to deter deer browsing is *regular application*! If you miss just one, you may see a lot of deer damage. *Whatever deer repellent you consider using, inquire about its active ingredient, and make sure you understand if and how the product has to be mixed, how it has to be applied, and how often it has to be reapplied* so you understand exactly what you need to do and when.

Whenever people have said to me, "I tried such-and-such deer repellent, and the deer ate everything anyway," I have always asked whether the repellent was reapplied at the frequency required; in nearly every case, the response was, "Well, no, maybe I did miss an application or two." The fact is, if you don't have time to apply a deer repellent, you don't have time for a garden. Applying deer repellent is the *least* time-consuming task among the multitude of chores a garden requires.

A few last tips about deer repellents. If they are liquid, they must be stored over winter where they will not freeze. This is true for *all* liquid garden products, whatever their purpose. Liquid repellents that freeze and then thaw may not have the same consistency they did originally, which may prevent them from passing through sprayers without clogging. It may also diminish their efficacy by causing chemical changes. Put a note in your calendar to take all liquid garden products inside to a frost-free area at the appropriate time, and you won't have to replace those products in spring.

Also, at least initially, it might be more effective to apply repellents to your entire garden rather than just the plants you expect deer to browse. I know of a garden that had a severe deer-browsing problem. One year, the gardener sprayed all the "usual suspects" (hostas and daylilies, primarily) with deer repellent in May, once those plants were mostly leafed out. What did the deer do? Within a week, they'd sampled everything *else*, including many plants considered reliably deer resistant: astilbe, goatsbeard, toad lily, purple coneflower, and more. That was the first time I'd ever heard of those plants being browsed! It was a real eye-opener.

The point of spraying everything is to train the deer to think that everything in your garden is unpalatable. After a year or two of that, try cutting back on the repellent, applying it to just the most tempting plants.

Fencing and More

Not all methods of deer deterrence involve the application of products to the garden. For example, there are devices that use motion sensors to spray water or produce noise to scare away deer, but I don't have enough experience with them to vouch for their usefulness.

Fencing, both stockade and electric, is an obvious way of preventing deer browsing by keeping deer off your property altogether. The upside of fencing is that you no longer have to be tied to a schedule of applying and reapplying a product. The downside is cost, not to mention the fact that stockade and electric fencing aren't permitted in all communities and do tend to give houses the look of fortresses or prisons.

A very effective method of keeping deer away, but one available to only a few of us, is a free-running dog. A fenceless boundary (also known as "invisible containment") that allows your dog to pester deer whenever they approach your property line, day or night, will effectively keep deer away. There are many obvious downsides to this solution: not everyone can or wants to own a dog; not everyone can have a fenceless boundary; giving your dog access to the outdoors at night when deer are most likely to be active may not be safe for the dog because of larger predators, such as coyotes; a dog chasing deer at night will probably bark, irritating the neighbors; and the problems go on and on. However, for a very small number of people, the family dog may be the only deer deterrent necessary.

I should add that *your* presence on and around your property daily is a strong deer deterrent. All wild animals seem to be cognizant of the habits of people if they must live close to them. In my area, I have observed that the owners of weekend homes usually have a much more severe problem with deer browsing than do year-round residents.

Although some deer will come rather close to people who are sitting quietly outside, no wild deer will stick around when approached by a person waving his or her arms and making loud noises. Let deer know that you don't want them in your garden, and they'll get the message. Of course, this alone won't do the job unless you're prepared to keep sentinel 24/7, but every little bit helps!

Admittedly, finding the right combination of methods to control deer browsing can be a frustrating process. Whatever you decide to try, be aware that one method by itself may not be enough (except in the case of fencing). You may have to use multiple products, or you may have to alternate methods, switching between different products or devices to keep deer "on their toes." Only experimentation will tell. *Above all, you must start early in the growing season and keep at it.*

Before we leave the topic of deer, I want to strongly discourage all gardeners from planting hostas, daylilies (not a shade plant, anyway), and other plants for which deer have a strong preference by roadsides! Attracting deer to areas alongside automobile traffic creates a terrible hazard for both deer and people. For planting in roadside areas, there are plenty of plants that deer are likely to ignore.

MANAGING SHADY AREAS

It's worth spending a moment talking about how to manage shady areas. Shade cast by trees is something that can be controlled or even eliminated (although I strongly urge you to think twice about the latter course). Your options for controlling shade are basically three: (1) thinning the whole planting (that is, selectively removing some trees); (2) thinning the crowns of the trees without removing any entirely; and (3) limbing up branches.

Obviously, thinning an entire planting will reduce shade in a fairly permanent way. If some trees in a grove are sickly and likely to die soon anyway, removing them makes sense for multiple reasons. Many homeowners in the Northeast have had to remove ash trees in the past decade or so because the trees have been in decline.

Thinning the crowns of trees will temporarily lighten shade, but in the long run, this does not effectively improve gardening conditions because eventually, the trees will replace the growth cut out, and the shade will once again increase. However, there might be other good reasons for thinning the crowns of trees, including crossing branches or limbs that are unhealthy.

Removing trees and thinning crowns are operations that should be performed only by a licensed and insured arborist because these are dangerous jobs that require skill, knowledge, and appropriate equipment.

Limbing up branches is the practice of removing just the lowermost branches of a tree—ideally a very small number of branches—in order to create a certain look, to enable walking upright underneath, to eliminate conflicts with neighboring structures or traffic on paths and driveways, or to slightly reduce shade. This is not unhealthy for the tree (if done correctly) and can solve a lot of problems. Many trees, especially deciduous trees, naturally limb themselves up as they age, so the practice is not even particularly "unnatural."

Limbing up is something that many homeowners can do without having to call in an arborist. Describing the process is beyond the scope of this book, and if it's not something you already know how to do, then for your sake and the tree's sake, you should probably call in someone more qualified to do the work. But it is something that many homeowners can learn how to do.

Now a word about a much more complicated issue: the root zone of trees. Trees, of course, have roots. The closer to trees you try to garden, the more you will encounter their roots. It's important to disturb tree roots as little as possible. Doing otherwise can harm a tree's health or even kill it.

Mature trees sometimes have exposed roots radiating out from the trunk. Under certain circumstances, you can add soil to such areas to provide a root zone for smaller plants, but tree roots may encroach on this soil, eventually displacing the plants you put there. Adding more than a few inches of soil may even kill the tree. Use caution when covering tree roots with soil, and do so only after researching the tree well! It's always a good idea to consult an arborist before doing anything that could harm a major tree.

SOIL BASICS

When you build a house, you start with the foundation. When you build a garden, you do the same . . . but in the case of a garden, the foundation is the soil. Unless your lot just naturally has deep, fluffy soil, you may need to do something to improve it.

The subject of soils could fill a book all its own, but gardeners don't need to know more than a few basics. In hilly or mountainous areas, soils are frequently *thin*. Thin doesn't mean that the soil isn't fertile—it just means that there isn't a lot of it. Soil washes off hillsides over time, so it never has a chance to accumulate to any great depth in hilly areas. This is one reason that exposed ledge (bedrock) is such a common sight on New England hillsides despite the fact that new soil is being generated all the time, as vegetation decomposes on the forest floor, and as rocks weather. You may find deep soils in major valleys, such as the Connecticut River Valley, because valleys are where the soil that washes off hillsides goes!

People often confuse thin soil with *poor* or *infertile* soil. Poor soils are those that have few nutrients—or at least few nutrients in a form readily available to plants—regardless of how deep they are. Most woodland soils are naturally fertile enough to support most shade plants, although they may be hard to garden in (a different thing altogether) because they're filled with stones or tree roots.

Many soils are categorized as either *clayey* or *sandy*. Clayey and sandy are self-descriptive terms: clayey soils (or just *clay* soils) have lots of clay particles in them, and sandy soils have lots of sand in them.

Clay soils are heavy and hard to dig, and once they are wet, they may stay wet longer than is ideal for plant growth. Plant roots can have difficulty penetrating them, although once a plant is established in a clay soil, it may do quite well.

The good thing about clay soils is that they are generally better than sandy soils at hanging on to nutrients. However, the nutrients that are present may not be available to plants for reasons that are beyond the scope of this book to explain.

Sandy soils are just the opposite. If you've ever been on a beach, you know that water drains very quickly from pure sand. Soils with too much sand tend to dry out more quickly than most plants prefer. What's more, because sand contains no nutrients, sandy soils tend to be poor.

Not surprisingly, sandy soils are often found in coastal areas, but it's possible to find clay soils along the coast and sandy soils inland, so you should always have your soil tested to determine its type. Ask your state's Cooperative Extension service how to have your soil tested. Soil testing for gardening purposes is generally very affordable.

I would be remiss if I didn't mention an obvious, but fairly unimportant quality of many Northeast soils, especially in upland areas: they are *rocky*. The rocks in our soils are simply an inevitable consequence of the fact that much of the Northeast is covered by an eroding mountain range: the Appalachians. The Berkshires, the Green Mountains, the White Mountains, and most other mountains in this region are all part of the greater Appalachian chain. Small rocks in the soil are a nuisance, but they don't really affect plant growth substantially and certainly don't signify any kind of soil deficiency. Of course, large rocks below the soil surface *can* create an unfriendly environment for plants by limiting rooting room, so you may need to remove some rocks from your soil. If your soil is extremely rocky, then passing it through a hardware cloth screen is probably the fastest way to make it garden fit.

Improving Your Soil

So far, we've identified some common qualities of soils in this region and the problems associated with them. If your existing soil isn't too awful, you always have the option of going with the flow, and limiting your garden to plants that can live with what you've got. But that might not result in a very satisfying garden. What if you need to make some alterations?

If your soil is thin, you need to add more soil by purchasing a high-quality screened topsoil or a screened topsoil-compost mix (screening removes significant rocks). Topsoil is not a soil amendment. You use topsoil when you don't have much soil; you use an amendment when you have enough soil, but your soil is of inadequate quality. When you add topsoil, you can't just dump it on top of the existing soil and be done with it. The topsoil should be incorporated into the top few inches of the existing soil using a tiller or other equipment, or by hand. If the soil is on any significant grade, it should also be lightly compacted to prevent it from washing away. Always buy soil from a reputable retailer, always inspect topsoil before purchasing it because there are differences in quality, and never consider using "fill" as a cheaper alternative. If you are unsure how to evaluate the quality of a topsoil, your local Cooperative Extension office may be able to help by testing a sample and providing you with an analysis.

If your soil is either too clayey or too sandy, you can improve it by adding a high-quality soil amendment. An amendment is something that is high in mostly decomposed organic matter. Its primary purpose is not to add nutrients, but to make the soil more *friable*. To be very non-technical, friability is the crumbliness of soil when you handle it.

When you amend a clay soil, you "unlock" its preexisting fertility, allow plant roots to penetrate more easily, and permit water to drain at a more ideal rate. Amending a sandy soil not only makes it retain water a little better, but also improves its fertility.

Most plants like conditions (soil quality, air temperature, soil moisture—just about everything, really) that are moderate, and amendment will take both clay soils *and* sandy soils in that direction.

Earlier I noted that the primary purpose of an amendment is not to add nutrients, but rather to make soil more friable. However, virtually all amendments contain some nutrients, and this turns out to be important. The fine line gardeners must walk is this: how to improve the friability of the soil without overloading it with nutrients that might become a source of water pollution. Why an excess of nutrients is dangerous is explained in the chapter titled Fertilization, where nutrients are discussed in more detail.

So, gardeners should choose soil amendments carefully. One amendment to consider is compost. For many years, it was truly difficult to find commercial sources of compost. Fortunately, that situation is changing. As the benefits of compost become more widely known, it's getting easier and easier to find compost for purchase, both by the bag and in bulk.

Compost is excellent for improving friability, but its nutrient content is variable, and that's an issue. The problem, basically, is that there isn't just one thing called "compost." Commercial compost may be made from any combination of autumn leaves or animal manures or grass clippings or tree bark or a host

How Much Compost (or Mulch) Do I Need?

Let's assume that you need either compost or mulch for your garden. If you require only a small quantity, you can get away with buying a bagged product. But if you need a lot, it's much more economical to buy in bulk, by the cubic yard. When sold this way, garden products such as compost and mulch are called *bulk goods*. Although retailers usually just drop the "cubic" part of "cubic yard" and refer to "yards" of compost or other bulk materials, it's still a measure of volume, not length.

A cubic yard is the volume contained in a space measuring 1 yard by 1 yard by 1 yard. Because that's the same as a space measuring 3 feet by 3 feet by 3 feet, a cubic yard contains 27 (3 by 3 by 3) cubic feet. If you spread out a cubic yard of mulch or compost on the ground at a depth of exactly 1 foot, it will cover an area measuring 27 square feet. If you spread it out at one-half the depth (6 inches), it will cover an area twice as large, or 54 square feet. And if you spread it out at a depth of 3 inches (one-fourth of 1 foot), it will cover an area four times as large, or 108 square feet. At a depth of 2 inches, a cubic yard would cover 162 square feet.

To calculate how many yards of any bulk good you need, first measure your garden. If it doesn't have nice, straight lines to make measuring easy, just make your best estimate. Come up with a rough square footage for your garden.

Now, decide how deeply you'll be spreading your bulk material. A typical depth for mulch is 2 inches. Using the example just given, you know that you need to order 1 cubic yard of mulch for every 162 square feet of garden space. If your garden measures 1,050 square feet, divide 1,050 by 162. You'll get 6.48 for an answer. Round up that number to the nearest whole number, and you'll get 7 yards. Many retailers of bulk goods will let you order half yards, so in this example, you could also round up just slightly to 6 and one-half yards, but they don't cut it any closer than that.

of other ingredients. Depending on its composition, compost may contain enough nutrients to be a pollution source if applied in large quantities. Yet, large quantities might be needed to improve friability enough to make a difference to your plants.

There is an alternative to compost, but it's not for everyone. Aged horse manure is also an excellent soil amendment. How old is aged? Generally, one year old or more. If it smells like manure, it's not old enough. If it doesn't smell like manure, but smells more like soil, and if it's very crumbly, it's old enough. Other animal manures are also good as long as they are well aged and from noncarnivorous animals.

In contrast to compost, I know of no commercial sources of aged manure (although it's almost sure to be a component of any compost you buy). That means getting aged manure directly from farms. There is a downside to this. Because the farm isn't a commercial compost-producing operation, piles of manure aren't necessarily turned, sterilized, or otherwise treated. With manure from a farm, you get what you get, and you can't expect any particular standard of quality or uniformity. The manure may be full of weed seeds or even some farm trash. The upside is that it's probably free, especially if you haul it away instead of asking the farmer to bring it to you.

All in all, if you can possibly afford commercial compost, use that in preference to free manure unless you are *very* confident of the manure's quality.

Leaf mold (shredded leaves that have aged for six months or so) and aged sawdust (but not from pressure-treated wood, and not fresh sawdust!) can be used in larger quantities than some composts, but they aren't usually available commercially. Sphagnum peat is another option without a lot of nutrient content, but it lowers soil acidity, may alter the soil's wettability, and is prohibitively expensive for amending an entire garden. Some people also regard sphagnum peat as a nonrenewable resource and therefore avoid it. (I use it only for preparing planting holes for acid-loving plants, and I use it only in conjunction with compost, not on its own.)

So, what's a gardener to do? I can't give you a rule of thumb because soils vary too much for one blanket recommendation. Instead, your best bet is to get your soil tested, asking for recommendations to improve soil structure and discussing the results, if necessary, with a local Cooperative Extension educator or soil scientist.

If you're thinking of adding commercial compost (or any other amendment that might be high in nutrients), it should be tested, too. Actually, commercial compost suppliers should be having their product tested independently, and they should be willing to share the results with you. Alternatively, you can do your own testing. Contact your local Cooperative Extension office for instructions because testing methods vary by state. With both soil test and compost test results, you'll have plenty of information at your disposal for the Cooperative Extension educator to use to advise you.

Keep in mind that if your soil is such that it requires a large quantity of an amendment to improve its friability meaningfully, you can do the work in multiple stages over the course of a year or more, incorporating small amounts of amendment each time and then letting earthworms and microbes go to work for several months before repeating the procedure.

Soil amendments must be thoroughly incorporated into the top foot of soil. What's more, because tillers don't penetrate that deeply, in order to be done right, adding a soil amendment really should be done manually, by turning and mixing the soil and the amendment with a shovel. This is one job where you don't want to try to cut corners. If you have to hire help to get the job done, do it. Money spent at this stage will come back to you in spades later.

When I give talks on shade gardening, at this point someone in the audience always raises a hand to ask anxiously, "Do you have to amend the soil *before* planting?" Alas, yes . . . unless you're willing to empty your garden of plants and then put them all back in after the amendment is complete.

If your garden is already established and you've come to the conclusion that your soil needs amendment, your options are limited. You can deconstruct your garden one small area at a time, replacing the plants after improving the soil. Or, you can embark on a long-term effort to improve the soil slowly through judicious mulching and turning of soil where you can do so without damaging plants, letting nature take its slow course toward eventual improvement. Slow improvement is better than none.

pH

A basic trait of soils is pH (pronounced "pee-aitch," just as if you were reading the letters). It's a measurement of acidity or alkalinity. Though you really don't need to understand what pH is, you'll want to have at least a passing understanding of how plants react to it.

The pH measurement scale runs from 0 to 14. A soil with a pH of 7 is called *neutral*; a soil with a pH lower than 7 is called *acidic* or *sour*; and a soil with a pH higher than 7 is called *alkaline* or *sweet*. Although soils in the Northeast are generally acidic for a number of reasons, there are many isolated pockets of neutral or alkaline soil, especially in areas underlain by limestone. Don't assume you have acid soil! A standard soil test will include a pH measurement.

Like many other things about soils, pH can be changed—but only temporarily. Products that will lower soil pH (make it more acidic) include soil sulphur and fertilizers such as Holly-tone and Miracid that are formulated for acid-loving plants.

Lime is the product most commonly used to raise soil pH (make it more alkaline). Have you ever wondered why you're told to lime your lawn? It's because turf grasses prefer soil that is more alkaline than the soils that occur naturally in much of the Northeast. Liming the soil creates better growing conditions for grass, helping it to be healthier, but the effect isn't permanent. The pH of your soil will eventually migrate back to its natural state. That's why you have to lime your lawn repeatedly.

The same is true of soil acidifiers: you must reapply them regularly in order to maintain the artificially lowered pH.

Most ornamental perennials want a soil in the neutral range, which is generally considered a pH between 6 and 8. If your soil doesn't fall into this range, you may find that certain plants won't perform well for you even if all other garden conditions are favorable. In that case, you'll need specialized advice from your local Cooperative Extension office or other resources.

MULCH

There is a common misconception that shady areas don't need to be mulched as much as sunny ones because they aren't exposed to the drying effects of direct sunlight. In fact, shady areas can be even drier than sunny areas because of competition from tree roots and other factors. It's wise to mulch all of your gardens.

Shredded leaves make an excellent and inexpensive mulch. I know some gardeners who collect their *neighbors'* leaves in order to have more to shred for their own gardens! There are both electric- and gas-powered shredders to get the job done. The best tip I can offer is to shred leaves in batches, raking them up soon after they fall and when they are dry and still largely intact. Do an hour of shredding every weekend through autumn rather than trying to do it all at once after all the leaves have fallen. You'll just have a mess on your hands by that point. And although you can try to rake up last year's leaves in spring and then shred them, they'll probably be soggy and matted and won't shred as well (but they'll still be fine for composting.) If you have a time crunch in autumn, one thing you can do is bag autumn leaves and store them in a dry place for shredding at a later date.

Another choice for mulching your shady perennial garden is compost, especially if you can find a commercial source that is low in nutrients. Most gardeners have never used or thought of compost as a mulch. Because for many years it was nearly impossible to find large quantities of compost to purchase, gardeners got into the habit of mulching with what *was* available, which was a variety of products made from waste tree bark from the timber industry. The vast majority of mulches available at garden centers are still one form or another of processed bark.

Bark can be processed in several ways to make mulches that vary from large "nuggets" to a fine, shredded fluff. Bark mulches provide a good barrier to help prevent the erosive action of rainfall, and they help minimize evaporation of moisture from the soil. They can also look very attractive, and are sometimes offered dyed, for those who aren't happy with strictly natural tones.

One of the main reasons I'm recommending shredded leaves or compost as mulch—in preference to bark products—is that this book focuses on perennial gardens, not landscapes composed of trees and shrubs. Compared with perennial gardens, trees and shrubs require very different maintenance regimens. Once you plant a tree or shrub, you may prune it and do lots of things to its branches, but you rarely disturb the soil around it except minimally, to remove weeds. Most perennials, on the other hand, require division. They can "migrate" in a way that most woody plants do not. As a consequence, the soil in perennial gardens is frequently disturbed as plants are lifted and divided or rearranged.

This difference in maintenance regimens is the reason I find shredded leaves and compost to be the best mulches for perennial gardens, though a bark mulch may be a perfectly good choice for woody plantings. If you incorporate large quantities of undecomposed bark mulch into the soil of your perennial garden when performing routine maintenance, you can create a temporary (but still potentially serious) problem called *nitrogen deficiency*. Essentially, by putting undecomposed organic matter into soil, you provide soil microbes with a great big meal. The "digestion" process requires nitrogen, and because that nitrogen isn't in the bark mulch, it comes from the soil. As the food source dwindles, this nitrogen is returned to the soil, but the temporary lack of it may have set back your garden plants because nitrogen is so critical to plant growth. If you use compost or shredded leaves as mulch in your perennial garden, you avoid this problem.

Another difficulty with bark mulches is the way they are typically used, or rather, the way they are typically *mis*used. Most gardeners want the mulch in their gardens to look "fresh" all the time, but any bark mulch will begin to weather the day it is applied. Soon it loses its fresh look, yet it hasn't really decomposed. When a gardener then applies more bark mulch over top of the old, a problem can arise. When bark mulch is piled on too thickly, it decomposes at an ever-slower rate. Although you might think that this is a good thing—after all, you're getting more "life" out of your mulch—it's not! The mulch can form a crust that actually prevents enough water and air from reaching the soil, and that's not a healthy situation for plants.

Tip: Buying and Applying Bulk Compost or Mulch

When you have compost or any other bulk material delivered to your house, it will usually arrive by dump truck. Select a spot for the product to be dumped where the driver can raise the bed of the truck without hitting overhanging branches, electrical lines, or other wires. Before the driver arrives, spread a large tarp where the material is to be deposited, weighing down the edges with rocks if the wind threatens to carry it away. Cleanup of the area will be much easier than if you'd had the material dumped directly on your driveway or on a verge—all you have to do is sweep off the tarp, dry it, and fold it for storage.

Avoid dumping bulk goods on your lawn if possible, regardless of whether a tarp goes under them. You can't leave a heavy pile of mulch or compost on grass for more than a couple of days, so you are forced to move it quickly. If the weather doesn't cooperate and you can't spread your materials for a week, then you may have a patch of dead grass underneath.

Lastly, if it rains before you finish the job, cover any materials waiting to be spread with another tarp—and make sure there are no holes in it. Moving wet mulch or compost is easily three times the work as moving the same materials dry.

Unless you own your own truck and don't mind filling it up with dirty materials, you'll want to have purchases of bulk materials delivered to your property. The delivery fee, usually modest, will save you a great deal of time and aggravation, so consider it money well spent.

You *want* mulch to decompose! I know that's a tough idea for many people to accept after years of thinking about mulch in a very different way—as a sort of semipermanent "set of clothes" on the garden. But consider this: in a woodland, nature replenishes organic matter every year when trees lose their leaves or needles, which fall to the ground and begin to decompose, forming a natural mulch. It isn't necessarily good for the mulch you put on your perennial garden to last longer than nature's mulch does: one season. This is one reason that my first recommendation for mulch is shredded leaves. Plus, it solves the leaf-disposal problem.

So, rather than judge a mulch based on how long it lasts, judge it based on how healthy an environment it creates for your garden plants. These are two entirely different—and sometimes diametrically opposed—things. Shredded leaves or low-nutrient compost as a mulch will create the best growing environment for your perennial garden, and because these materials decompose quickly, they must be reapplied every year. I know that having to do something *more* often might seem undesirable, but giving plants the environment they need will pay off in the long run by reducing failure.

Another misconception about mulch in general, whether shredded leaves, compost, bark, or another material, is that it will stop weeds from growing. It's true that mulch will lessen the number of *seeds* that *germinate*, but it will do little to stop established perennial weeds from emerging underneath. Established perennial weeds will simply come up through any kind of mulch you put down, just as your garden plants do. Perennial weeds must be pulled up by the roots or they will return again and again.

What's more, although mulch will lessen the number of weed seeds that germinate and grow through the mulch, it won't eliminate them. What it *will* do is make them much easier to pull, because they will root largely in the mulch rather than in the denser soil underneath. No matter what kind of mulch you use or how much you put down, *you will still have to weed*.

The ideal depth for a layer of mulch is 2 inches, although depth is more critical for bark mulches than for shredded leaves or compost. Putting down a thicker layer of a bark mulch in an attempt to "smother" weeds is not beneficial to your garden plants for the reasons already given: the mulch can start to block water and air, leading to unhealthful conditions.

The main functional disadvantage of shredded leaves and compost, when compared to most bark mulches, is that they can be more easily displaced by water on a slope. However, significantly sloped areas are not appropriate for cultivated gardens in the first place. They may be suitable for *naturalizing*, but not for intensively maintained gardens. Significantly sloped areas should be left undisturbed, or else terraced with retaining walls, which effectively reduces them to a series of areas each having negligible slope; in this case, the lightweight nature of shredded leaves or compost as mulch is not an issue. And when you naturalize a woodland area, there's no need to mulch, because presumably you'll be letting the leaves lie where they fall in autumn.

FERTILIZATION

If you begin caring for your shade garden as I've suggested, you may find that you don't need to fertilize. There are a couple of reasons for this. First, when compost and shredded leaves (especially compost) are used as mulch, they also act as a fertilizer. Second, the plants recommended in this book are not so-called heavy feeders. Their nutritional needs are ordinary, and most soils can supply them.

Fertilizer isn't a fix-all. It won't make up for too little light or water, inadequate soil preparation, or a lack of maintenance. It can help only if all the other conditions in a garden are as they should be.

Nonetheless, there may be occasions when fertilization is necessary. In that case, this "intro to fertilizer" should help you select the one you need.

Fertilizers are typically labeled prominently with three numbers. These numbers stand for the nitrogen, phosphorus, and potassium content of the product, in that order. The order never varies. These numbers are often referred to as the fertilizer's NPK, because on the periodic table of elements, nitrogen is designated as N, phosphorus as P, and potassium as K.

Nitrogen, phosphorus, and potassium are so essential for plant growth that they are referred to as primary *macronutrients*. All other nutrients are considered either secondary macronutrients or *micronutrients*.

Gardeners are sometimes unsure of how to express themselves when shopping for a fertilizer, so here's an example. If you were at your local garden center, you might say to the salesperson helping you, "I need a fertilizer with an NPK of three five seven," and this would appear on the fertilizer's label as 3–5–7.

A typical fertilizer formulation is 10–10–10, meaning that it contains equal amounts of the three primary macronutrients. Miracle-Gro is a well-known product that comes in a 10–10–10 formulation, although it comes in other formulations, too (that is, there are several Miracle-Gro products, not just one). A 10–10–10 fertilizer is considered a general-purpose fertilizer suitable for most needs.

Plants use nitrogen mainly for leafy growth. A plant lacking nitrogen might be stunted or might exhibit chlorosis (extreme yellowing of the leaves).

Although it's essential for your plants to have adequate nitrogen for their growth, an excess is undesirable. Nitrogen runoff from lawns and gardens is a major source of water pollution. Soil can't "store" nitrogen, so anything beyond a moderate amount is a waste; plants can't take it up before rain leaches it away. For this reason, use great caution when applying a fertilizer containing nitrogen near any stream, river, or body of water.

Phosphorus is critical for flowering, and that's why many fertilizers meant to encourage heavy blooming will have a high P number. But remember that most perennials bloom only for two to three weeks anyway. They don't need to be showered in phosphorus for the whole growing season in order to bloom well. Still, you may want to give annuals some supplemental phosphorus because they bloom for months at a time.

Finally, there's potassium. Plants need potassium for a wide range of functions, but you'll probably never find yourself applying a fertilizer specifically for its potassium content unless a soil test indicates that you should.

Not all fertilizers contain *all* the primary macronutrients, and this may seem slightly confusing. Any one of the NPK numbers may be 0. Bone meal, for example—a traditional bulb fertilizer—contains no nitrogen and no potassium, but is rich in phosphorus. A bag of bone meal might be labeled 0–10–0.

Probably the greatest confusion about fertilizers revolves around the two words *organic* and *inorganic*. The word *organic* as applied to fertilizer doesn't mean quite the same thing that most people mean when they talk about, say, organic food.

An organic fertilizer is one that must be broken down chemically in the soil before its nutrients can be taken up by plants. An inorganic fertilizer is typically one whose nutrients are available to plants immediately.

You're probably wondering what determines which kind to use. It depends on the desired effect. An inorganic fertilizer is the best choice when a plant is suffering from a deficiency and needs quick help. It's also my choice for use on annuals because you want them to start flowering quickly after planting. In contrast, you use an organic fertilizer when you want food to be released to your plants over time, providing a steady stream of nutrients. Sometimes the appropriate feeding regimen is a combination of organic and inorganic fertilizers. If you have any doubt about whether to fertilize your garden or what to use, your best resource is your local Cooperative Extension office. Depending on the exact nature of your question, the staff may need you to have a soil test before they can make a recommendation, and they should also be able to advise you on how to have that done.

The most important piece of advice I can offer about fertilizer is to always use the appropriate formulation for the situation! If you apply a fertilizer with substances your plants don't need, not only are you paying for something that will go to waste, but you might be contributing to water pollution. If you use a general-purpose fertilizer at all, use it in moderation. Always follow label instructions when applying fertilizer, and never assume that more is better. Lastly, before you apply any fertilizer, I encourage you to think carefully about where the water that runs off your property goes. Protecting water resources is a basic responsibility we all share.

PLANT GALLERY

FINALLY, HERE IT IS—the heart of this book! The Plant Gallery features the plants I most highly recommend for landscaping use in the shade in the Northeast. In an earlier section, About the Plants Recommended in this Book, I listed the criteria I used to decide which plants to include and which plants to exclude. Because it's not humanly possible to be absolutely objective, I acknowledge that to some degree, my choices reflect my personal tastes and biases. Likewise, they reflect my imperfect experience—because no one's experience is ever perfect.

Other people would undoubtedly come up with a slightly different list, perhaps complaining that I overlooked some favorite plant. I can only reiterate that my choices were driven mainly by a desire to help people avoid the frustration that results from making less than ideal choices. So I was fairly aggressive in excluding plants I think might become problematic for people who just want a good garden but don't necessarily dream about spending all their time gardening.

A note about bloom times: even in the limited region covered by this book, local conditions vary a lot. My comments on bloom time are based on observations made at locations across northwest Connecticut. They will shift somewhat depending on readers' exact latitude and proximity to the ocean or other major bodies of water such as Long Island Sound, as well as metropolitan areas such as New York City and Boston.

My principal reference book—the one I used to verify terminology and more—was the *American Horticultural Society A–Z Encyclopedia of Garden Plants.* I recommend that every serious homeowner-gardener invest in at least one such book. It will serve you well for decades and never become completely or even mostly obsolete.

The plants profiled here are organized in a novel way. Most gardening books present plants in an alphabetical list by Latin name, but I took a different approach. First, I divided plants into two broad groups: (1) those that will grow well in deeper shade, and (2) those that perform satisfactorily in light shade only. I did this so that readers with very challenging conditions could find what they need without having to sift through descriptions of plants they ultimately couldn't grow.

Then, within the section on plants for deeper shade, I have presented them in this order:

1. Backbone Plants	4. Bulbs
2. Accent Plants	5. Ferns for Border Use
3. Spring Ephemerals	6. Ferns Best for Naturalizing

Although all ferns are backbone plants, it's useful to group them separately because we tend to use them differently from flowering plants in the garden. (If you need to, use the index to refer to earlier sections of this book where terms such as *backbone plant* and *naturalizing* are defined.)

I repeat the same order in the section on plants for light shade only, with the exception that ferns are omitted because they are all suitable for deeper shade.

This is followed by a section on plants for special situations, in which entries are further subdivided into perennials for naturalizing, perennials for shady rock gardens, and perennials for cool, moist, but well-drained spots.

What's the benefit of this approach? Well, as one example, if you're a gardener with very shady conditions, all the information you need is in one place: the section on plants for deeper shade. You don't have to search through all the entries looking for the ones that apply to you.

If you're a gardener with lighter shade, or a mix of types of shade, you should be able to use all the plants presented in both sections, because a plant that will grow well in very shady conditions will also grow well in light shade.

And although plants that I think are suitable *only* for naturalizing are in a special section, plants that *can* be used for naturalizing appear throughout the Plant Gallery. The rule of thumb is simply this: *any native plant is suitable for naturalizing an area that offers the conditions in which it wants to grow, as long as you feel you can contain it on your own property.* I do not recommend using nonnative plants for naturalizing; past experience has shown that too many of them eventually become the focus of expensive statewide or regional eradication efforts. A list of plants native to eastern North America appears at the back of this book.

In the same way, the short section on perennials for rock gardens highlights plants I consider suitable *only* for rock gardens. Many other plants in this book are also suitable for rock gardens, but they appear elsewhere because they have broader garden application. At the end of the Plant Gallery, you'll find several lists (such as plants suitable for shady rock gardens) intended to help gardeners with specific needs quickly identify the plants that can best meet those needs without having to sift through every entry here.

A quick observation: because plants like to defy categorization, it's hard to group them by function, as I've done. I've grouped them according to the ways in which I think most people will (or sometimes *should*) use them, but that doesn't mean their role in every garden is determined always and forever. When in doubt about how best to use a plant, experiment, but try out your idea on a small plot of soil before committing to a large area.

The spring ephemerals presented a special challenge. For instance, it's hard to say whether trillium should be considered a spring ephemeral. Its leaves usually persist until late summer, but because it's unlikely to be visible in the garden by Labor Day, I decided it was best to place trillium and similar plants in a category that didn't oversell their charms so readers wouldn't try them and then have an unpleasant surprise.

Lastly, it will undoubtedly occur to many readers that some well-known shade-adapted plants do not appear in this book. These include Japanese pachysandra (*Pachysandra terminalis*), lily-of-the-valley (*Convallaria majalis*), bishop's weed (*Aegopodium podograria*), and chameleon plant (*Houttuynia cordata* 'Chameleon'). They are excluded because they are all what I consider garden troublemakers: nonnative plants with serious potential for invasiveness and extreme resistance to eradication without the use of herbicides. For any situation in which you might consider growing one of these plants, a superior choice exists, and I want to encourage the use of the superior choice.

There are also a few plants I would *like* to have included in this book, but couldn't—either because I have not personally had enough success with them to recommend them to others, or because finding a source for them is extremely difficult or impossible. Lady's slipper orchids (*Cypripedium*) come to mind. I would dearly love to have them in my own garden, and I have tried to grow them, but I haven't yet found the key to success. Perhaps in a future edition . . .

PLANTS FOR DEEPER SHADE

Backbone Plants

If shade gardening were a board game, this would be the square that says "Start Here!" Remember that I've defined backbone plants as the ones I think have the greatest potential to perform well over a long season for most gardeners. I recommend you use backbone perennials to fill 75 to 80 percent of your garden.

Groundcovers are backbone plants pretty much by definition because you can fill 100 percent of a garden space with one of them and call it "job done." You'll find a list of plants that can be used as groundcovers with other plant lists at the end of this book.

Japanese Anemone · Tall Garden Anemone

Japanese anemone (*Anemone vitifolia* 'Robustissima') is among the last of the shade perennials to flower.

Tall garden anemones have two traits that distinguish them from the majority of shade plants. First, rather than blooming in spring, they start flowering in mid- to late summer and continue through early autumn. Second, they are relatively tall. These two qualities make them must-haves for any gardener attempting to create a long-season shade garden or any shade border with a lot of depth.

Although there are many such anemones (more on this to follow), 'Robustissima' is widely available and reliably cold hardy at least to Zone 5. 'Robustissima' has shell-pink flowers that float atop delicate, yet self-supporting stalks, and its leaves are like those of grapes; other cultivars can have deeper pink, white, or double flowers. Its foliage emerges later than that of most perennials, but it quickly grows into an attractive bushy clump 30 to 36 inches tall and about 24 inches wide. In flower, the plant can reach 5 feet in height.

Use 'Robustissima' in the middle of a deep border or at the rear of a narrow border. It will withstand moderate shade and still flower well. More sun (up to full sun) yields more flowers, but also encourages plants to spread in some gardens. One downside of tall garden anemones is that deer are also fans of their excellent qualities (which apparently include gastronomic ones) and will show their appreciation in the usual way!

Another downside of tall garden anemones is that they are a taxonomically confused lot, and it's rather a pity that the very first entry in this Plant Gallery has to give the lie to the idea that using Latin plant names allows you to identify plants with accuracy! Plants in this group may variously be identified as *A. x hybrida*, *A. japonica*, *A. tomentosa*, *A. vitifolia*, or *A. hupehensis* (this last is considered Chinese anemone). I usually call the whole lot Japanese anemones, as most gardeners do, and because these plants are almost always offered for sale as named cultivars, it really shouldn't matter to gardeners what the rest of the name says.

NOTE: Japanese anemones have a wide range of light tolerances. In other words, they can be grown in both shade and sun. As a shade plant, Japanese anemones are probably functionally hardy only to Zone 5. I'm aware that some people have successfully grown them as far north as Zone 3, but this is probably only possible in sun. Without sun, far-north gardeners may find it difficult to get Japanese anemones to bloom before frost cuts them down.

Aruncus spp. and cvs.

Goatsbeard

Varies | USDA ZONE

A mature goatsbeard (*A. dioicus*, Zone 3) is an impressive plant. It looks for all the world like a giant astilbe, and was once categorized in that genus. Checking in at a height of 48 inches tall and wide in leaf, and up to 6 feet tall in flower, it's one of the very biggest plants for the shady border.

Goatsbeard produces creamy-white blooms in mid-June. It has dense and attractive foliage, adding to its utility as a plant for anchoring the rear of a border. It can tolerate moist soils but does not require them, and has a tenacious, wide-spreading root system. Although it divides well, large, old plants can be hard to dig, especially if grown in clay.

A young goatsbeard plant will get tall quickly but will take several seasons to put on girth, so you may want to buy a half dozen plants and group them together as if they were one plant in order to get a "presence" from your goatsbeard sooner. The only problem with doing this is that goatsbeard is dioecious. As I explained earlier, that means that individuals are either male or female. If you have both in your garden, you may find yourself with lots of seedlings, so you may elect to grow just males or just females. (Males seem to me to have ever so slightly

Impressive in bloom, goatsbeard (*Aruncus dioicus*) is one of the largest plants available for the shady border.

better flowers, but the difference is negligible.) To tell males and females apart, you have to observe them after flowering. The females will set seed rapidly, but the flower stalks on males will just wither away.

Goatsbeard is one of those shade plants that can also be grown in full sun in the North. If you do that, I recommend pairing it with peonies and early roses.

Although goatsbeard is generally considered immune to disease and pests, I have witnessed leaf spotting and early, rapid defoliation from an unidentified fungal condition. If this is left untreated, the vitality of the plant will be compromised over the course of several years. Send a sample of any affected plant to Cooperative Extension for identification, and treat as recommended. Goatsbeard also seems susceptible to viruses. Cut out any foliage infected with a virus and discard it in the trash, not the compost.

On occasion you may see other types of goatsbeard offered at nurseries, including cultivars of *A. dioicus* (to me, these seem indistinguishable from the species); *A. aesthusifolius* (Zone 4), a truly dwarf species with finely cut leaves and a height in flower of only 12 inches; and hybrids that grow to an intermediate height of about 24 inches. *A. aesthusifolius* in particular is good for rock gardens in shade and sun, or it can be used at the very front of a lightly shaded border, where it will give the impression of a dwarf astilbe. It is very drought resistant.

USDA ZONE Varies

Asarum spp.

Wild Ginger

I can't say enough good things about native wild ginger (*Asarum canadense*, Zone 2). Hands down, it is my very favorite groundcover. Fast spreading yet easy to control, it produces a dense, 4-inch carpet of matte-green, heart-shaped leaves every spring. It is completely deciduous, dying back to the ground after frost. There is no need to remove the dead foliage, which will decay quickly on its own.

Some gardeners may be unfamiliar with the advantages a deciduous groundcover can offer. First, because their leaves die back every autumn and are completely replaced the following year, deciduous groundcovers look fresh and new in spring while evergreen groundcovers can look tattered after a rough winter.

Second, removing fallen tree leaves from a deciduous groundcover can be much easier than it is with an evergreen one. You can simply rake stray fallen leaves off a planting of native wild ginger in spring without getting your rake

Native wild ginger (*Asarum canadense*) is a superior native deciduous groundcover that can also be used in the border.

bound up in persistent stems, as happens with evergreen groundcovers. The wild ginger's own dead leaves (if any are left by that time) will detach and come away with the tree leaves without pulling the ginger roots out, as can happen with other deciduous groundcovers that root more shallowly or hang on to their old foliage more tenaciously. This makes it an ideal groundcover from a maintenance standpoint.

Native wild ginger is also a nice plant for the border, where large clumps at the very front of the garden look neat and lush in front of taller plants with contrasting foliage, such as hellebore. Like lady's mantle, ginger is an ideal neutral companion plant.

Native wild ginger's blossoms are insignificant, but interesting to look at once. To find them, look under the leaves at the crown of the plant, at ground level, soon after the foliage emerges. The fuzzy, ballooned sacs with three recurved, maroon "petals" are the flowers. Their unusual appearance gives rise to a picturesque but little-used common name: little brown jugs.

Formerly hard to find and expensive, native wild ginger has become much easier to acquire in recent years and more affordable, although it will still come at a premium compared to very cheap groundcovers such as Japanese pachysandra. Also worth growing in the border is European ginger, *A. europaeum* (Zone 4), which features waxy, leathery, dark-green leaves. This species does not shed its old leaves as easily as the native species does, making it unsuitable for use as a groundcover in any area where tree leaves fall in significant quantities.

Aster spp. and cvs.

White Wood Aster · Blue Wood Aster

White wood aster (*Aster divaricatus*) is ideal for naturalizing difficult spots such as driveway verges.

The Northeast is aster country, home to many native species of these starburst flowers for sun and shade. Two of the best for low-light conditions are *A. divaricatus* (white wood aster, Zone 4) and *A. cordifolius* (blue wood aster, Zone 5). Both are ubiquitous along shaded roadsides, where their masses of tiny flowers open in August and early September, announcing the end of summer and the coming change of seasons.

White wood aster is naturally compact, growing 18 to 24 inches high, and blue wood aster is 36 to 48 inches tall. White wood aster has dark-green, maroon-tinted foliage and mahogany-colored stalks, but blue wood aster is uniformly green. Both are surprisingly disease resistant. At summer's end, they'll show barely a sign of the mildews and scaly, bare ankles that can afflict the tall, sun-loving asters. In contrast, the foliage of the woodland asters will be relatively clean and remain intact until frost.

Both of these asters are attractive but understated plants for most of the growing season. Then, suddenly, they're spectacular! True to its name, the flowers of white wood aster open white with a small yellow eye, but as temperatures drop, they mature to a delicate pale lavender. The blossoms of blue wood aster are usually a pale, bluish-purple right from the start.

Both of these asters are also fairly rapid spreaders—blue wood aster principally by seed, and white wood aster principally by runners. Because excess plants are easy to pull out and are native, I recommend them without hesitation, even considering their spreading nature.

It's fairly common to find the *A. divaricatus* cultivar 'Eastern Star' and the *A. cordifolius* cultivar 'Avondale' offered for sale. Personally, I can't distinguish them from the species from which they're derived.

For many years, these asters suffered from the malady of the familiar—underappreciation—which made them hard to find for purchase. More recently, they've gotten favorable press, and their good qualities are getting some attention.

In the wild you'll often see them growing among hay-scented ferns, Christmas ferns, Solomon's seal, and any number of other high-quality native plants. These asters make great companions in naturalized landscape settings, but don't be afraid to plant them in the border too. Blue wood aster in particular looks breathtaking alongside Japanese anemone, which blooms at the same time, but it might need a little staking to help keep it upright when it gets top-heavy with flowers. I haven't found that it responds too well to pinching, although I think that's still worth a try. White wood aster goes with everything and needs no staking. However you use these asters, you'll appreciate their profusion of blooms at a time of year when little else is happening in shade gardens.

The asters mentioned here were recently reclassified taxonomically, so in newer references you may find *A. divaricatus* listed as *Eurybia divaricata* and *A. cordifolius* as *Symphyotrichum cordifolium*.

The airy sprays of blue wood aster (*Aster cordifolius*) usher in the late-season shade garden.

Carex spp. and cvs.

Sedge

An unusual edging plant for shade is Japanese variegated sedge (*Carex siderostica* 'Variegata').

Sedges are often mistaken for grasses and frequently lumped with the grasses in plant catalogs. Although they are distinctly different, it's true that they offer the ornamental qualities of small grasses while growing far better in low light.

Japanese variegated sedge (*Carex siderostica* 'Variegata,' Zone 5) grows to about 10 inches, producing thick masses of strap-like, white-striped leaves that will gracefully adorn the very front edge of a small garden bed or outline a path. It spreads moderately but roots shallowly, and it can be controlled easily by simply removing any stray crowns with a spade. Its leaves emerge very early in spring and can look a little worn by the end of the season. Insignificant flowers come out with the leaves, but deadheading is not necessary. Slugs can mar the leaves if their populations are high.

Most sedges prefer moist soil but will be perfectly happy in ordinary soil conditions. Japanese variegated sedge is completely deciduous; remove all dead foliage in late winter, or do nothing, and just let the new growth cover it.

A small but growing number of interesting sedges, including native ones, are available from specialty nurseries. I'm actively experimenting now with this group of plants, but my own experience is unfortunately too limited for me to make specific recommendations. Some may be best suited for naturalizing or specialized use, as in streamside environments, but others may prove to be worthy additions to more cultivated spaces. I can say that I've seen *C. appalachica* and *C. pensylvanica*, both native species probably hardy to Zone 3, used to beautiful effect as groundcovers as well as in combination with other plants. This is one genus just now being fully explored and exploited for garden use, so expect to see lots of new offerings in coming years. Some additional sedges that are widely available are covered in the section on plants for lighter shade.

Bugbane is notable as potentially the very tallest perennial for shady spaces. *C. racemosa* (Zone 3), a native species, grows to about 36 inches in leaf and can be 7 feet or taller in flower! Obviously, its proper place is at or near the rear of your border. Its creamy-white flowers are borne in 12-inch bottlebrushes atop wand-like, naked stalks. When the flowers are backlit by rays of sunlight, it becomes strikingly obvious why one common name for this plant is fairy candles. Because there's not much but empty air between the foliage at the bottom of the plant and the flowers at the top, the blooms show up best against some sort of darker backdrop, such as a line of trees. Despite its height, the plant's stalks are generally self-supporting, but don't tempt fate: avoid placing it in exposed, windy sites.

Many reference books refer to this species as "fragrant" but fail to mention that not everyone cares for the smell. It is the perennial equivalent of paperwhites in this regard. I like the smell of paperwhites, but many people do not. So, give this plant a whiff when it's in flower in the nursery. If you find the scent a bit overpowering, either plant it far enough away from your house for the fragrance to disperse, or try one of the other bugbanes with a less "thick" perfume.

Other bugbanes are more compact versions of *C. racemosa*. *C. simplex* 'White Pearl' (Zone 4) is about 6 feet tall in flower but slightly bushier, with somewhat smaller and blunter flower spikes on shorter stalks, and its fragrance is less noticeable.

Several bugbanes ('Hillside Black Beauty,' 'Brunette,' 'Atropurpurea,' and others, Zone 4) feature burgundy leaves. Although they are shade tolerant, I recommend growing them in some direct sun (all bugbanes are quite sun tolerant) to enhance the depth and longevity of their coloration. In too much shade, they will fade to a rather muddy green by midseason. Bugbanes with burgundy leaves sometimes have flowers lightly tinged pink; they look exceptional next to companions with gold leaves, gold variegation, or strong blue-green foli-

One of the tallest plants for shade is summer-blooming bugbane (*Cimicifuga racemosa*).

age, such as the shrubs *Spiraea* 'Magic Carpet' (gold) and *Hydrangea arborescens* (blue-green), and large gold or blue hostas.

Regardless of color, all bugbanes have good-quality, finely cut and ornamental foliage when they are not in flower and are not susceptible to any significant pest or disease. With more light, bugbanes will bloom more profusely, but they are still well worth growing even in significant shade.

USDA ZONE 5

Epimedium spp. and cvs.

Bishop's Hat

With great foliage and unique flowers, bishop's hat (*Epimedium x rubrum* is shown here) works well as both a border plant and a groundcover.

Epimediums are exceptionally good plants in every way. They are superlative deciduous groundcovers, well adapted to significant shade and dry conditions. Easy to grow, they flower abundantly and spread moderately fast, yet they're easy to control. These plants are among the few things in life that sound too good to be true . . . but *are* true!

Epimediums bloom beginning in early April, before or as their leaves emerge. Dangling flowers, which have a complex shape often described as "spider-like," are soft yellow, golden yellow, white, pink, purple, or orange, depending on the species or cultivar you choose. The flowers and the first flush of leaves will be 8 to 10 inches tall. After flowering, epimediums may produce a second, taller flush of leaves up to a height of 15 inches. When new leaves first emerge, they may have a russet coloration that will fade to medium green in a few weeks.

Use large clumps of epimedium (six to ten plants) at the front of the border, or mass them as a groundcover. You can trim away last year's foliage in March if you want an exceptionally neat look and a clean backdrop for the flowers. Or, do nothing and let the new growth conceal the old. I have never observed any pest or disease on epimedium, and it can even be grown in full sun if it is not allowed to dry out.

Epimedium "roots" are rhizomes—fleshy, starch-storing organs underground, from which actual roots branch off. When they start to grow beyond where you want them, just take a spade and cut off the excess. Although epimedium doesn't *need* division, you can take an established clump and spread it out over two or three times the area it originally occupied, and it will fill in well the first season, making it an economical plant.

Some common and recommended epimediums include *E.* x *rubrum* (pink flowers, very floriferous, and said to be slightly more cold hardy than others, to Zone 4), *E.* x *versicolor* 'Sulphureum' (butter-yellow flowers), *E.* x *perralchicum* 'Frohnleiten' (golden-yellow flowers and semi-evergreen foliage that can remain good looking through mild winters), and *E.* x *youngianum* 'Niveum' (white flowers and an overall smaller, shorter plant than the others mentioned here).

Like many plants, white snakeroot is an excellent plant but better for some uses than others. It would be an ideal border plant if not for its tendency to self-sow immodestly. Shade does put the brakes on its reproduction somewhat, so the best advice I can give is to try it in moderation and see how it behaves in your garden. It's a native plant and extremely common throughout the Northeast, so control is an issue not so much of keeping an exotic plant at bay as of keeping your garden from becoming a monoculture.

White snakeroot emerges a little later than many perennials, but quickly grows anywhere from 24 inches to 48 inches (always taller than wide) depending on exact conditions. It produces a dense crop of leaves finely toothed at the margins, attractive more for their substantiveness than any singular quality. Its stalks are an attractive mahogany color. In August and September, a froth of white flowers provides a late-season nectar source for bees and other insects (who will show their appreciation) for several weeks.

No less valuable for being common, white snakeroot (*Eupatorium rugosum*) blooms late and profusely.

In a naturalized setting, combine white snakeroot with *Aster divaricatus* and largish native ferns for a subtle yet pleasing late-season combination that will reassure you that summer isn't really over, even if it's past Labor Day. In a more cultivated setting, white snakeroot makes a great companion for just about anything.

White snakeroot grows admirably well in both shade and sun. A little leafminer (tiny insects that tunnel between the upper and lower leaf layers) damage to the leaves can be expected by late summer, but I've never seen this become disfiguring. 'Chocolate' is a cultivar with a burgundy leaf, but this trait diminishes more and more as the shade in which it's grown gets deeper and deeper.

Deadheading white snakeroot is a bit tricky because it's one of those plants that seem to release mature seed even as they continue to flower. The only way to prevent it from spreading seed is to simply cut the flowers off after a few weeks, even if you'd rather not from an aesthetic perspective. Unwanted seedlings develop tenacious roots quickly and can't be removed by mere pulling; you'll need a trowel or spade. Get to them as early in spring as possible to make the job a little easier.

This species was recently reclassified as *Ageratina altissima*, so you might see it under either name in books and catalogs.

Geranium macrorrhizum and cvs.

Bigroot Geranium

Only a very small number of geraniums grow in shade, and of those that do, bigroot geranium stands head and shoulders above the others. Fragrant, flowery, and endowed with fine foliage, bigroot geranium deserves much wider use than it currently enjoys. It's one of the very best deciduous groundcovers, tolerant of dry shade but equally happy growing in full sun, and quite showy in all circumstances. I wondered why I rarely saw bigroot geranium in nurseries, and started asking around. Professional growers told me that it is difficult to grow in pots and prone to crop failure in certain years, but I can assure you that once it's established in the ground, it's tough as nails.

Bigroot geranium is one of the first perennials to show growth in spring, but it doesn't really fill out until early May. It looks like one of the "scented geraniums"—actually members of the genus *Pelargonium*—that we in the

Bigroot geranium (*Geranium macrorrhizum*) makes a dense, colorful groundcover in moderate shade.

North grow as annuals. Its fuzzy, medium-green and aromatic leaves form a dense mound 12 inches high. When bruised, or when warmed by high air temperatures on hot days, the plants exude a spiced honey fragrance, and in fall they color up irregularly, with some leaves turning red while others remain green.

White, soft-pink, or magenta flowers (depending on the cultivar) held just above the foliage appear in late May and early June. Bright light encourages more flowering, but bigroot geranium still flowers moderately even in considerable shade, especially after it is well established.

It's difficult to remove autumn leaves from a planting of bigroot geranium because the plant's rhizomes are easily disturbed by tools, so I recommend using it as a groundcover only in areas where removal of fallen leaves by hand is manageable, or where you are comfortable simply leaving them in place to be concealed by the geranium as it leafs out in spring. You can also use it in groups of six to eight at the front of the border, where it drapes nicely over edging or stepping stones. If it grows out of bounds, just cut off the excess with a spade; it will rip out easily.

Bigroot geranium's availability fluctuates. As already noted, in some years it can be hard to find. In other years, it's readily available. Even if you don't see it in your nursery, ask about placing a special order, because this plant just isn't on some people's radar screen . . . but it ought to be.

Helleborus spp. and cvs.

Hellebore

Hellebores (*Helleborus x hybridus* is shown here) are typically the very first perennials to bloom in the spring shade garden.

Hellebores are probably the best shade plants you've never heard of . . . or maybe the best shade plants you've just gotten to know. Long obscure, they are finally gaining in popularity and expanding in variety, and none too soon: they hold the distinction of having the longest ornamental season of any shade perennial.

Hellebores are generally the first perennials to bloom in northern gardens. In late March, they send up fleshy stalks that unfurl around the first of April to reveal large, compelling flowers. Those of *H. x hybridus* (formerly often called *H. x orientalis*, Zone 5 at least) are extremely variable, ranging in color from pure or creamy white through apple green, light pink, and mauve to deep plum, often with intricately speckled throats. As the flowers dangle about 15 inches above the ground, the leaves emerge. Large, thick, leathery, deep-green and lush once fully opened, the leaves have several sharp lobes radiating outward from a common point.

As the flowers mature, they fade to a greenish-ivory color in much the same way that hydrangeas do. The flowers remain on the plant, still looking reasonably good, until their seeds burst out of their pods around late June. The foliage stays attractive and generally unblemished until frost.

Other hellebores are variations on this theme, with some having more finely divided leaves, different proportions, double flowers, or a specific flower color instead of a mixture. I recommend starting off with *H. x hybridus* for several reasons. Its foliage is among the best of its genus, if not necessarily the most unusual, and it's winter hardy over a large part of our region. In short, this is a reliable plant, and it makes sense to me to start with a plant unlikely to disappoint. If you fall in love with the idea of hellebores, then branch out. *H. niger* (Zone 4), *H. argutifolius* (Zone 6), and *H. foetidus* (Zone 6) are some other hellebores that often can be found in better nurseries.

It used to be that *H. x hybridus* was offered only in a mix of flower colors.

When you purchased these plants in the nursery, you had no idea what color they would be (hellebores must be three to five years old before they flower, and nursery plants were usually too young to have anything but leaves), but this wasn't a bad thing. Personally, I have always found mixed-color plantings to be the most interesting. In recent years, however, single-color selections have largely replaced them, so that now you often find plants labeled *H.* x *hybridus* 'Pink Lady' or something similar. I haven't achieved the same success with the named cultivars I've tried as with *H.* x *hybridus*, which, ironically, is getting difficult to find. When you purchase your first hellebores, be sure to read the label carefully so you know what you're getting, and take the time to do a little research on the side if you have any doubts. Mixed-color groups are still offered sometimes under various names.

Because hellebores start growing so early in the year, they are prone to damage from fickle winter weather. One recent December was so mild that hellebores that shouldn't have started blooming until April were up and at it at Christmas! When winter finally did arrive—as it always does, eventually—the newly opened blossoms were killed by cold, leaving few flowers for the normal spring display. I have taken to leaving old hellebore foliage on the plants for winter protection until April, and if the emerging plants grow up through this insulating layer in March and a bitter night is predicted, I heap a bunch of fallen tree leaves from the previous autumn on top until the danger is past.

Use hellebores in groups of five or more at or near the front of the border, or mass them in small areas as an alternative to a groundcover. They are trouble-free plants but will rot in waterlogged soil, so be sure to provide adequate drainage. In most years, expect a fair crop of seedlings underneath the parent plants unless you deadhead them before seeds ripen.

Hosta spp. and cvs.

Hosta · Plantain Lily

USDA ZONE **3**

As ornamental shade plants go, hostas are unsurpassed. How good are they? Well, were it not for the unfortunate fact that hostas are among the trio of plants that deer find irresistible (along with tulips and daylilies), no gardener would need anything other than hostas to have an excellent shade garden. That's how good.

Hostas offer an extraordinary variety of sizes, shapes, leaf colors, and var-

Plants for
Deeper Shade

97

Hostas are quintessential shade plants, offering unsurpassed foliage variety as well as showy summer flowers.

iegation. From petite golden 'Kabitan' (topping out at 6 inches) to gargantuan green-and-cream *H. montana* 'Aureomarginata' (as wide as a small table when mature), there is a hosta for every shade garden. Although thought of as foliage plants, hostas also produce lovely and abundant displays of pale lavender or white flowers in early to midsummer. *H. plantaginea* and its cultivars are even subtly fragrant.

It's important to know that not all hostas that are variegated when they first emerge in spring will retain their color all season long. Some, although not most, will rather rapidly fade to green as summer progresses; *H.* 'Fortunei Albopicta' is an example. If you want stable variegation, do a little research before making your purchase.

Exposure to light can play a big role in the exact shading of a hosta's leaves as well as the rapidity of its growth and the size it ultimately attains. As a very general rule, hostas with a lot of variegation do best in light to moderate shade, but those with green and blue leaves can take deeper shade. Brighter light will *not* stop a variegated hosta from fading to green by early summer if that trait is in its genes.

Some hostas have a slightly stiff posture—they are the riding academy students of the plant world. They have a definite vase shape and hold fairly rigid leaves well above the ground. The leaves of other hostas are more pliable and cascade, forming a thick skirt of foliage that skims the ground around the perimeter of the plant. A few hostas are intermediate between these two very different looks, but most fall into one of these two aesthetic categories.

Like most plants, hostas look best when mature. Because it can take eight to ten years for a large hosta to reach its full size, I advise purchasing them in the biggest size you can find and afford. Luckily, 2- and 3-gallon specimens of many selections are frequently available.

Vigorous hostas will need division about every five years, because their centers will die out as growth expands outward. Slow-growing hostas may not need division for many years.

If you grow hostas, you will almost certainly have to take measures to prevent deer browsing. Slugs also have a taste for hosta leaves. Hostas with thick, corrugated leaves are more resistant to slug damage than those with thin, smooth leaves.

There are hundreds of worthwhile hostas, and which one(s) to grow is largely a matter of taste. A few of my recommendations follow. All of the variegated ones mentioned will retain their variegation all season long without fading to green, although some variation in the variegation over the course of a growing season might occur. Assume flowers are lavender unless otherwise noted. When a hosta is described as a "sport" of another, that means that it is a natural mutation of the "parent" hosta and will share many of the original's traits, probably differing only in leaf color.

Gold and yellow variegated hostas. 'Golden Tiara' is low growing, displaying a dense cluster of roundish leaves having a lemon-lime combination of a green heart and a neat, bright-gold margin. Its leaves cascade. If I had to choose one small- to mid-sized hosta for the average garden, 'Golden Tiara' would be it. A related hosta, 'Emerald Tiara,' has the reverse variegation, while 'Grand Tiara' has a very wide gold margin and a central green zone that is more of a stripe.

In coloration, 'Shade Fanfare' looks like a slightly larger version of 'Golden Tiara' but is more upright in stature, and its leaves are slightly puckered. It really glows in the shade, and it grows very satisfactorily even in light levels that would inhibit other hostas with significant gold variegation.

Larger yet, 'Gold Standard' is an old cultivar that, in many ways, is still the gold standard for variegated hostas. Each leaf has a broad gold heart and the thinnest of green margins. Its leaves cascade.

'Great Expectations' is my favorite large yellow hosta and my favorite hosta overall. Its leaves have a clear yellow (as distinct from gold) heart with a blue-green edge and broken patterns of blue and green in between. They have a somewhat puckered texture and a moderately rounded shape. The plant has a definite vase shape, holding its leaves parallel to the ground and making a magnificent display. Flowers are white. If it grows very slowly for you, try moving it to a spot with lighter shade. If you like this look but need a smaller hosta, try 'Paul's Glory.'

H. montana 'Aureomarginata' is one of the very largest hostas you can grow (any hosta with the species *H. montana* in its lineage will be very large). Its leaves have a green heart that appears to have been painted on a gold or yellow margin, with distinct brushstrokes visible. The margin bleaches to a creamy white to one degree or another as the season goes on. The leaves are somewhat puckered and have a distinctly pointed tip. This hosta can be grown in morning sun (an eastern exposure is ideal), in which case the variegation will bleach quite a bit. Flowers are white.

If the two previous hostas are just too large for you, try 'Wide Brim.' Its coloration is similar, but its leaves are rounder and the plant has a low, broad growth habit. *H.* 'Fortunei Aureomarginata' is a very old, common, and affordable hosta that is well worth growing. Each leaf has a green central zone ringed by a neat gold margin. It is intermediate in stature and an excellent, all-purpose, medium-sized hosta that will complement any companion.

'June' has the royal mien of 'Halcyon' (discussion follows) and is a variegated sport of it. The two planted together make a beautiful combination. Leaves are gold with brushstrokes of blue around the edges. For best color, grow it in bright light; in low light, the entire leaf has a distinctly bluish cast that spoils its look.

If an all-gold hosta is what you're after, 'Sum and Substance' is one of the best very large hostas, and 'Gold Edger' is a good smaller selection. The color of the former ranges from chartreuse to greenish-gold depending on light conditions, and it's hard to predict except to say that it tends to green out if placed in too much shade. It's very sun tolerant, and its leaves are quite puckered. 'Gold Edger' has pointed leaves with a smooth texture and works well with 'Hadspen Blue' (discussion follows) as a companion.

White variegated hostas. 'Francee' is an old standby in this department, and for good reason. It is medium sized, with lance-shaped green leaves set off by a bright white margin. It would look good next to any other hosta.

Very similar in appearance to 'Francee' is *H.* 'Undulata Albomarginata.' It is perhaps the single most useful hosta for gardeners who need to fill a large area, because it is very attractive, affordable, and readily available, and increases in size rapidly.

'Patriot' was probably the most popular hosta in the country a few years ago and certainly could have a place in any shade garden. Medium sized, it has somewhat elongated, dark-green leaves with a broad, pure-white margin. Imagine the reverse variegation of 'Patriot' with a floppier growth habit and you've got 'Night Before Christmas.' It is a sport of 'White Christmas,' whose nearly all-white leaf with a thin green margin gives it a radical look more reminiscent of a caladium than a hosta.

'Ginko Craig' (and yes, that is the right spelling) is a very small hosta whose leaves never top 8 inches. It looks very much like a dwarf version of 'Undulata Albomarginata' and is equally adaptable in any space where it will not get lost. It forms more of a colony than a clump, so it is useful as a groundcover for very small areas. Finally, 'Diamond Tiara' is like 'Golden Tiara' (mentioned earlier) but with a white edge, and 'So Sweet' is very similar.

Fine foliage offers months of ornamental value, whereas flowers last only days or weeks.

Blue hostas. Probably the most widely grown blue hosta is *H. sieboldiana* 'Elegans.' It has given rise to any number of variegated sports, one of which is 'Great Expectations' (mentioned earlier). Consequently, it is basically identical to 'Great Expectations' except for color. 'Elegans' has dusty-blue leaves the size of dinner platters and is a classic in every sense. Other good large to very large blue hostas include 'Big Daddy,' 'Blue Angel,' and 'Blue Mammoth.' Although hosta purists would shudder to read this, for the average gardener they are fairly interchangeable. Many of the large blue hostas have flowers that are white or such a pale lavender that they appear white.

'Frances Williams' is another very large and deservedly classic hosta. Its heavily puckered leaves have a blue heart with an apple-green margin, giving it a variegation that is colorful yet not overly bold. It will complement any other hosta.

'Halcyon' is a medium-sized hosta with a regal bearing and an extremely vibrant powdery blue color. Its leaves have a slightly elongated shape and a lot of substance. The complete lack of waviness or puckering makes each leaf look exceptionally elegant and formal.

'Hadspen Blue' is a great all-purpose, medium-sized blue hosta. Its leaves are a rather dark blue that coordinates perfectly with its abundant lavender flowers, and it has a pleasing fullness. Its stature is intermediate. 'Blue Wedgewood' is similar.

Green hostas. Don't forget to include these in your garden. Not only are they worthwhile in their own right, but they'll provide contrast to variegated and blue hostas, enhancing their effect. 'Royal Standard' is an excellent cultivar that's been around for decades and is easy to find. It's notable for two reasons. First, it's one of the final hostas to bloom, in August-September instead of June-July. This makes it a natural choice for gardeners who are trying to extend flowering in their shade gardens through the late-summer months. Second, its pure-white flowers are exquisitely fragrant. Plant this hosta near seating areas and drink in its heavenly scent! Gardens of almost any size, small or large, can accommodate it because of its moderate proportions (15 to 18 inches tall and about 24 inches wide). Try using a purple-flowered *Tricyrtis* as a companion, because it generally starts blooming just as the hosta is peaking, and the two together make a wonderful late-season combination.

'Guacamole' is technically a variegated hosta, but its coloration is subtle except in very bright light, and I think the eye really parses it as green. It's aptly named, because its very rounded, glossy leaves are exactly the color of mashed avocados and look good enough to eat! Its flowers have the same fragrance as 'Royal Standard,' thanks to their common lineage from the species *H. plantaginea*.

Finally, there is petite *H. lancifolia*. True to its Latin name, this hosta has lance-shaped, deep-green leaves with an attractive sheen on short stalks. It hugs the ground and makes an excellent, if ordinary, mound of foliage about 12 inches high and 18 inches wide in virtually any type of shade. Deep-lavender flowers in midsummer complete its appeal. This hosta increases at a remarkably fast rate, making it a good option for gardeners on a budget. I frequently see it in plantings around older houses, where it probably got its start as divisions passed from neighbor to neighbor. I couldn't recommend it more highly. Although it isn't hard to obtain, you might have to ask your local nursery to special order this hosta because it is often overlooked in favor of more showy selections.

Despite all these specific recommendations, I've just barely scratched the surface of hostas. A smorgasbord of choices is available to any gardener with the interest and ability to grow a wide range of these superb shade plants.

Yellow waxbells will be a favorite with any shade gardener who appreciates bold foliage and plants that take care of themselves. There are two common species in the nursery trade, *K. palmata* and *K. koreana*. Most gardeners will find them interchangeable. Both produce tiers of fairly large, maple-shaped leaves and grow to about 30 inches tall and 36 inches wide at maturity. In late summer they bear large, pendant, bell-shaped flowers in a cheery yellow that shows up well in shade and against the plant's black stalks. Overall, yellow waxbells gives the impression of cascading softly over itself like a gentle waterfall.

Yellow waxbells can be a little hard to integrate into small gardens. The plant emerges on the late side, well after most shade perennials are actively growing. Despite that, a mature plant will get quite large by late summer. It needs a big chunk of space, but doesn't actually fill it out until July or so. An effective way to grow it in gardens where its "late arrival" will be conspicuous is among self-sowing forget-me-nots, which will flower early in the season and die off at just the time when yellow waxbells fills out. In large gardens, I recommend massing it alongside other similarly architectural plants such as *Rodgersia*. A bank of yellow waxbells in front of a long row of *Hydrangea arborescens* (or blue *H. macrophylla* for gardeners along the coast) is a particularly lovely combination for midsummer onward when many other shade plants are past their peak.

Above all, remember that a small, young specimen of yellow waxbells will look gangly for a few years, but after about five growing seasons, it should be full, bushy, and impressive. Like many good things, this plant needs time to develop.

Few shade plants are more impressive than a mature specimen of yellow waxbells (*Kirengeshoma* spp.).

If you need a dense groundcover that isn't overly vigorous, try native *Pachysandra procumbens*.

Everyone knows pachysandra; the problem is, they know the wrong one! The one we all should be growing is our native species, *P. procumbens*. The one we've all inherited from previous generations of gardeners is its evil twin, Japanese pachysandra, *P. terminalis*.

You may already have picked up on the fact that I discourage the use of Japanese pachysandra. This isn't because it's not a fine plant. It is, in fact, beautiful and adaptable (if so overused that it's also banal). I understand completely how and why Japanese pachysandra came to be so widely planted. It's one of those plants that seems like a problem solver: a great way to fill a lot of real estate cheaply. But I've come to the conclusion that this plant causes more problems than it solves.

The basic problem with Japanese pachysandra is that it's the cockroach of the plant world. I have no doubt it would be the first plant to revegetate Earth after a global catastrophe. Unfortunately, it just doesn't know when to stop, and it doesn't know its own strength. Controlling the spread of Japanese pachysandra is a really tough job that basically requires the use of a physical barrier because the plant produces such a thick, impenetrable mat of rhizomes that hacking through it can be nearly impossible. If planted behind a rock retaining wall, Japanese pachysandra will grow right through it and eventually push it apart. So although I admire Japanese pachysandra the way one might admire anything undefeatable, I don't want it around me.

Pachysandra procumbens, on the other hand, is more manageable. In appearance, it's a kissing cousin of Japanese pachysandra. The principal differences are that *P. procumbens* is deciduous and its leaves have a matte (rather than glossy) surface and display a subtle mottled pattern instead of uniform green. In behavior, however, it's more tractable, spreading the way you want a groundcover to do, but not becoming a menace to society.

The main drawback of using native pachysandra is its cost. Japanese pachysandra is so widely grown (and cheaper to produce because it grows like wildfire) that it dominates the market. But I've seen the price of the native alternative decrease through the years, and I strongly encourage paying extra money up front for what I see as a better plant in the long run. If you think you'd like to try this plant and are willing to buy in quantity, contact a nursery with a good native plant section in winter (winter is when retail nurseries place their orders with growers) and ask for pricing for spring delivery. You might be pleasantly surprised. It will probably come bare root.

Polemonium spp. and cvs.

Jacob's Ladder

USDA ZONE
4–

There are several species, hybrids, and named culti- vars of Jacob's ladder, but of all the ones I've tried, I keep coming back to *P. reptans*, a somewhat diminutive species native to eastern North America. Just 8 to 10 inches tall, it's a charmer for the front of the border or the informal woodland garden. One of the things I like about it is that it's pretty much the same height in leaf and in flower. Some other Jacob's ladders put up very tall flower stalks but must be cut back to 10 inches after flowering; this makes it harder to find the right spot for them.

Thanks to leaves composed of many small leaflets, Jacob's ladder looks delicate without being quite ferny. Medium-blue flowers held just above the foliage appear in late April and May. If adequate moisture is main- tained through the summer, the foliage can continue to look reasonably good until fall, but drought or periods of hot, humid weather can make it shrivel up.

The blue froth of Jacob's ladder (*Polemonium reptans*) is a head turner in spring.

In recent years, some variegated *Polemonium* selec- tions have been introduced to the market. If you want that look, I'd suggest *P. reptans* 'Stairway to Heaven' or 'Touch of Class' in preference to *P. caeruleum* 'Brise d'Anjou,' which I have not found to be particularly robust. Variegated Jacob's ladder can look nice interplanted with similarly variegated *Lamium* cultivars. Various hybrids are also available now, as well as a cultivar with purplish leaf accents called 'Heaven Scent.' I expect the options to expand in coming years, and experience will sort out which ones are best for Northeast gardeners.

USDA ZONE ZONE

Varies

Polygonatum spp. and cvs.

Solomon's Seal

Because one of the essential elements of a good garden design is contrast—contrast in leaf color, leaf shape, flower presentation, and more—and because shade gardeners, more so than sun gardeners, must rely on foliage interest, a plant such as Solomon's seal, with its extraordinary stature, is a must-have.

A clump of Solomon's seal looks like a group of synchronized swimmers or dancers gracefully bending in unison. All the stalks in a planting arch in roughly the same direction, typically toward the brightest source of light. This regal, regimental arrangement is so unlike that of most other plants, which often present their leaves in crowded mounds or mats, that Solomon's seal automatically contrasts with all but a tiny number of similar plants.

The foliage of Solomon's seal is so attractive that if the plant didn't flower at all, it would still be worth growing, but nature wasn't stingy in this case. In May, the underside of each stalk is adorned with dangling white bells, often with green markings. The flowers look very similar to those of snowdrops, the spring bulb.

P. odoratum 'Variegatum' (also called *P. falcatum* 'Variegatum,' Zone 4) is the Solomon's seal most commonly found in nurseries. Its stems start out pink, fading to greenish-white as the season progresses, and its leaves are variegated with white brushstrokes along the margins. It grows to 24 inches.

The native species *P. biflorum* (Zone 3) and most other kinds of Solomon's seal have plain green leaves that are no less ornamental than those of their variegated relative. The ones most commonly offered for sale look similar to each other but vary in height from 9 inches (*P. humile*, Zone 5) to 48 inches or more (*P. biflorum* var. *commutatum*), and specialty growers offer some distinctly different variations on the Solomon's seal theme.

Unfortunately, there is some confusion about the identity of some Solomon's seals both among taxonomists and in the nursery trade, and I've had the experience of buying one, only to find it quite different from what was described. So

The arching stems of Solomon's seal (*Polygonatum odoratum* 'Variegatum' is shown here) add grace to the shade garden.

buy potted plants at the nursery to be certain about what you're getting, or else discuss this issue with your mail-order supplier before ordering. The one exception to this is *P. odoratum* 'Variegatum,' which is consistently labeled correctly.

Solomon's seal looks best in sizeable clumps of fifteen or so plants positioned just behind the front row of plants in the border or woodland garden to help conceal the naked base of its stalks. You can also try underplanting it with a noncompetitive groundcover such as *Vancouveria* or *Lamium*. It's nice with ferns and epimediums, and very tall types are stunning behind annual dragon wing begonias. When choosing a spot for planting, pay careful attention to the directionality of the light. If you want the stems to arch toward a pathway, for instance, the brightest light must arrive from that direction. Otherwise, the stems may bend away from the path or parallel to it, and that may not be the effect you intend. Planting near the wall of a house or outbuilding usually results in the stems arching away from the wall (which blocks light), and that's how they look best.

Deer may browse Solomon's seal more or less enthusiastically, so you might have to apply a repellent, but otherwise all species are easy to grow, and here's a tip: when your Solomon's seal is in bloom, be on the lookout for hummingbirds hovering near the ground to feed on its nectar—a very special sight!

If you're a gardener with a taste for plants that shimmer in the shade, there's probably a lungwort in your future. Lungwort leaves can be adorned with anything from a tentative splash of irregular white dots to a full-on sterling plate, or anything in between, or both at the same time. If lungworts were people, they'd be the sort of people who wear plaids and stripes together and think nothing of it.

In addition to their adventurousness in attire, lungworts are one of the very first perennials to bloom in northern shade gardens. Around April 1, their first flowers will open on short stems just in time to lure the first bees of the season. These stems slowly elongate as new leaves emerge and the plant fills out.

Lungwort flowers often have the curious quality of being pink in bud yet opening blue, a trait that's given rise to a rarely used common name: bride and groom plant. But if you prefer your lungworts without a color identity crisis, plant breeders have created selections that do not change color, such as 'Pierre's Pure Pink.' There are also a few white-flowered selections, 'Sissinghurst White' and 'White Wings' being the most common.

Some lungworts are understated. *P. rubra* (Zone 5) has quite ordinary leaves with no variegation and coral-pink flowers that never show a hint of blue. (Curiously, though, the *P. rubra* cultivar 'David Ward' has the leaf coloration that fits the more classical definition of *variegated*—white margins.) 'Little Star' has cobalt-blue flowers and very slight speckling of the leaves. At the other end of the spectrum, 'British Sterling' is an example of what a lungwort can do when it tries: a Rorschach test in white on green. Other lungworts, notably those with some *P. longifolia* ancestry, have leaves that are decidedly lance shaped and stiff instead of broad and somewhat lax, adding to the considerable variety of lungwort looks.

The one weakness of many lungworts is a susceptibility to powdery mildew. You can apply a fungicide as a preventative (left untreated, the plants may decline and eventually die) or grow one of the resistant types. *P. rubra* shows no hint of the disease, but the straight species is rather plain looking. 'Margery Fish' has long been recommended for its clean foliage and classic lungwort appearance: broad leaves, moderate speckling, and pink buds evolving into sky-blue flowers. Many selections and hybrids of *P. longifolia* (Zone 5) also show good resistance.

Most lungworts (*Pulmonaria*) feature speckled foliage that can look good for an exceptionally long season.

My personal favorite is 'Roy Davidson,' with moderately speckled, lance-shaped leaves and icy-blue flowers. Inquire about new mildew-resistant selections wherever you plan to buy your lungworts.

Because lungworts are small—8 to 12 inches tall in or out of flower—use them at the front of your border, where lady's mantle, astilbes, and low-growing ferns make attractive neighbors. Selections with particularly good leaves can even be massed as a groundcover in small areas with companions such as *Astilbe* 'Sprite.' Lungworts are very suitable for informal gardens and look especially nice scattered along rustic pathways. They prefer not to dry out, so be sure to provide water as needed. Cutting off spent flowers in early May, nipping the flowering stalks off at ground level, helps maintain plant vigor, and the grooming improves their appearance.

NOTE: the lineage of many lungworts is so complicated that it's impossible to give a general cold hardiness rating. Rely on local nurseries and arboreta for recommendations for your area.

When you want a large plant to make a bold statement in the shade, turn to *Rodgersia*. Growing 24 to 30 inches tall in leaf and 48 inches tall in flower, it takes up some space, and each of its palmate leaves, resembling those of a horse chestnut tree, is the size of a serving platter. With a look that borders on the tropical, it's sure to draw attention.

A rodgersia's idea of heaven would be a streamside setting; it thrives in consistently moist soil. But unlike a lot of moisture-loving plants, it will not wilt and droop with just average soil moisture. It will look just fine as long as genuine drought never sets in.

Rodgersia is well worth growing for its foliage alone, and if that's all you need, it will grow beautifully in significant shade, which is why I placed it here in the section devoted to plants for very low light. But if you also want to enjoy a full-fledged floral display, light shade is best. In bright but indirect light, rodgersia will reward you with thick, sturdy stalks topped by tall pagodas of creamy-white or smoky-pink flowers that exude a sweet but subtle perfume.

R. podophylla has white flowers and the most ornamental leaf of all the rodgersias, each having a saw-toothed terminal edge. 'Rotlaub' is a cultivar with eggplant-hued leaves that reputedly holds its color well; try fronting it with Japanese painted fern for a great foliage pairing. Actually, in any rodgersia planting, regardless of the species, some leaves typically emerge burgundy but usually fade to green within a few weeks.

R. aesculifolia is the most common rodgersia. Its leaves have a smooth profile and its flowers are white to pale pink. For reliably pink flowers with a dusky quality, grow *R. pinnata* 'Superba.'

You can mass rodgersia to fill a space all by itself, but it also works well in the second tier of the border, especially if grown among other plants of stature, such as large hostas, goatsbeard, and the like. If happy in its location, it increases rapidly from rhizomes yet is easily controlled and needs little care other than containment. But do give it plenty of room.

Rodgersias (*Rodgersia podophylla* is shown here) are notable for their highly ornamental, serving-platter-sized leaves.

Very few people who read this book will ever grow sweet box, yet it's a fine plant for certain limited applications. It's actually a dwarf shrub that suckers and can be used as an evergreen groundcover. But it's hard to find and very expensive, and it grows so slowly that you basically have to plant it at the density you ultimately want, because at the rate that it spreads, you might not be around to see it fill in!

Despite all these drawbacks, sweet box is still desirable. It has very dark green, glossy, tapering leaves, flowers like tiny white sparklers in spring, and dark-blue berries late in the season. It makes me think of a miniature *Leucothoe*, although the two plants aren't even in the same family.

You'd think that sweet box wouldn't hold up well under heavy snow loads, but it handles them admirably, which is a definite plus at northern latitudes. So, if you have the budget and the patience, sweet box can be an unusual and very classy alternative to other groundcovers for small spaces.

Exceptionally slow growing, sweet box (*Sarcococca hookeriana* var. *humilis*) is nonetheless an excellent groundcover that will survive the darkest spots.

Smilacina spp.

False Solomon's Seal

As you might expect from the name, false Solomon's seal strongly resembles true Solomon's seal (*Polygonatum*). The two plants are almost identical in size and form (about 24 inches tall with arching stems), but the flowers of *Smilacina* are borne very differently. Instead of pendant bells, the plant produces a fluffy panicle of creamy-white flowers at the tip of each stalk. Sometimes these droop, and sometimes they are held basically upright. They turn into ornamental, pale-red, darkly veined fruits reminiscent of gooseberries. False Solomon's seal leaves are medium green; although I have heard reports of variegated sports, I've never seen one for sale.

Give false Solomon's seal time to mature before expecting too much of it. It can be diminutive when its rhizomes are young and small, but over time, plants will develop into strong, impressive colonies. Although it is quite tolerant of significant shade, light shade and/or a couple of hours of sun a day will result in larger, more floriferous, and faster-maturing plants. Use it as you would true Solomon's seal, planting in groups of a dozen or more, remembering that stalks will generally arch in the same direction.

Because it is one of those woodland perennials with bare ankles, false Solomon's seal benefits from interplanting with a suitable companion. You can try *Lamium* or any of the other mat-forming, nonaggressive groundcovers discussed

The white seafoam flowers of false Solomon's seal (*Smilacina*)
become red berries in late summer.

in this book, but you can also try *Aster divaricatus*. The false Solomon's seal blooms in June while the aster is still rather short and not a distraction. Later in summer, the aster elongates and blooms from August onward, making this pairing a nice complement of two natives that can coexist indefinitely despite the aster's rather aggressive nature.

S. racemosa (Zone 4) is the species usually found in the gardening trade, but occasionally *S. stellata* (Zone 5) is offered for sale. There seems to be no consensus in the trade as to what the difference between them might be, and although my reference book of choice gives a different cold hardiness for the two species, I suspect they may often be mislabeled. *Smilacina* has been rechristened *Maianthemum*, so you may find the plants under either name.

Stylophorum diphyllum	5	USDA ZONE
Celandine Poppy		

Celandine poppy is a plant I hesitated to include in this book. It's an aggressive self-sower that most gardeners will not be able to keep within bounds. Although pulling unwanted seedlings when they're small is pretty easy, deadheading is the preferred means of control because in addition to producing lots of babies, offspring can show up yards away from the parent plant. It's too easy to overlook plants that come up on the margins of your property, meaning that celandine poppy can overwhelm a neighborhood in just a few seasons if left to go to seed.

So ask yourself, "Am I really going to find time every May from now to eternity to clip off all the fuzzy little celandine poppy seedpods?" If the answer is "no" (be honest!), and if you value the goodwill of your neighbors, don't grow celandine poppy. However, for the truly diligent it can be a nice part of your gardening toolkit.

Celandine poppy emerges very early in spring and grows quickly into a dense, 18-inch mound of heavily lobed, grayish-green leaves. In short order, it produces a good crop of extremely cheerful flowers like giant buttercups. By the end of May, flowering will have petered out and you'll see many, many prominent, fuzzy seedpods that will make you think of the air bladders of some aquatic animal. If you judiciously allow celandine poppy to seed around, it will fill in those clumsy little gaps that seem to spring up in any garden. Follow up your deadheading by hand pulling any extra seedlings the following spring, allowing only those to remain that genuinely have a purpose in your garden.

The cheerful buttercups of celandine poppy (*Stylophorum diphyllum*) will shine for many weeks in spring.

When bruised, celandine poppy exudes a brilliant yellow sap that is a mild skin irritant, so be sure to wear gloves when handling the plant. The sap will also stain skin and clothing, so don the dirty-work duds to do your deadheading.

One last caveat: it's easy to confuse celandine poppy with greater celandine, *Chelidonium majus*, especially before or after flowering when you have only leaves by which to judge (the flowers are more easily distinguished). Greater celandine is an equally aggressive spreader, but decidedly nonnative, and to add insult to injury, it's not even as attractive. *Stylophorum* is at least native to the East Coast, although not to the Northeast. If you decide to try celandine poppy, be sure you're really getting *Stylophorum*, not *Chelidonium*!

<table>
<tr><td>USDA ZONE
ZONE</td><td>5</td><td>*Tricyrtis* spp. and cvs.
Toad Lily</td></tr>
</table>

Somewhat similar in size and shape to Solomon's seal, false Solomon's seal, or even a small bamboo, *Tricyrtis* is one of the few shade plants to bloom in autumn. It bears intricate, orchid-like flowers along or at the ends of its stalks in September or October. These corsage-worthy blossoms are white or yellow, usually with complex purple markings that give rise to the rather homely common name toad lily.

Toad lily looks best when massed in a large clump. If starting with plants in standard 5-pint nursery pots, you might want to group as many as a dozen together, but six makes a good start. They will need little more than a suitable spot and time to establish themselves.

Most toad lilies are 24 to 30 inches, in or out of flower. Position them behind something low growing and broad leaved, such as a line of small hostas, both for the effect of the complementary foliage and to conceal the somewhat uninteresting base of the toad lilies. Toad lily stems are somewhat fragile and easily snapped, so be careful when performing maintenance around them.

Any of the late-summer flowering and fragrant hostas descended from *H. plantaginea*, such as 'Royal Standard,' makes a superb companion for toad lily. Both plants entice gardeners to get close: the hostas so you can breathe in their perfume even more deeply, and the toad lilies so you can marvel at the complexity of their exquisitely precise flowers. This wonderful conjunction happens because the flowering times for these two plants overlap, with the toad lily taking over as the hostas fade.

Plant collectors go out of their way to get rare toad lily cultivars, but the average gardener will do just as well with the three or four types usually offered in nurseries. Often these are identified with just the genus *Tricyrtis* and a cultivar name, such as *T.* 'Sinonome' or *T.* 'Miyazaki.' Most are derived from *T. hirta*, the most cold-hardy species. Occasionally, you might find a variegated toad lily with a white margin rimming its leaves. I recommend just purchasing the one(s) you find most appealing, but be careful to check cold hardiness when purchasing toad lilies via mail order because some are winter hardy only in much warmer climes than ours.

Although toad lilies are generally deer resistant, I have seen them get topped in some locations (maybe as a result of hostas planted nearby?), so it seems to depend on the taste buds of the local deer population. Take precautions if you have any doubt.

The complex flowers of toad lily (*Tricyrtis*) are a highlight of the shade garden in autumn.

Inside-out flower (*Vancouveria hexandra*) is a fine-textured groundcover whose leaves are held in layers.

It's surprising to me that this delicate, lacy groundcover is not more widely known, because it's a useful ace up the sleeve for gardeners who need a noncompetitive groundcover. A native of the Pacific Northwest, *Vancouveria* looks right at home on this side of the continent. Its thin, fragile stems support layers of small, prettily lobed, duckfoot leaves that give the impression of mounded green lace. Tiny white flowers, like those of shooting star (*Dodecatheon*) only smaller, dangle above the foliage on wiry stems for a brief spell in early June. They are highly reflexed, giving rise to one of the most evocative of all common plant names: inside-out flower.

Vancouveria spreads slowly to an indefinite width, but as I've noted, it is noncompetitive. This is extremely useful because other plants with bare ankles can grow up through it without being harmed by its association. I recommend planting it underneath *Disporum*, *Polygonatum*, and the like, especially because these plants are unlikely to shade it into oblivion. It would make an ideal companion for jack-in-the-pulpit, which goes dormant early and is hard to use in the garden unless it's paired with something like *Vancouveria*. And although as a general rule I discourage mixing groundcovers, I've observed inside-out flower and *Galium odoratum* coexisting happily. It's also a suitable choice for narrow little spaces where you just want something low care but green.

In the Northeast, *Vancouveria* is deciduous, and because it is so delicate, it requires no cleanup in spring. The remnants of last year's growth will disintegrate quickly on their own. Shallow rooted, *Vancouveria* is easy to control because its rhizomes are not so brittle that they break apart when dug. If it eventually grows out of bounds, just run a spade along the desired edge, and either tease the unwanted plants out of the soil using a garden fork, or cut them up into moveable pieces for transplanting elsewhere.

Inside-out flower shows up in nurseries now and then, but most gardeners will probably have to purchase it via mail order; better nurseries may be able to special order it.

Periwinkle is one of the two most common groundcovers to be found growing in the Northeast—the other being Japanese pachysandra—so I doubt any reader will be unfamiliar with this plant. I don't encourage its use, but I don't find it as objectionable as Japanese pachysandra because it is easier to control.

Periwinkle is a trailing, evergreen plant with long, thin stems and small, glossy, entire leaves. It grows rapidly and roots wherever a node (a spot where a leaf emerges from a stalk) touches the ground. Although white-flowering (and, less frequently, raspberry-flowering) forms are available, blue is its characteristic flower color, so much so that we even refer to that shade as "periwinkle blue." You can also purchase forms with white or golden variegation.

Though I have seen woodland gardens where periwinkle is managed as a somewhat rangy perennial in combination with other plants, I think that's a lot of work. Periwinkle's tendency is to spread, so it's most *easily* used as a solitary groundcover. It should be closely monitored to prevent it from spreading into the unmanaged landscape.

Periwinkle is generally sold either bare root or rooted in shallow flats. After planting, it may experience a brief period of shock and temporary dormancy. Keep it adequately watered, and it will leaf out when it's ready.

Periwinkle (*Vinca minor*) is a common groundcover that makes a reasonable compromise between vigor, cost, and controllability.

Waldsteinia spp.

Barren Strawberry

Barren strawberry (*Waldsteinia*) is a great option for shallow-soil areas in need of a groundcover.

Barren strawberry is the last of the "undiscovered groundcovers" I would like to see in wider use. True to its common name, it looks like a wild strawberry but produces no edible fruit. It forms a 2-inch mat of glossy, deep-green, semi-evergreen leaves that remain free of pests and disease all season long, and it sports single, golden-yellow buttercup flowers in April.

Barren strawberry roots in very shallow soil, is drought tolerant, and does not compete aggressively; this makes it ideal for underplanting specimen trees, including delicate native dogwoods (*Cornus florida*). It might even be able to survive under Norway maples, although I've never tried that. If conditions are adequate—and it doesn't need much—barren strawberry will spread steadily but remain easy to control with nothing more than a little spadework.

The only possible drawback to barren strawberry is that it's difficult to clean fallen tree leaves out of it. A leaf rake can uproot the plant, but with some care the job is doable. Alternatively, use a low-powered leaf blower for leaf removal.

Barren strawberry's own leaves will remain through the winter but will probably look slightly tattered by March. There is no need to cut back last year's growth because new leaves arise quickly in April and simply overgrow the old.

There is a species native to the East Coast (*W. fragarioides*, Zone 5), but the species most frequently offered for sale is the exotic *W. ternata* (Zone 3), probably because it is said to be more cold hardy. The two species appear to be interchangeable from an aesthetic standpoint, but I encourage using *W. fragarioides* if you can find it and if it will grow in your area.

Accent Plants

These accent plants for deeper shade should be used in borders to comple-

ment backbone plants, or as filler for fullness at the back of garden spaces, or

to help make the transition from cultivated to uncultivated landscapes. Each

entry specifies the use(s) for which each plant is best suited.

Corydalis spp.

Fumitory

5 USDA ZONE

The two most common and adaptable fumitories are *C. lutea* (yellow fumitory) and *C. ochroleuca* (white fumitory). Both are delicate, frilly plants good for filling small gaps between other, more principal perennials at the front of your shade garden. Forming a 12-inch mound of living green lace, they put a finishing touch on the border, much like fancy trim on a piece of clothing. Yellow fumitory bears small yellow flowers in abundance, appearing more or less constantly all season long beginning in May. White fumitory is its white-flowered counterpart.

Their principal drawback, as well as their principal charm, lies in the fact that they self-sow freely. Generally, I don't recommend plants that self-sow with abandon because of their tremendous potential for invasiveness, but I consider the fumitories an exception because gardeners who make a little effort to control them will find that their utility outweighs their fecundity.

If you'd like to soften the look of a dry-stone wall with soil pockets or a dry-laid patio, one of the fumitories could be the answer. Their tendency to self-sow into spots far too small to be planted with a trowel, and their preference for well-drained conditions makes

Yellow fumitory (*Corydalis lutea*) self-sows freely to fill hard-to-plant niches.

them a natural for those difficult spots. Because they also like to grow directly in gravel walkways, thin soil, and scree, they are one of the few shady rock garden plants.

Within a year after putting even just one fumitory in your garden, you'll probably have many seedlings. When young, they transplant exceedingly well. You can move a full-sized plant by simply cutting off all or nearly all of its foliage before moving it. It will produce a new flush of leaves in no time. Extra seedlings pull out almost effortlessly, and hoeing works if you have a really big crop. I have to reiterate that control of escaped seedlings is essential, or you'll soon have a population explosion.

There are other fumitories that gardeners find very desirable for their blue flowers, yet these are liable to be disappointments. When it comes to perennial *Corydalis* (this doesn't apply to the spring ephemerals in the same genus), I always say this: if it's blue, you probably will be, too . . . after it dies out.

That said, even the reliable yellow and white fumitories are "short-lived" perennials, although you may never notice because they'll produce plenty of progeny to take the place of the parents.

USDA ZONE 5

Disporum maculatum

Nodding Mandarin

This excellent North American native plant is almost entirely unknown in gardens, yet now that I have grown it for many years, I can't imagine being without it. Probably the only reason it's not widespread in the nursery trade is that it's slow to develop and doesn't seem like much when it's just a young thing in a small pot. It takes about five years in the ground before reaching its stride.

Nodding mandarin is a May bloomer. It produces unique, dangling white flowers with twisting petals, dark speckles, and yellow anthers that remind me of twirling ballet dancers. The foliage is reminiscent of *Polygonatum* or *Smilacina* in that arching, jointed stalks bear alternate, entire leaves; but instead of solitary stalks, nodding mandarin produces a mass of stalks from a central crown, and they branch and arch away in all directions to form a symmetrical vase shape with a layered texture. A mature nodding mandarin is a very fine woodland plant.

Because of its shape and size (30 inches tall and 24 inches wide when well established) and the sparseness of leaves on the bottom few inches of its stalks,

Nodding mandarin (*Disporum maculatum*) is an unusual and highly desirable native woodlander.

nodding mandarin should be planted in the second tier of plants in a border. Front it with something small and airy such as *Corydalis lutea* or accent it with annual impatiens. Alternatively, underplant it with a very low-growing and nonaggressive groundcover.

Nodding mandarin will self-sow in very small numbers—be on the lookout for seedlings in May. Give each plant adequate room because, unlike many plants, one large but solitary nodding mandarin specimen looks better than a mass of smaller ones. Instead of grouping them, repeat them throughout your garden.

Slugs and snails have a taste for nodding mandarin foliage, so inspect your plants regularly for the skeletonized leaves and slime trails that signal mollusk predation. A non-yucky way to control slugs is to place a scrap piece of plywood (perhaps 12 inches square) at the base of the plant on which they're feeding. Early in the morning, turn the plywood over and you'll probably find some slugs clinging to the bottom. Take it over to the compost pile and brush the slugs off. Voilà!—slug control without the disgusting bits. Setting up a toad house in your garden can also do wonders.

Nodding mandarin is a plant you will have to special order or purchase by mail from specialty nurseries dealing in woodland plants, but it is worth seeking out and patiently cultivating.

Spotted geranium (*Geranium maculatum*) naturalizes well with other natives, such as sensitive fern (*Onoclea sensibilis*).

Spotted geranium (*Geranium maculatum*) is the best of our native geraniums. Its leaves, produced somewhat sparsely, have a classic, deeply cut geranium shape. In June, fresh, pink flowers with a slight purplish tinge cluster atop 18-inch stems. The whole plant is a bit on the slim side, wispier and less dense than the other geraniums mentioned in this book, and needs to be planted in quantity in order to look good.

In the wild, spotted geranium mixes with anything and everything, and although it has the ability to hold its own even with aggressive cohorts such as sensitive fern, I've never seen it overwhelm a neighbor. Spotted geranium is a charming plant in a naturalized setting or a very informal woodland garden where it can be allowed to spread at will along with *Phlox divaricata*, trillium, Jacob's ladder, our short native Solomon's seal (*Polygonatum biflorum*), and smallish ferns.

If given a little sun, spotted geranium does become a more substantial plant. 'Espresso' is a cultivar with bronzy leaves and pale-pink flowers, but because I've never had the opportunity to grow it, I don't know how well its color holds up in shade.

An alternative is dusky cranesbill (*G. phaeum*), a slightly oddball plant. Its other common name—mourning widow—arises from the rather somber purple flowers it usually sports. These are not to everyone's taste, yet they can look very attractive, especially next to more brightly flowered neighbors or gold- or blue-leaved hostas. In every other respect, dusky cranesbill looks like what we expect from a geranium, with finely divided leaves and beaked blossoms. Cultivars with white or lighter pink flowers are available. All are about 24 inches tall in flower and bloom in June. Its foliage may decline after flowering, so some grooming might be needed.

Hepatica · Liverwort · Liverleaf

Varies

USDA ZONE

I have grown liverwort for about three years now, and I am in love with it. It's become one of my favorite plants and my personal harbinger of spring. If you have a fondness for other little woodland wildflowers, such as trillium and Dutchman's breeches, you'll like liverwort, too.

H. acutiloba (Zone 4) is probably the most widely available liverwort; I sometimes see *H. americana* (Zone 3) offered for sale, too. They are very similar in appearance, and both are native plants. Only 4 inches tall in leaf and flower, they are truly charmers.

Like so many early-spring wildflowers, liverwort puts up blossoms before leaves. In mid-March, each crown will produce eight to ten sweet, single little flowers with a central explosion of stamens. Liverwort is coy, keeping its flowers closed on overcast days. Flower color changes with the light, sometimes appearing icy white, sometimes pale violet, and sometimes light pink. And the flowers change color as they mature, usually fading to white if they didn't start out that way.

The simple but delightful flowers of liverwort (*Hepatica acutiloba*) come and go before the plant's leaves unfurl.

When the flowers are spent, fuzzy furled leaves with three lobes open to display mottled patterns on a waxy surface. These remain as tiny foliar accents in the garden for the whole season.

Because of their diminutive size, plant liverworts in groups of three or more at the very foreground of a small border, or scatter them by the dozens or hundreds throughout an informal woodland garden, benignly neglecting them so they can slowly increase their numbers through the years. Don't confuse *Hepatica*, whose common name is liverwort, with *the* liverworts, one of the three plant groups making up the bryophytes.

Goldenseal (*Hydrastis canadensis*) shows off its stoplight-red, late-summer fruits.

Goldenseal is a native plant better known to herbalists than gardeners. Some people might initially grow it for its ecological value and as a curiosity rather than its ornamental qualities. Goldenseal has an interesting history as a medicinal plant overharvested for economic reasons. Consequently, goldenseal is much less common in the wild than it once was.

Goldenseal is a small plant (12 inches tall by 8 inches wide) with coarsely rugose (wrinkled), almost bumpy leaves with a dull surface. Each plant produces a solitary, white, sea anemone–like flower in spring. These mature into globular fruits much like those of kousa dogwood, turning stoplight red in late July or early August. By September, the seeds have dispersed, and left to their own devices, a high percentage of seeds will germinate the following spring.

Although I've placed goldenseal in the accent plants category, that doesn't mean I recommend using it only as a foil for other plants. If not for the tendency of its foliage to decline late in summer, I would call goldenseal a backbone plant. It looks best massed in groups of thirty or more individuals spaced quite closely. Starting with just a half dozen plants and letting them self-sow (offspring will come up very close to the parent plant), you'll get an impressive little colony after seven to eight years.

Goldenseal is tolerant of medium to high soil moisture. Although temporarily dry conditions won't kill the plant, they can result in early dormancy, less vigorous growth, and a withered appearance.

Goldenseal is best used in informal woodland gardens. Native plant collectors will surely prize it, and it looks right at home next to other natives such as trillium, twinleaf, Solomon's seal, white wood aster, and the like. Goldenseal is not a garden center plant, but is certainly available via mail order and at any nursery with a decent native plant section.

Twinleaf is a native plant that some gardeners, myself included, find absolutely endearing. Whether it will ever catch on in a bigger way, I can't predict, but I do encourage every shade gardener to give it a try. Thomas Jefferson is said to have had a special fondness for the plant and to have grown it widely at Monticello, which is the reason for its Latin name.

Twinleaf emerges in late March or early April, pushing pink-hued stalks through the soil soon after spring thaw. In no time at all, each plant produces a handful of simple, cheery white flowers that remain open for only three to four days before their petals drop. At the same time, twinleaf's characteristic symmetrical, butterfly-shaped leaves unfurl and spread out into a tiny canopy only 12 to 15 inches tall. The spent flowers are followed rapidly by unique seedpods in the shape of an inverted pear but with a hinged lid reminiscent of Nantucket baskets. These pop open in early July and disperse their seeds, after which the plant can go dormant—but will not necessarily do so—at any time. Because of the uncertainty it exhibits about early dormancy, I debated long and hard about whether to call twinleaf a spring ephemeral or an accent plant. Finally, I placed it here because it at least has the potential to look good through the summer months.

An ideal way to use twinleaf is to place it near yellow fumitory or native bleeding heart. Those plants have finely divided leaves that contrast pleasingly

Leaves like oversized butterflies and pristine white but short-lived flowers are typical of twinleaf (*Jeffersonia diphylla*).

with the broad "butterfly wings" of twinleaf and will also help conceal the small gap it may leave if it goes dormant early. Deer have a taste for twinleaf and may browse it if they find it, so treat it as you would a hosta with respect to applying repellent. Twinleaf may self-sow in very small numbers. Be on the lookout for seedlings in early May, no more than a few feet from the parent plant.

Twinleaf is still hard to find in nurseries, and mail-order sources specializing in native plants may be the best option for purchasing it. Once in your garden, it will become a finer foliage plant with each passing season. It needs about five years to come into its own, so give it lots of time before deciding what you think of it.

Lamiastrum galeobdolon and cvs.

Yellow archangel · False Lamium

Yellow archangel (*Lamiastrum galeobdolon*) is a shallow-rooted spreader with long-lasting flowers in late spring and early summer.

Lamiastrum resembles *Lamium* and is occasionally even identified as *Lamium galeobdolon* in the trade. I'll leave it to the taxonomists to duke out its actual identity, and I'll focus on the difference between the two in garden utility.

Yellow archangel is a low-growing rambler often offered for sale in the form of the cultivar 'Hermann's Pride,' with leaves featuring pleasing, variable, and understated silvery variegation. Like *Lamium*, it creeps along and roots wherever a node touches the ground, and flowers principally in late May and early June. In contrast to *Lamium*, its flowers are a soft yellow.

For use as an actual groundcover, I think *Lamiastrum* is superior to *Lamium* because it's a slightly more substantial plant and its foliage holds up better over the course of the summer. The downside of *Lamiastrum* is that, as a more vigorous plant than *Lamium*, it has the potential to become a bit of a pest if left to grow unchecked.

I don't recommend using yellow archangel to cover large swaths of ground anyway, because of the difficulty in removing fallen leaves from it in autumn (another trait it shares with *Lamium*). It roots shallowly, so raking it is impossible, and a leaf blower is the only real option. Perhaps the best way to use it is as a subtle but effective filler allowed to spread throughout a small stand of medium-sized ferns, where it will fill in more quickly than *Lamium* and its color scheme will be complementary rather than contrasting.

Deadnettle is a low-growing, prostrate plant that will root shallowly everywhere a node touches the ground. It's called a "nettle" because its leaves resemble those of the onerous stinging nettle, but never fear—its stems lack that plant's biting barbs, and its growth habit is entirely different. (I have always assumed that the "dead" in deadnettle's name is used in the sense of "inactive" or "harmless.")

Deadnettle is grown for both its foliage and its hooded flowers. Leaf variegation takes two forms: nearly white with a thin green margin, or medium green to chartreuse with a white stripe down the center. Deadnettle's numerous, small, pale-pink, purple-pink, or white flowers whorl around short, blunt, upright stalks, first appearing in May and returning, on and off, throughout the summer. The whole plant is only 3 inches tall in leaf and 6 inches tall in flower.

Although often called a groundcover, deadnettle is really not very useful for covering substantial areas because it frequently looks a little ratty in the heat of

Show off deadnettle (*Lamium* 'Shell Pink' is shown here) to best effect by allowing it to drape over rocks.

midsummer. There are other plants that make far superior groundcovers in the usual sense of that word. Instead, I suggest using deadnettle as an underplanting for other perennials that lack a lot of leaves at ground level. Underneath tall, vase-shaped and widely spaced hostas (*Hosta sieboldiana* 'Elegans,' for example), nodding mandarin, or Solomon's seal, deadnettle can make a carpet of attractive leaves and keep its companion plants cleaner by preventing soil or mulch from being splattered upward by rain. In return, the shelter of the taller plants may

Plants for
Deeper Shade

keep deadnettle from developing the moth-eaten look it can get when exposed to too much sun or abuse from weather.

Deadnettle also looks exceptionally good at the very front of a planting atop a rock retaining wall, which many of us Northeasterners have. Tuck small pieces of deadnettle in between taller foreground plants, and allow it to drape over and soften the edge of the wall. This placement will also show off its flowers to best effect. If it gets longer than desired, just clip away the excess. Deadnettle is very amenable to pruning and shaping. If it does get ratty for a time, don't worry—fresh foliage will come along soon.

Popular cultivars with white leaves include 'White Nancy' (white flowers), 'Beacon Silver' (purplish flowers), and 'Pink Pewter' (pink flowers). Two good selections with chartreuse foliage are 'Aureum' (purplish flowers) and 'Beedham's White' (white flowers), while 'Shell Pink' has green-and-white variegation and soft-pink flowers.

USDA ZONE 4

Lysimachia nummularia 'Aurea'

Golden Creeping Jenny

Golden creeping Jenny (*Lysimachia nummularia* 'Aurea') adorns the base of summersweet (*Clethra alnifolia*) shrubs.

If you're familiar with this as a common container plant, generally sold as an annual in 4-inch pots, you may be surprised to learn that it's winter hardy throughout much of the Northeast. That said, I recommend its use in the ground only in limited circumstances, because it is a plant with the potential to become a pest.

Golden creeping Jenny is grown for its foliage. In containers, it's used as a "spiller," draping several feet in the course of a season. In the ground, it forms a dense, 1-inch mat of brilliant golden leaves. In contained spaces, it can be used as a groundcover to fill in around taller perennials that suffer from "bare-ankle syndrome."

Its bright leaf color in the shade is quite striking, but it looks best as a contrast to plants with green leaves, so use it in moderation or it will no longer seem as remarkable. Any excess plants you pull should be bagged and thrown in the trash; composting them will probably just lead to a creeping Jenny invasion.

Sweet Cicely is a plant I recommend with extreme caution. It has the potential to spread rapidly by seed and should be religiously deadheaded. It's somewhat self-regulating, though: if grown in too much shade, it won't flower—hence, no seed. So, if you're happy with just the leaf, you can grow this plant in deeper shade, but if you want flowering, you will have to give it light shade.

In light-shade situations, sweet Cicely's 2- to 3-foot mound of ferny leaves can grace the garden airily. In May, white, umbelliferous flowers reminiscent of Queen Anne's lace will appear on stalks held well above the foliage. The leaves and seeds of sweet Cicely have a pleasantly pungent anise fragrance.

The licorice scent of sweet Cicely (*Myrrhis odorata*) adds another dimension to the shade garden beyond flowers and foliage.

Be aware that at least two other plants go by the name sweet Cicely, but they are not as highly ornamental, so be sure to purchase this plant by Latin name, not common name, or you might be disappointed.

Bursting forth with profusions of star-shaped flowers in May, the two species that share the common name woodland phlox—*P. divaricata* and *P. stolonifera*—are plants I look for every year with anticipation. Sweetly simple yet seductive, they are among the truest signs that spring is not just coming, but here to stay.

Woodland phlox's flowers may be blue, pink, pale plum, or white. Its leaves are quite ordinary (although one selection of *P. divaricata*, 'Montrose Tricolor,' has foliage outlined in white and pink), forming a low mat 6 to 8 inches tall and creeping moderately wherever light is adequate and competition is not too fierce. Out of flower, it's not unattractive but also not impressive—it's liable to fade

Plants for
Deeper Shade

Woodland phlox (*Phlox divaricata* and *P. stolonifera*) can spread through the years to produce a sea of flowers in spring.

into the background. So this is not really a border plant, but rather an excellent choice for naturalized areas and informal woodland gardens.

Getting woodland phlox to work well in your garden can be a little tricky, but it's worthwhile in the long run. The key to using woodland phlox to good effect is to interplant it with suitable companions. Allowing it to meander around the base of ferns and other small plants that will not overwhelm or overshadow it is a good approach. You can allow patches of noncompetitive wildflowers such as jack-in-the-pulpit to grow right through woodland phlox without detriment.

An especially lovely effect can be achieved by planting swaths of different colors of woodland phlox adjacent to one another, contrasting, say, a pale and icy-blue selection ('May Breeze') with periwinkle ('Blue Moon') and purple ('Plum Perfect') neighbors. It's also excellent under upright deciduous azaleas that flower around the same time.

Uvularia grandiflora

Merrybells

U. grandiflora is another member of that group of sweet native woodland plants that also includes Solomon's seal and nodding mandarin. Like its kin, it sends up the slenderest of stalks, leafless at the bottom and fragile looking, yet capable of piercing through the thickest blanket of last year's leaves. These delicate, 15- to 18-inch stems then bend gracefully to take on the shape of a candy cane before producing dangling yellow bell-shaped flowers at their tips in May.

Dangling yellow blossoms give rise to the delightful name merrybells (*Uvularia grandiflora*) for this native wildflower.

Uvularia works best in informal woodland gardens. It can be used in more structured gardens, but it only really holds its own in those settings if an entire mature clump is transplanted into the garden, or if you have the patience to grow it for five or more years. Starting from one merrybells plant in a standard 5-pint nursery pot, it will take at least that long to get a clump dense and showy enough to be a real contributor to your garden. Other species of *Uvularia* can be running rather than clump forming, so I recommend sticking to the species mentioned here. Deer sometimes browse *Uvularia*, and it can suffer from slug damage.

Viola spp.

Violet

Varies | USDA ZONE

I list violets here with some hesitation. Although violets are certainly well adapted to shade and lovely, they do have two major drawbacks. First, most violets are rampant self-sowers, and second, it's quite hard to dig out unwanted plants. I could overlook the former problem if it weren't for the latter one; but anyone who has tried to weed out excess violets, only to have the plants' top growth come off in his or her hand while the tenacious rhizomes stay stubbornly behind in the ground, knows how frustrating violets can be.

But if you use them for naturalizing, you don't really have to worry about those problems. In fact, they could work to your advantage. My one caveat is that you'll have trouble keeping violets from cropping up *everywhere*. If that's okay with you, go with violets. If you think you'll end up frustrated, this is one plant best avoided.

For naturalizing, I suggest using native species only. There are so many of these, many adapted to very specific conditions (such as moist soil), that if you really want to find the perfect violet for your garden, you should probably consult a botanical society in your state for more detailed information. Here

The Northeast enjoys a wealth of native violets, including *Viola labradorica*.

are a few of the more common ones to consider: *V. biflora* (yellow flowers, Zone 4), *V. canadensis* (white flowers, Zone 3), *V. labradorica* (classic purple flowers, Zone 2), and *V. pedata* (two-toned purple-and-white flowers and a finely divided leaf that's also ornamental, Zone 4).

You might find that there are already lots of violets on your property. Many species are native to this part of the world, and several others were introduced and have escaped into the wild. If you have one of those rare violet-free lots and would like to try growing them, you might start off with *V. canadensis* or *V. labradorica*, two of the easiest native species to buy. Alternatively, you shouldn't have too much trouble finding a neighbor or gardening buddy with some violets to share!

For anyone unfamiliar with this ubiquitous plant, violets are mounding plants typically 4 to 12 inches tall that produce a dense growth of green or plum-colored heart-shaped leaves. Violet (what else?), white, yellow, or bicolored flowers perfect for nosegays generally start in June.

One last note: the violets I'm referring to here are *not* the same as the garden pansies sold by the millions at every garden center and grocery store each spring, although they are certainly related. Most pansies are neither reliably winter hardy in the North nor particularly shade tolerant. For naturalizing, use one of our native perennial species.

Spring Ephemerals

These are plants that go dormant during late spring or summer, making them one-or two-season plants. Remember to position them so the gap they leave in the garden will be filled in by a neighboring plant or won't be noticed.

Arisaema spp.

Jack-in-the-pulpit

4 USDA ZONE

Just as Clara Smith's poem "Jack in the Pulpit" is a classic of children's literature, the plant that inspired it is a classic of the Northeast woods. Jacks (for short) are queer little plants, remarkably variable and ineffably charming. Somehow, their very oddness (like opossums in the animal kingdom) is what makes them delightful. If someone asked me to design a private shady nook for a child, the first thing I'd think of planting is jack-in-the-pulpit, because if ever there was a plant that looked like it should be a home for a fairy (or the inspiration for a poem), it's this one.

Jack in the pulpit
Preaches to-day,
Under the green trees
Just over the way. . . .
Green is his surplice,
Green are his bands;
In his queer little pulpit
The little priest stands.
CLARA SMITH

A. triphyllum is our most common native species. It puts up one to three stalks (up to 24 inches tall on an established plant, but likely to be much shorter on a youngster), each one topped by a three-part leaf that looks nearly identical to those of trillium. Soon after, flowering parts with an unusual spathe-and-spadix arrangement appear, the spathe (the "pulpit" part; the spadix is the "preacher" part) often boldly striped with some combination of apple green, white, and deep chocolate brown. Over the course of the summer, the seeds develop innocuously until suddenly in late August, a flash of brilliant crimson close to the ground catches your eye, and you realize that the jack's leaves have gone dormant, revealing a drumstick of impossibly red berries. Let them lie where they fall, and the following spring you'll probably have a crop of seedlings that can be moved with ease to populate other garden nooks and crannies.

Plants for
Deeper Shade

If you're a jack fan, you'll also want to try *A. dracontium*. Exotic though it looks, it is a Northeast native. It's a larger plant with a somewhat different leaf whose spadix is topped by a long, whip-like protrusion that inspired some imaginative gardener to dub it "green dragon" plant.

Jacks grow almost anywhere they are left undisturbed. They tolerate dry soil but are also happy in moist areas. Interestingly, for a plant so thoroughly associated with the woods, they also love growing in sun and become truly impressive with enough light. As plants that go dormant early, they need to be interplanted with ground-covering companions such as native wild ginger or leafy things that will fill in the gap when jack has gone to bed. They are truly easygoing, no-care plants that will bring a smile to your face every time you see them.

The extraordinary spathe-and-spadix flowers of jack-in-the-pulpit (*Arisaema triphyllum*) charm young and old alike.

Corydalis solida and cvs.

Spring Fumitory

This is another of those plants that seem to be on no one's radar, and I'm at a loss to explain why. *C. solida* is quite hardy, deports itself sweetly, comes to the garden well dressed in feathery gray-green foliage topped by flowers of a unique dusky-purple hue, and vanishes after making its contribution to the landscape with absolutely admirable rapidity. In short, it's what we all wish our guests would be, so why don't more gardeners grow it? It's a mystery to me.

Really, this spring ephemeral is a little beauty. It closely resembles Dutchman's breeches (*Dicentra cucullaria*) in size (6 to 8 inches), season of bloom (April), foliage (feathery), and floral presentation, except for the fact that its smoky-lavender flowers are distinctly not in the repertoire of a *Dicentra*. Because of their sameness-yet-difference, these two plants make nice garden companions. Alternate groupings of them around early-emerging plants with bare ankles, such as hellebore and baneberry, to create a carpet of pastel purple and pink that will conveniently fade just as the long-season perennials are filling in. *C. solida*

Spring fumitory (*Corydalis solida*) is ferny, fleeting, and fascinating.

is also excellent in the rock garden, where it will tolerate three seasons of dry conditions with aplomb during its dormancy.

C. solida grows from very small tubers that need no special care. Once planted, they'll never need you to do a thing for them. The plant does seed a bit, but only close to home. If the flower color of the species isn't to your liking, look for the legendary light-red cultivar 'George Baker' (a legend mostly because no one is sure if they have the real thing) or other cultivars that bloom pale pink or white.

Dicentra spp.
Dutchman's Breeches · Squirrel Corn

USDA ZONE **4**

Every bit worthy of its giggle-inducing name, Dutchman's breeches (*D. cucullaria*) is a true treat of spring. It's a tiny, delicate native plant with dangling white flowers that do indeed look like upside-down, ballooning pantaloons strung out on a laundry line to dry. I challenge anyone to look at them without being utterly charmed!

If not for its very early season of bloom and rapid onset of dormancy, Dutchman's breeches could easily be confused with *D. eximia* or a *Corydalis*. All three

The pantaloon-shaped flowers of Dutchman's breeches (*Dicentra cucullaria*) never fail to delight.

are, in fact, related, belonging to the same plant family. They share the same highly divided, lacy foliage and fleshy, easily damaged stems, but there the resemblance ends. Dutchman's breeches emerges as early as March, grows about 12 inches tall and wide, blooms in April, and disappears in May. Another species, *D. canadensis* (squirrel corn), is very similar but harder to find as a nursery plant.

Given enough years to naturalize and a spot it prefers, Dutchman's breeches can form enormous, noncompetitive colonies. Many hikers lucky enough to go for a walk in the woods at just the right time of year have been stopped in their tracks by the sight of thousands of Dutchman's breeches sweeping across hillsides and down ravines. I have seen native stands growing equally well in both damp and well-drained soil, alongside streams as well as on dry, rocky slopes. Interestingly, though, the seeds of Dutchman's breeches are apparently spread by ants in a symbiotic relationship, so quite possibly the occurrence of large colonies in some locales and smaller ones in other locales depends on more than just soil and drainage.

Whatever the exact combination of conditions required for Dutchman's breeches to spread, you can't go wrong using them in naturalized plantings with clumping ferns that will fill in just as the frilly foliage of Dutchman's breeches is waning. They are equally sweet in the border, ideally clustered around late-emerging perennials such as hostas, particularly slower-growing varieties that do not need frequent division.

Like virtually all spring ephemerals, Dutchman's breeches need no special care once planted. Just be sure to get out into the garden early enough to enjoy their brief but special show.

Dodecatheon spp.

Shooting Star

The species of shooting star native to eastern North America, *D. meadia*, is one of our more impressive spring ephemerals, perhaps second only to Virginia bluebells in showiness. In April, a mound of substantial, strap-like leaves emerges from the ground, followed in May by naked 16-inch-tall stalks that erupt at the top into a little shower of heavily reflexed white flowers on long pedicels.

Obviously, someone felt the flowers were reminiscent of shooting stars, but what they really remind me of is badminton shuttlecocks streaking downward! Whatever you see when you look at them, you'll enjoy the sight.

Shooting star looks best scattered irregularly along the edges of pathways through your woodland garden. Several other species are native to North America but are principally from the West Coast. Some have bright, purplish-pink flowers but otherwise offer no advantage over our eastern species.

Shooting star (*Dodecatheon meadia*) is a spring ephemeral whose name describes the fireworks impression its flowers give.

Erythronium 'Pagoda'

Pagoda Trout Lily

'Pagoda' is an *Erythronium* hybrid bred to be much bigger and showier than species such as our native *E. americanum*. Rather than repeat my general description of trout lilies here, I'll refer you to the entry for *E. americanum* under Plants for Special Situations. Imagine something three times as large in every way, and you've got 'Pagoda.'

'Pagoda' blooms in April and early May. Unfortunately, many people report that deer browse it. Because it's a member of the Liliaceae (a plant family that

The dangling, recurved flowers and mottled leaves of hybrid trout lily (*Erythronium* 'Pagoda') are among the most unusual of any spring ephemeral.

also includes true lilies and daylilies, both deer favorites), this isn't surprising. You may not even notice a bit of deer browsing in a naturalized stand of *E. americanum*, but you'll definitely notice it if your 'Pagoda' trout lilies get topped! Apply repellent if you anticipate that this will be a problem on your property.

Mertensia virginica

Virginia Bluebells

Virginia bluebells are nothing less than the royalty of spring ephemerals. Large, showy, and colorful, they put on one of the very best spectacles of any spring-blooming plant, with all the rich costuming you'd expect in the court of a queen.

Virginia bluebells break ground very early in spring. Their tightly furled leaves look like tiny burgundy cabbages when they first emerge, but as they grow, they quickly morph into medium-green, fleshy oblongs that resemble the leafy green vegetable sorrel. In no time, they produce profuse clusters of dangling blue bell-shaped flowers on 18-inch stems, blooming for several weeks in late April and early May. (They also come in a white-flowered form that is uncommon but not impossible to find.)

Once flowering ceases, and almost before you have time to notice, they close up shop. Their leaves yellow rapidly, and the plants have gone completely dormant by mid-June. They'll spend the remainder of the year as inscrutable, seemingly dead but really just dormant rhizomes nestled just below the soil surface. Incredibly, their entire aboveground life cycle is barely two months long.

The amazing rapidity of their growth and "demise," along with their large size and showiness, make Virginia bluebells very border friendly. Their leaves don't need to hang around the garden for months to store enough

Perhaps our showiest native spring ephemeral is Virginia bluebells (*Mertensia virginica*), a natural companion for old-fashioned bleeding heart (*Dicentra spectabilis*).

energy to ensure flowering the following year. Virginia bluebells put on their spectacular display and then vanish—a gardener's dream!

Virginia bluebells spread readily by seed, moving outward from an original planting at a speed of 1 or 2 feet a year. This is generally a welcome tendency, because however many you have, you will almost assuredly want more.

Virginia bluebells' sky-blue flowers are an effective counterpoint to yellow daffodils, and gardeners with borders in both sun and shade can take best advantage of this artful duo, planting the sunny areas with clumps of daffodils and the shady ones with masses of bluebells. The result will be breathtaking!

Another natural companion is old-fashioned bleeding heart, whose brilliant pink or clean white flowers reach their peak simultaneously with those of Virginia bluebells, although the bluebells will go dormant months before bleeding heart. If you try this combination, use hostas, ferns, or other late-emerging plants to fill in the areas occupied by the bluebells in May.

USDA ZONE **3**

Sanguinaria canadensis and cvs.

Bloodroot

First, let me dispense with this plant's alarming name. Bloodroot is so called because if you snap one of its roots in half, it exudes a reddish sap that resembles blood. Undoubtedly, the roots have been the means whereby many a practical joke was perpetrated, but aboveground, there's nothing creepy about this plant.

Bloodroot emerges from the ground in April with its leaves clasped around 4-inch stems and a central, brilliant white single flower. Once open, the leaves display heavily cut but rounded lobes, and the flowers sport bright-yellow stamens. At some point during summer (I've seen it go dormant early, and I've seen it go dormant late, and I don't know why this varies so much), it all vanishes until the following year.

The creepy name of bloodroot (*Sanguinaria canadensis*) belies the plant's spotless white flowers and bold leaves.

Bloodroot is odd and a little homely, yet simultaneously cute. It self-sows moderately over time to produce loose colonies. It's not well suited to a border where it has a tendency to seed into other perennials, but it's nice in an informal woodland garden where it's fun to let things pop up where they may. Bloodroot also grows densely and beautifully in full sun. A double-flowered cultivar, 'Flore Pleno,' is rare but available from specialty growers.

Trillium spp.
Trillium

Varies | USDA ZONE

Trilliums are prized woodlanders with a small but devoted following. They are deceptively simple plants with a certain *je ne sais quoi* that some gardeners find irresistible. Several of the world's loveliest trilliums are native to our Northeast woods, and although they are very sensitive to changes in their environment and must be treated with care, many are actually quite easy to grow.

Trillium produces a small number of 8- to 12-inch stalks with three whorled leaves at the apex. From the center of the three leaves, a single flower emerges in April or May. Depending on the species, the flower may sit upright or it may nod, sometimes to the point of being hidden beneath the leaves. It may look as abstract as some sort of alien pod or be classically flower-like. Trillium blossoms are typically bright white, garnet red or sulfur yellow, and trillium leaves may be an ordinary green or mottled like a toad. Sessile trilliums in particular (those that present their flowers in an upright posture) tend to look like a work of carefully folded origami, which is undoubtedly part of their allure.

You'll eagerly anticipate the odd beauty of wake-robin (*Trillium erectum*) every spring.

Large-flowered trillium (*T. grandiflorum*, Zone 5) may be the most ornamental of all trilliums, and fortunately it is a snap to grow. Just give it a nice spot with rich but well-drained soil at the base of a deciduous tree and without too much other competition, and it will thrive. A double form called 'Flore Pleno'

A colony of great white trillium (*Trillium grandiflorum*) is the most prized possession of many a shade gardener.

is available, as is a pink form (var. *roseum*). *T. erectum* (wake-robin, Zone 4), *T. cuneatum* (Zone 6), *T. luteum* (Zone 5), and *T. sessile* (Zone 4) are several more trilliums that are not too demanding.

A nice way to display trillium is in a little "trillium corner" where clumps of several different kinds are interspersed with *Uvularia* and other delicate spring-flowering woodlanders with similar needs. Some or all may go dormant by midsummer, so interplant with begonias or caladiums to fill in the space for the remainder of the season.

People grow trilliums because they are fascinating, odd, collectible, sculptural harbingers of the coming summer, reminders of childhood walks in the woods, and for dozens of other reasons. Whatever your reason for growing them, patience is key. They are slow to increase, which is the reason nursery-propagated plants can be quite expensive—they require five or more years of cultivation from seed before they are large enough to sell. Buy only from reputable growers and always ask about the provenance of the plants.

Bulbs

As I explained earlier, I recommend that bulbs be added to a garden only after the garden has gone through one or two growing seasons and its design has been finalized. That way, the bulbs won't interfere or get lost if the garden is rearranged.

Also recall that the bulbs that do well in shade are minor bulbs. With the possible exception of bluebells (see "Bulbs," in "Plants for Light Shade"), plant minor bulbs in larger groups than you would major bulbs, but not as deeply, and put them where they can be appreciated despite their small size.

Crocus spp. and cvs.

Crocus

Varies
USDA ZONE

Crocuses are the second earliest of the minor bulbs, typically blooming in March right after the snowdrops come to light, and they are one of the first to offer colors other than white. Only about 4 inches tall, they produce little chalice-shaped flowers in brilliant shades of yellow, blue, violet, and pink (in addition to white) that often feature vivid contrasting veins or bicolored markings. Bloom time is very short—only a few days—but crocuses have a simplicity and vivacity that's powerfully cheerful and an effective antidote to the winter blahs, so plant them close to your house.

Crocuses are usually offered by species and cultivar name. Although there are differences between crocus selections—some have larger flowers, and bloom time and cold hardiness vary—for the average gardener, spring-flowering crocuses can be viewed as a pretty monolithic bunch. As plants they are all fundamentally

Of all the early spring bulbs, crocus (*Crocus*) offers the widest range of colors.

the same size and all bloom very early, so just choose the colors you like best from among the crocuses cold hardy in your area.

Crocuses can spread fairly aggressively. *C. tommasinianus* has a well-deserved reputation as a self-sower. A bunch of it planted on a hill will, left to its own devices, create a downslope delta of offspring in a few years. Rather than deadhead these miniscule plants, make a pass in spring when the crocuses are in bloom to remove any strays from places they shouldn't be. In all likelihood, you'll notice the seedlings only when they are in flower, so make a point of being diligent about this task.

Winter aconite (*Eranthis hyemalis*) presents its flowers in a uniquely decorative way.

The "winter" in winter aconite's name is a dead giveaway that this bulb is among the very first to flower—generally as soon as the snow melts. It's a great addition to any setting where you might have crocuses and snowdrops.

Small in scale, like all minor bulbs, winter aconite tops out at about 3 inches. People love it for its slightly unusual presentation. Instead of the strap-like leaves so common to bulbs, it produces a solitary (but large for the size of the plant), bright-yellow buttercup flower surrounded by a not-quite-Elizabethan ruff of a leaf "collar."

Winter aconite is said to require adequate moisture even during the summer months when it's dormant, so it may have its limitations for rock garden use, but in woodland soils it does well consistently. It's also said to self-sow, but I have not had this occur to any significant degree, so I think of it as one of the better-behaved spring bulbs.

Galanthus spp. and cvs.

Snowdrop

Varies | USDA ZONE

Snowdrops are so called because they miraculously appear, already in bloom, as the snow melts in earliest spring. From 6 to 8 inches tall, they have charming, pendant white flowers with olive-green markings and gray-green, strap-like leaves. Unlike crocuses, their flowers are fairly long lasting, looking good for several weeks before fading. Also unlike crocuses, they should be deadheaded before their seeds ripen to prevent them from carpeting the garden, which will not look as good as it sounds! Or, allow them to naturalize within a controlled space, deadheading the perimeter plants to contain them.

There are several species and many named cultivars of *Galanthus*; the most common is *G. nivalis* (Zone 3), but at the risk of offending snowdrop aficionados, I'll offer my opinion that they are all interchangeable from

Snowdrops (*Galanthus*) will often appear in flower under melting snow drifts.

the average gardener's perspective, at least from an aesthetic standpoint. Unless you are particular, use whichever kind you come across in your plant shopping expeditions, as long as it's winter hardy in your area.

Scilla spp. and cvs.

Squill

Varies | USDA ZONE

By far the most common squill is Siberian squill (*S. siberica*, Zone 5, usually offered in the cultivar 'Spring Beauty' but also available in a white form, 'Alba'). In late March, it puts forth bright-green, chive-like leaves that broaden to look more like blades of grass, followed quickly by 5-inch stems topped by a small number of pendant, intensely true-blue stars. It goes dormant almost as speedily as it appeared, vanishing by late May.

Most other squills hardy in our climate are similar. Through specialty bulb

Plants for
Deeper Shade

Siberian squill (*Scilla*) offers the first burst of blue
in the early-spring shade garden.

catalogs, you might come across *S. bifolia* (Zone 3), whose flowers are more purplish and face outward or upward, and its form *rosea* (also called *carnea*), which is the palest of pale pinks. *S. tubergeniana* (also called *S. mischtschenkoana*, Zone 6) is a squill whose milky-white flowers have blue midribs and appear even earlier than those of Siberian squill. Along the coast where conditions are milder, gardeners might be able to grow *S. pratensis* (also called *S. litardierei*, Zone 6), which looks more like a grape hyacinth than a squill and also blooms at a time of year (May) more typical of grape hyacinths.

Squills are rampant spreaders that should be grown in limited numbers and deadheaded to keep them from seeding. This can be tedious on a plant as small as a squill, but it is imperative, or in a few short years every perennial in your garden (as well as your lawn and just about everything else, possibly up to and including your sock drawer) will be infested with squill bulbs. If you know that you won't have the patience or time to do this job, you're better off not growing squills.

These are the ferns whose growth habit makes them good neighbors and therefore suitable for use in a shady flower border. They clump rather than run, and they may never need dividing. Don't overlook them because they don't flower! These ferns are graceful, undemanding, and rewarding—what more can you ask of a plant?

Adiantum pedatum

Northern Maidenhair Fern

USDA ZONE 3

This delicate, lacy fern is the boreal counterpart to the South's *A. capillus-vernus*, the maidenhair fern many people know and grow as a houseplant. Every bit the equal of its tender relative in attractiveness, *A. pedatum* is cold hardy and a fairly common resident of northern woodlands.

Maidenhair fern is an iconic plant of the Northeast woods. The shape of its unusual, reflexive frond—it curves back on itself—and its ebony stalks (*rachides*, technically) make it unique.

This fern increases in size slowly, so it's one of those plants worth buying big if you can afford to and if you can find it in gallon containers. However, in those rare locations where it is very happy, it can be extremely vigorous and will produce an extensive colony over time.

Maidenhair fern grows 12 to 18 inches tall, and because its stalks are quite naked at the bottom, it's best placed behind something low growing with good, persistent foliage, such as native wild ginger, a short hosta, a dwarf astilbe, or epimedium. Alternatively, allow *Lysimachia nummularia* 'Aurea,' *Lamium*, *Gallium odoratum*, or something similar to wander at its base.

Maidenhair fern (*Adiantum pedatum*) is the most elegant of our native Northeast ferns.

Athyrium spp. and cvs.

Japenese Painted Fern · Lady Fern

The ghostly shades of Japanese painted fern (*Athyrium niponicum* 'Pictum') make a counterpoint to native wild ginger (*Asarum canadense*).

By far the most commonly grown *Athyrium* is *A. niponicum* 'Pictum' (Zone 5), commonly called Japanese painted fern. It's absolutely unique in its appearance, with grayish-blue fronds having complex shading and pink accents that are strikingly lovely. Growing to about 12 inches tall, its lax habit gives it a spread of about 24 inches.

Its best quality—its stunning coloration—makes placement a bit challenging. Although it doesn't look *bad* next to anything, it can look unspectacular next to some companions and utterly natural next to others. It's not always obvious why certain combinations work and others are just mediocre, so experimentation is key. In my experience, this fern looks best next to plants with foliage having a strong blue or gray component (lady's mantle, blue hostas, native wild ginger, twinleaf, the shrub *Hydrangea arborescens*, and, if planted in light shade, *Heuchera americana* 'Dale's Strain' and the shrub *Spiraea* 'Little Princess'); plants with pink, pale-blue, or violet flowers (*Geranium maculatum*, *Phlox divaricata*); and plants whose finely cut foliage matches the fern's, even if every other quality is different (*Dicentra eximia*, especially the pink-flowered form). It's also effective massed as a groundcover and used as a foreground for taller, upright ferns such as interrupted fern.

Unless massed, Japanese painted fern should be planted in groups of three or five. One solitary painted fern just doesn't look right somehow, unless it's a large specimen. Although this fern is a clumper, it is so vigorous that it's sure to need division every few years except when used as a groundcover, in which case there's no reason not to let it increase in size indefinitely.

In recent years, other cultivars have been introduced with more pink or burgundy tones or other variations on the basic 'Pictum' mold. All are worth trying.

The other common *Athyrium* is *A. filix-femina* (Zone 4), known as lady fern for the graceful impression made by its vase-shaped form and finely divided fronds. John Mickel, formerly of the New York Botanical Garden and a noted fern expert and author, wrote in his book *Ferns for American Gardens*, "This is probably the most variable species in the world, with more than three hundred named English forms." Most, of course, are available only through specialty growers. The species itself is not too hard to find at any nursery with a decent fern selection. Reaching 18 inches tall, it's useful wherever you need a fern of moderate size and upright stature.

Cyrtomium falcatum

Japanese holly fern

Although every reference book says that Japanese holly fern is winter hardy only to USDA Zone 6, it has thrived on my Zone 5 property for over a decade without extra winter protection and despite the stress of having been transplanted twice. At the very least, I can say that gardeners in coastal areas should have no trouble growing it, and its unique beauty makes it worth a try for inland gardeners willing to roll the dice.

Each of the principal divisions (technically, a *pinna*) of a Japanese holly fern frond is entire and resembles a stiff, glossy holly leaf, hence the plant's common name. In addition, each pinna has a faint, net-like pattern on its surface, although this is noticeable only on close inspection.

Japanese holly fern is a medium-sized fern, growing to about 18 inches tall but holding its fronds laxly to spread about 24 inches. It looks best massed in groups of about three to six or more, planted closely to give a full, lush effect. It looks especially graceful draping over rocks or next to pottery placed in the garden for ornament, or against a backdrop of gold-variegated hostas. Its fronds are persistent, so if you're a stickler for neatness, cut off the previous year's growth in late winter.

Japanese holly fern (*Cyrtomium falcatum*) looks right at home next to fetterbush (*Leucothoe fontenisiana*).

Plants for
Deeper Shade

Dryopteris spp. and cvs.

Wood Fern · Autumn Fern · Male Fern

Marginal fern (*Dryopteris marginalis*) is one of the best in a genus of exceptionally statuesque ferns.

The genus *Dryopteris* is a treasure trove for Northeast gardeners. It probably contains more useful, attractive, and winter-hardy members than any other genus. As a group, they are known as the wood ferns. Although some wood ferns will not survive northern winters, if you're going to experiment with new ferns in your garden, look to this genus first for strong contenders.

Marginal wood fern (*D. marginalis*, Zone 3) is a major component of the natural woodland herbaceous layer in the Northeast, and one of the very best ferns overall for garden use. It is shaped like an elegant, wide-mouthed vase, and it's large enough (30 inches tall and 24 to 30 inches wide across the top) to have presence. Its frond is classic, with divided pinnae and a gentle taper from base to tip. It's what people see in their minds when they think "fern."

Use marginal wood fern either singly or in small groups in the middle of the border, or to fill in and merge with the natural setting at the rear of an informal woodland garden. Its fronds are moderately persistent, and you may want to go to the effort of removing them in winter or early spring.

There are at least a half dozen other wood fern species worth trying. *D. australis* (Dixie wood fern, Zone 5) is the tallest in the group, supposedly capable of growing to 5 feet (although it hasn't for me). Its stalks have an almost military bearing, growing nearly vertically. Its pinnae, on the other hand, orient themselves parallel to the ground, resulting in a "Venetian blind" effect. Because these plants are so narrow, plant them very closely—only 12 inches apart.

In contrast, *D. cycadina* (black wood fern, Zone 5) is wider (24 inches) than it is tall (18 inches). It's an Asian species with fronds that are thick and also somewhat waxy, which gives them weight and substance. Somehow, one solitary black wood fern just doesn't look right to me. I recommend planting it in quantities of a half dozen or more. It works well in small spaces and spots where its fronds can arch gracefully over the edge of a wall, a path, or decorative boulders.

D. erythrosora (autumn fern, Zone 5) and the very similar *D. purpurella* (Zone

5) are both notable for their colorful fronds tinted purple and bronze when they first emerge. Their fronds are markedly triangular in outline and are held very stiffly at about a 45-degree angle. Their rigidity makes them a bit difficult to place in the garden, but try positioning them at the foot of a major tree, fronted by something dense, low, and leafy, such as epimedium.

D. filix-mas (male fern, Zone 4) has the potential to become one of the thickest, densest, and most impressive ferns in your garden. This is a fern to grow as a specimen, scattering individuals alongside paths that wend through the woods. Start with the largest plants you can find, because you'll almost surely prefer them that way. Many forms of male fern are available—some with frilly, crested tips—but be careful when making your purchase because some forms have a sparse appearance very *un*like what I've just described.

Osmunda claytoniana

Interrupted Fern

As the years go by, I grow fonder and fonder of this adaptable, well-behaved clumping fern named for the spore-producing portions of its fertile fronds that "interrupt" the leafy growth. As ferns go, it is early to emerge, unfurling bright, fresh, apple-green colored fronds in April. Its hue changes to medium green by early summer, and then again briefly in autumn, when it turns a particularly fetching clear yellow before dying back to the ground for winter. Its fronds are not at all persistent, so if you don't get around to cutting away last year's growth, the dead fronds will decompose quickly on their own.

Use interrupted fern in the garden just behind epimedium and other low-growing plants and alongside arching plants such as *Polygonatum* and *Smilacina*. It's great as part of a green "screen" to help define the rear of planted areas, and it's very effective for naturalizing dry

Interrupted fern (*Osmunda claytoniana*) is named for the fruiting organs that "interrupt" its fertile fronds.

areas that cannot support the moisture-loving ferns. Try interspersing randomly spaced groups of it with masses of smaller Christmas fern and *Aster divaricatus* for an easy woodland understory. Interrupted fern is one of our larger native ferns, reaching 30 inches in height and somewhat less in width, with a habit that is pleasingly informal without being downright lax.

Polystichum spp. and cvs.

Christmas Fern · Shield Fern

Like *Dryopteris*, the genus *Polystichum* contains several excellent ferns for northern gardens, including what might be the single most useful fern of all: Christmas fern, *P. acrostichoides* (Zone 3). This diminutive (12 to 18 inches tall) native grows densely with a very upright bearing rendered less stiff by fronds with a tendency to curl under gracefully at the tip. Its pinnae are dark green and glossy, and its fronds are so persistent that they are a frequent food of deer in winter. Don't worry, though—Christmas fern is not bothered by four-legged browsers during the growing season.

Christmas fern is ideal for bordering walkways or providing attractive foliage contrast to flowering plants at the front of the border. It's extremely common in our woodlands, even on dry, rocky slopes, an indicator of its excellence as a naturalizing plant for those challenging conditions. If I could grow only one fern, it would be Christmas fern; I can't recommend it highly enough.

My other favorite species in the genus is *P. setiferum* (Zone 5), which comes in many forms, most of them wider than tall and with the same stockiness of Christmas fern but more finely divided pinnae, giving a lacier look. 'Divisilobum' is among the best. Decidedly horizontal in its growth habit, its fronds have the habit of curving to the right or left charmingly. Many other forms have crested tips, and gardeners with a taste for the unusual will definitely find a lot in this species to interest them.

Other shield ferns worth trying if you come across them include *P. braunii* (Zone 3) and *P. polyblepharum* (Zone 5), both of which are medium sized and semi-evergreen with stiff, glossy, deep-green fronds. They are highly suitable for mixing with broad-leaved evergreen shrubs, but they should have some mat-forming groundcover such as *Waldsteinia* growing underneath because their upright vase shape leaves the ground exposed around their crowns. Groom them by removing last year's fronds in late winter.

There's a spot for Christmas fern (*Polystichum acrostichoides*) in every shade garden.

Ferns Best for Naturalizing

These are ferns whose vigor makes them suitable only in naturalized settings where their roaming tendency actually works to your advantage. Remember that many of the native ferns I've already suggested for border use are also perfectly good for naturalizing—they just won't spread the way these ferns will.

Dennstaedtia punctilobula

Hay-scented Fern

Hay-scented fern (*Dennstaedtia punctilobula*) is a problem solver when you need a spreading fern for naturalizing.

If you've ever hiked in the woods and seen thick swaths of a delicate fern occupying dappled glades under breaks in the trees, you've probably already been introduced to hay-scented fern. In situations like that, it's not uncommon for all the fronds in a hay-scented fern colony to face the same direction, as if lined up in a regiment. In locations where the light is more generous, fronds can turn any which way.

If you run your fingers along hay-scented fern's fronds (carefully—they're easily broken), you can pick up a little of the grassy, fresh smell for which this common native is named. Hay-scented fern grows thickly, and its ability to hold soil on a slope is moderately good despite its fragility. For added interest, try interplanting it with native *Aster divaricatus*, a combination nature often employs, too. These two spreading plants are about the same size (21 inches tall) and equally aggressive, so they can coexist indefinitely.

Hay-scented fern is one of the few ferns to show appreciable fall color, turning an attractive straw yellow in October before being cut down by frost.

This aggressive moisture-lover is perhaps our most common native riverside fern. So named because its fronds have the elegant drape of ostrich plumes, ostrich fern is lovely, and it's tempting to use it for general landscaping; but in cultivated areas, this fern is only for gardeners with the time and determination to control it yearly. John Mickel, the renowned fern expert, notes in his book *Ferns for American Gardens* that 6 original plants in his garden had grown to more than 700 in fifteen years, and that he gives away more than 100 plants every year! In a naturalized setting, however, ostrich fern's vigor can serve a useful purpose: it's ideal for controlling streamside erosion, and will generally set its own boundary wherever the moisture dries up.

Ostrich fern grows 36 to 48 inches tall and has an upright, graceful, narrow vase shape. It spreads via long underground stems that give rise to daughter plants at a considerable distance from the parent plant. If uncontrolled, ostrich fern will produce enormous colonies. Drier conditions slow its spread, and it will not grow at all in a persistently parched location. Its fronds persist moderately through the winter.

Ostrich fern (*Matteuccia struthiopteris*) is a superb naturalizing fern for waterside spots.

Of all our native ferns, sensitive fern has one of the most distinctive fronds: each looks like a stylized Christmas tree stamped out of apple-green dough with a lettuce-edged cookie cutter. The plant's sweet appearance belies a tough, aggressive nature: this is a fern that could eat many garden plants for lunch. It's a

Plants for
Deeper Shade

The fronds of spreading sensitive fern (*Onoclea sensibilis*) have a unique Christmas tree outline.

moisture-lover with a rangy habit that you've probably seen many times growing in ditches or shallow swampy areas where water gathers and persists.

In those circumstances, sensitive fern can be found growing with other common riparian plants such as skunk cabbage, horsetail, ostrich fern, and cinnamon fern. Unlike these frequent companions, though, it is also a common inhabitant of relatively dry and sunny roadsides. The message is clear: sensitive fern is anything *but* sensitive; it can tough out a wide range of conditions.

Sensitive fern grows to a height of about 18 inches and meanders to an indefinite width.

Its fronds arise along a thick, sinewy, creeping and branching rhizome that winds itself around and among any other plants nearby, a growth habit it will exhibit wherever it grows, wet or dry. Because many other plants would succumb to sensitive fern's invasiveness, a good rule for using it is to emulate the example nature sets. In a naturalized setting where water is usually present to some degree, interplant it with the cohorts just listed. In drier spots, it can coexist nicely with *Geranium maculatum*. Try other companions at your (or really, *their*) own risk!

Osmunda spp.

Cinnamon Fern · Royal Fern

Similar in its overall look to ostrich fern, *O. cinnamomea* (cinnamon fern) is named for the fertile fronds that arise from the center of its crown, resembling huge sticks of the spice of the same name. Although many other ferns (including ostrich fern) also produce separate fertile fronds, those of cinnamon fern are the most distinctive and ornamental for the few short weeks they're present in early summer after dispersing their spores.

Cinnamon fern is a moisture-lover that will colonize a streamside area over time, but in slightly drier settings it is distinctly more restrained. Its needs are the same as ostrich fern's. It has a very upright profile and fairly narrow fronds, and grows to a height of 30 inches or more. Its fronds are moderately persistent.

If you have a year-round stream or a truly mucky spot on your property that never dries out, and you want a somewhat unusual-looking fern, *O. regalis* (royal fern) is the one for you. Its fronds have a distinctly leguminous look, as if the plant were half fern, half pea, delicate and airy. With adequate moisture, it should live up to its name, becoming a specimen 36 to 48 inches tall and wide with positively regal bearing.

The downside of royal fern is that its needs are *very* specific. In the wild, I have seen it growing only in bogs and along streams and rivers. It seems unwilling to grow even a few feet above the level of surface water. At the same time, it doesn't seem to want to be submerged in water. In standing or slowly moving water, it frequently grows on top of sedge hummocks. As with some other ferns I've mentioned here, my advice when planting royal fern is to follow nature's example. Alongside moving water, plant it at the bottom of the stream

Cinnamon fern (*Osmunda cinnamomea*) is a moisture-lover named for its striking cinnamon-stick-like reproductive organs.

bank at water's edge. In standing water, build up mounds of soil, planting royal ferns atop them and using suitable sedges around the perimeter. If you don't have enough water, don't plant it at all—it probably won't come back.

PLANTS FOR LIGHT SHADE

Backbone Plants

If shade gardening were a board game, this would be the square that says
"Start Here!" Remember that I've defined backbone plants as the ones I
think have the greatest potential to perform well over a long season for most
gardeners. I recommend you use backbone perennials to fill 75 to 80 percent
of your garden.

Groundcovers are backbone plants pretty much by definition because you
can fill 100 percent of a garden space with one of them and call it "job done."
You'll find a list of plants that can be used as groundcovers with other plant
lists at the end of this book.

In leaf, bugleweed is a very low-growing (1 inch), rapidly spreading groundcover. It produces a dense colony of leafy rosettes topped by 6-inch spikes of purple flowers in late spring. Many cultivars are available, but they all share the same basic look and growth habit. Most forms have some burgundy coloration to the leaf, but some were bred to enhance this trait. Rarely, you may find for sale a cultivar with pink flowers.

Bugleweed is highly invasive, as evidenced by the patches of it you frequently see in lawns, where it has escaped from some nearby planting. Although it looks charming newly planted in a small clump at the front of a border, it won't stay that way for long, so I think it's best used as a groundcover under a specimen tree, such as a crab apple, and closely monitored for errant behavior! It doesn't interplant well with anything else. I highly recommend a physical edging to control its spread. Dig out any stray plants with a dandelion weeder.

After flowering, bugleweed can be mowed with the mower blade on its highest setting as a deadheading shortcut.

Bugleweed (*Ajuga reptans*) is a compact spreading plant that also features short blue flower spikes in mid-spring.

Lady's mantle is a unique plant, understated at first glance, but destined for your highest esteem as you come to know it. The color, texture, and shape of its leaves set it apart from nearly any other cold-climate perennial. Taken together, its qualities make it the perfect "blender"—a plant that can complement and improve even the boldest companion without clashing. It's the first plant to try in those spots where nothing else seems to work from a design standpoint, and its ability to withstand moderate sun makes it a perfect plant for unifying landscapes with gardens in both sun and shade.

Shape is the attribute that catches your eye first: each leaf has an elegantly crimped edge like a scallop shell. Then, there is the color: a subtle gray-green that harmonizes beautifully with virtually all other hues. Finally, touching it, you will be entranced by its peach-fuzz softness. This *indumentum* (the term for the covering of tiny hairs on the upper surface of each leaf) catches and holds water droplets in such a charming

Lady's mantle (*Alchemilla mollis*) flanks the mouth of a path through the woods.

way that you'll find yourself going out into the garden after a rain shower just to look at the lady's mantle. In fact, in medieval times, water collected from lady's mantle leaves was reputed to have magical properties.

Even with this wealth of ornamental qualities, lady's mantle has more to offer. It produces masses of delicate yet sturdy chartreuse flowers starting in June; these are excellent for cutting and make a wonderful alternative to baby's breath in bouquets.

The standard garden lady's mantle is *A. mollis* (Zone 4), attaining a height of 12 inches in leaf and 18 inches in flower, and spreading via rhizomes to about 24 inches. Divide your plants when you notice their leaves looking "congested."

Use lady's mantle by positioning large clumps at regular intervals along the front of your perennial border. It can even be used to edge an entire bed. A dwarf species, *A. erythropoda* (Zone 3), is a good candidate for any rock garden that isn't too dry.

Bluestar (*Amsonia tabernaemontana*) is one of the most trouble-free plants you can find, and native to boot.

Bluestar is grown more often in sun than in shade, yet it will do well if it gets bright indirect light, especially from the south. It is slow to establish itself regardless of where it is grown, and will be spindly for its first few years in the ground. As it puts on girth, though, it becomes more impressive, eventually producing a bushy mass of willowy foliage on sturdy stems and loose clusters of pale, steely blue, star-shaped flowers in late May to early June. Although valuable enough in its own right, bluestar's height and density when mature also make it a valuable backdrop for smaller plants.

Whether to deadhead bluestar is a matter of personal preference. If not deadheaded, it may self-sow moderately, and seedlings can be a little tough to pull. On the other hand, because it doesn't naturally branch extensively, it will look a little "shorn" for a few weeks after deadheading until new growth covers the cuts. If you deadhead it, be sure to wear plastic or latex gloves because bluestar stems exude a sap that can irritate skin when cut.

Bluestar is not subject to any pests and is generally disease resistant. I have heard reports that it can suffer from rust (a group of fungal diseases), but I have never witnessed this. All in all, once it's well established, bluestar should be a solid contributor to your garden for many years to come. 'Blue Ice' is a dwarf cultivar that grows only about 10 inches tall in shade.

Astilbe

Astilbe is most notable as one of the few shade perennials to bloom during the summer months. If your goal is to have as many perennials as possible blooming in your shade garden from mid-June through early August, you'll need to rely heavily on astilbe.

Luckily, there are dozens of excellent astilbe cultivars, and although each one blooms for just two to three weeks, different astilbes can bloom at differing times. If you choose varieties carefully for overlapping bloom times, you can have at least one astilbe in flower for two entire summer months.

Astilbes come only in pinks, reds, and whites, but within that seemingly narrow range there is wide variety—from the pale, shell pink of 'Erika' to the saturated rose of 'Granat' and the purplish pink of 'Amethyst.' Reds and whites are both bright, with fewer distinctions of hue than among the pinks. Astilbes are more floriferous if given a few hours of sun, but will still bloom very well in up to moderate shade.

In light shade, astilbe (*Astilbe*) alone could carry the garden through midsummer.

Astilbe foliage is ornamental in its own right. Leaves are finely cut, medium green, and usually free of disease and pests. Height varies from 6 to 24 inches in leaf and 10 to 36 inches in flower. 'Sprite' is a common and excellent dwarf form.

Astilbes are fond of moisture but do not need it excessively. They require little maintenance other than division every three to five years. A decline in the quantity of flowers produced is either a sign that the plant is in too much shade or a sign that it wants division, so if the light level seems adequate, try division. Astilbes are rhizomatous, so when you dig them, what you will find is a bunch of finger-thick "roots." Cut away any parts of the rhizomes that seem dry and dead, and replant the rest, spacing them a few inches apart. Don't be surprised if you end up discarding three-quarters of what you dug up—that isn't unusual. Flowering should increase considerably the very next season.

Siberian bugloss (*Brunnera macrophylla*) is a forget-me-not look-alike, but a true perennial.

Despite having a name that suggests the sound of a sneeze, Siberian bugloss is a useful shade plant that is finally getting some appreciation. The species has rather plain rugose, heart-shaped leaves, above which it bears airy sprays of sky-blue flowers (a white form is available, but uncommon) reminiscent of forget-me-nots in late April and May. But in the last decade or so, a slew of exciting variegated cultivars have arrived on the scene to greatly expand the potential role of *Brunnera*. These new offerings have varying degrees of creamy-white or silvery leaf variegation, and all are worth trying.

The leaves of 'Variegata' have a green center with a wide, distinct, creamy-white margin; 'Hadspen Cream' is a virtual look-alike. 'Jack Frost' has a silvery-white leaf with green veining and looks very much the part of a caladium; 'Looking Glass' strongly resembles 'Jack Frost,' as does 'Mrs. Morse,' while having the distinction of white flowers. 'Langtrees' has a green center with silver spotting along the leaf edge; 'Emerald Mist' looks similar, but seems to have moderately more pronounced silvering, while 'Silver Wings' also has a silvery cast to the entire leaf and the thinnest of white margins. All healthy Siberian buglosses have strong, good-looking leaves that qualify them as foliage plants when not in flower.

I have noticed that variegated forms have a moderate tendency to "revert" to the plain green form of the species. If you see a portion of what is otherwise a variegated Siberian bugloss emerge with plain green leaves, separate that portion from the rest and replant it elsewhere. You may have to do a bit of this every year.

The warm glow of 'Variegata' and 'Hadspen Cream' is distinctly different from the cool silveriness of the other variegated cultivars, and these two groups call for differing garden companions. The creamy buglosses are best used with other plants having medium-green leaves or creamy variegation. The "frosty" buglosses are especially lovely next to blue hostas, twinleaf, nodding mandarin, deadnettle, and native bleeding heart. Siberian bugloss blooms simultaneously with, and is an excellent companion for, old-fashioned bleeding heart.

Siberian bugloss is never bothered by pests or disease, and will self-sow to a small degree (you may find a few seedlings at the foot of the parent plant every year). It grows to only about 12 inches in leaf (16 inches in flower) and should be used at the very front of the border. The first leaves to come up in spring may not be heart shaped, but those that emerge slightly later will be. Try using Siberian bugloss as the principal foliage plant in your garden, planting large clumps at regular intervals, alternating cultivars but probably restricting yourself to either the creamy types or the silvery types, both of which will go with the species. The repetition of shape but variety of variegation will create a cohesive yet visually interesting design element.

Ornamental grasses that will grow well in shade can be counted on the fingers of one hand, and the most impressive member of this small fraternity is northern sea oats. Perplexingly, it is almost always overlooked in lists of shade plants. Although it does not tolerate deep shade, it certainly does well enough with only bright indirect light to make it a definite garden "keeper" for fans of ornamental grasses.

Northern sea oats grows 24 inches tall in light shade and up to 36 inches when grown in some sun. In mid-spring it puts up a dense, erect clump of broad, fresh, green blades that arch over gently as they elongate. Toward the end of summer, airy green flowers will develop, catching chance breezes engagingly. They're attractive but not what you could call showy.

Northern sea oats (*Chasmanthium latifolium*), shown here in flower, is one of a tiny number of shade-adapted grasses.

Then, one day in September, you'll walk by the plant, notice an abundance of fat seedheads that look like they could grace a cornucopia, and say to yourself, "Where did *those* come from?" Unlike hakon grass, the only other grass I can recommend for shade, *Chasmanthium* has significant seedheads. The plant's large, pendant, wheat-like grains, dangling luxuriantly throughout the slowly cooling weeks of autumn, gradually turning from apple green to a rich nutty brown, are its best ornamental quality.

Delightfully, your enjoyment of northern sea oats doesn't have to end with the growing season. The seedheads make an excellent addition to dry arrangements for indoor display. Cut the stalks as they finish tanning, before inclement fall weather breaks the stems and disarrays the seedheads, and bring them inside. (In fact, deadheading is essential if you want to control the spread of the plant.)

There's no need to fuss with the seedheads—just put the cut stalks in a vase, allowing them to arrange themselves naturally, and leave them in a dry place until the last remaining moisture has evaporated and they feel papery. I've had bunches look as good ten or more years after cutting as they did their first winter. My only difficulty in keeping them indefinitely has been the attention of my cats, who love to bat at them because they rustle at the slightest touch!

USDA ZONE

3

Digitalis grandiflora

Yellow Foxglove

Yellow foxglove (*Digitalis grandiflora*) sends creamy spires skyward in June.

Although most foxgloves require a fair amount of sun to look their best, yellow foxglove is truly a shade plant. Despite its name, its flowers, borne in June, are more of an antique ivory or creamy white than a true yellow. It's a short foxglove, reaching 24 to 30 inches in flower but, like all foxgloves, having only a basal rosette of leaves. Yellow foxglove will self-sow to form colonies if not deadheaded, and offspring can crop up a fair distance from the parent plant.

Because it has a minimum of foliage after deadheading, perhaps the best way to use yellow foxglove is in small, irregular groups scattered here and there between other perennials toward the middle of the border where they won't draw too much attention after flowering.

Mayflower is a low-growing, spreading plant with little pinwheel leaves and a smattering of delicate white flowers in (can you guess?) May. I recommend mayflower with some hesitancy. Over time, it can develop into an effective groundcover for shallow soil in shade, but it's one of those plants you may regret ever introducing into your garden because ultimately, it can be all too effective—in other words, an aggressive spreader that's hard to control when it reaches the limit of where you want it.

You may wonder what I'm talking about because mayflower can take time to get established. But once it gets going, it increases at a good clip. The problem with controlling it is that its roots are fine and stretchy. When you try to pull them out, they tend to simply snap. Any little bit of root left in the soil simply regrows. You can start to feel as if the plant is thumbing its nose at you!

To control mayflower, you really need to separate any unwanted portion from the main planting by cut-

The whorled leaf of mayflower (*Galium odoratum*) distinguishes it from the denser look of most groundcovers.

ting a line with a spade. Then, slide the spade underneath the portion of the mayflower to be removed as if you were harvesting turf. Put this portion on a tarp and gently shake the soil off the roots, which you can then discard. (Don't compost them, or they'll grow in your compost pile). Do this on a day when the soil is neither too dry nor too damp, or the soil will not release well.

Although as a general rule I don't recommend mixing groundcovers, *Galium* and *Vancouveria* can look quite nice growing together. Each plant separately is a little "thin," so by combining them you get a denser look.

Although it seems as though mayflower would be perfect for interplanting with bare-ankles perennials the way I recommend doing with *Lamium* and several other plants, you might want to think twice about that. If and when you need to divide those perennials, you'll have a lot of difficulty teasing out the mayflower roots, and you may end up spreading it unintentionally.

Plants for
Light Shade

167

A gold Japanese hakon grass (*Hakonechloa macra* 'Aureola' is shown here) really jumps out of the shadows.

This pretty, billowy plant is one of the few true grasses with any shade tolerance. It looks for all the world like a broad-bladed cousin of the sun-loving fountain grass (*Pennisetum alopecuroides*). When the wind catches its blades and tosses them about, their graceful motion is engaging to watch and a pleasure to hear. In spots with light to moderate shade—it will pout a bit in deep shade—there is nothing else quite like it.

The species has a pleasant, olive-green cast to its leaves, while the more common 'Aureola' is a cultivar with radial gold stripes on its blades that really stand out in shade. A more recent introduction, 'All Gold,' is just that—all gold. You might occasionally run across other cultivars such as 'Albo-striata,' 'Albo-marginata,' and 'Albo-variegata,' all with varying degrees of white or yellow coloration. The aesthetic differences among these variegated selections may be minimal, so I'd recommend buying what you can find with ease rather than going to great effort to search out an obscure hakon grass in the hope of obtaining something different.

All types of hakon grass increase at a moderate rate, but because small plants look rather unimpressive, buy the largest specimens you can afford or buy several smaller ones, if that's all you can get, and plant them close together. Mature plants have very long blades that grow up and then cascade over to form a mound about 24 inches tall and 36 inches wide. Although it does produce spikelets of small flowers in midsummer, these are not significant. This is a plant to grow entirely for its foliage.

Position hakon grass where its blades can drape gracefully over rocks or, if you have a pond or stream, just above water's edge. It's very tolerant of a wide range of soil conditions, from dry to fairly moist.

Hakon grass can grow densely in light to moderate shade. It will survive in deeper shade, but at the expense of substance, producing airy sprays of blades instead of a massive mophead; and the greater the shade in which it's grown, the less likely it will be to flower at all. Give it the brightest spot you can, and use it as a counterpoint to plants with broad, green leaves, such as *Rodgersia* and hosta.

Lathyrus vernus and cvs.

Perennial Pea

5 USDA ZONE

This may be one of the best shade plants you've never heard of. A decade ago it was truly rare. I'm now seeing it in nurseries with some regularity, and I expect it to grow in popularity as people discover what a great plant it is.

Perennial pea is on the small side. Topping out at just 10 inches, it features divided leaves with lance-shaped leaflets and that characteristic leguminous look. When young, perennial pea is a bit sparse, but after many years in the ground it will become quite bushy. In late April and early May, a mature plant produces masses of distinctly pea-like flowers that are typically shaded from deep pink to violet blue, giving the appearance of purplish-pink from a distance. All-pink forms such as 'Rose Elf' are available as well.

If you don't deadhead the plant, the spent flowers will develop into fairly ornamental mahogany-brown seedpods. Plants will self-sow a little, but certainly not obnoxiously, so you won't create a headache for yourself by letting them go to seed to enjoy the pods.

In small gardens, perennial pea can look nice in groups as small as three, but in a larger garden, I like to see scattered groups of a dozen or more plants, each group composed of just one flower color but with pink and purple groupings alternating.

Perennial pea (*Lathyrus vernus*) offers a multitude of bright flowers in spring and interesting seedpods later in the season.

Plants for
Light Shade

169

Ligularia · Leopard Plant

Black stems contrast with tall yellow flower spikes on *Ligularia stenocephalla* 'The Rocket.'

Ligularias offer three qualities rare for shade plants: they are tall, yellow, and summer blooming. If you have a space that's right for them, they are sure to become a highlight of your garden. But having the right space is essential: although ligularias grow and bloom well only in light shade, they can wilt if exposed to any direct light, and they need moist soil.

The genus *Ligularia* includes many garden plants, but for most gardeners I recommend only two: *L. stenocephala* 'The Rocket' and *L. przewalskii*. 'The Rocket' has large, dentate, heart-shaped leaves and elegant black stalks topped by spires of golden-yellow flowers that open in July and continue into August. When happy, it will be full and up to 48 inches tall in leaf and 6 feet tall in flower. *L. przewalskii* bears similar flowers but is a bit shorter, with finely divided leaves that lend it a more delicate look. It tolerates average soil moisture better than any other species in this genus, making it my go-to ligularia.

Always mass these two ligularias. They are upright and slender by nature, and one solitary plant or even a small group will not make an impression. A cluster of eight to ten is a good minimum quantity. Use proportionately more for larger gardens.

A mass of 'The Rocket' will look reasonably dense and full, but *L. przewalskii* may need interplanting with companions to help fill out its bottom reaches. In very light shade, both common purple coneflower (*Echinacea purpurea*) and golden feverfew (*Tanacetum parthenium* 'Aureum') suit this purpose and bloom surprisingly well for plants normally thought of as full-sun perennials.

Other ligularias to try include *L. dentata* 'Othello' and 'Desdemona,' which look distinctly different from the ligularias already mentioned. They are much larger, bushier plants with leaves that make me think of water lilies and gigantic orange-yellow daisy-like flowers. These really do need the highest light levels possible without direct sun.

Whatever ligularia you try, siting it will be the most difficult part of growing it. The kind of spot you need is to the north of a line of trees, in the open with good light yet no direct sun, perhaps along a stream or natural drainage channel. Having such a spot with just the right amount of indirect light and adequate soil moisture is just a stroke of luck—if you have it, you have it, and if you don't, you don't. If you have it, though, ligularia is almost sure to have your friends asking, "What *is* that spectacular plant?"

Compact, neat, semi-evergreen and salt tolerant, lily-turf is a natural solution to a certain type of annoying landscape problem. I'm talking about the edging next to walkways, driveways, and curbsides along the road. These are spots often exposed to high levels of ice-melting salt in winter as well as heavy loads of plowed or shoveled snow. Lilyturf can withstand that punishment and spring back with grace when the weather warms. These same spots are often prone to significant deer browsing too, because access is so easy. Lilyturf is generally unpalatable to deer, making it less likely that these unpredictable animals will linger in high-traffic areas.

Lilyturf's strap-like leaves resemble those of daylilies and grow in a mound 12 to 18 inches tall and wide, rather like a thick shock of hair. Medium-green leaves are the norm, but several cultivars with gold or silvery foliage are available. In midsummer, lilyturf produces purple or white flowers that cling to short stems, looking much like grape hyacinths. The similarity is strong

Lilyturf (*Liriope*) is an old favorite for edging, and variegated selections can be used for a spot of color at the front of the border.

enough to suggest lilyturf and grape hyacinths as a natural plant pairing. This works especially well because lilyturf is somewhat slow to emerge in spring, so the spring bulbs provide continuity and are similarly deer resistant.

Although lilyturf is tolerant of deep shade in the South, it needs bright in-

Plants for
Light Shade

direct light at our northern latitudes, and is frequently grown in the sun here. Plants grown in moderate or deeper shade will often compensate for the lack of light by declining to flower, putting all their energy into vegetative growth.

It's important to distinguish between the two common species of lilyturf. *L. muscari* is noninvasive, and most of the named selections for sale in nurseries are derived from it. 'Big Blue' is the standard for a strong-growing, green-leaved, purple-flowered lilyturf, and 'Monroe's White' is its white-blooming counterpart. The leaves of 'Variegata' are striped with gold, complemented nicely by purple flowers. 'Silvery Sunproof' is similar, but with white replacing yellow in its coloration. Although lilyturf is most commonly used as a groundcover for small areas, clumps of *L. muscari* also make great accent plants at the front of the border.

L. spicata, on the other hand, spreads rapidly by rhizomes, and selections of this vigorous species should be used only where lilyturf is massed as a groundcover and appropriately edged to limit its spread.

Lilyturf needs nothing more than average garden conditions and can get by with no special maintenance. New foliage arising in spring will conceal last year's leaves, but if you prefer a neater look, take a few minutes to remove old leaves in late winter *before* new growth emerges. If you have a lot of lilyturf, one old trick is to mow it using the highest setting on your power mower. You'll still have to make a pass with hedge clippers or hand pruners to clean up the edges of the clumps manually, but mowing will cut down on the time involved.

USDA ZONE · Varies

Tiarella spp. and cvs.

Foamflower

To look at our native woodland foamflower in the wild, you wouldn't think a rock star was hiding inside, but plant breeders are apparently good at recognizing potential. The foamflowers you find in the woods are charming little plants with maple-like leaves and sparse, frothy flowers on short stems. The more outrageous of their descendants are positively rococo, with dramatically lobed leaves, often with striking maroon markings, and masses of flowers like a garnish of seafoam.

Yet, they still behave like their wild forebears. Most foamflowers form neat clumps of foliage about 6 inches tall. In early May, they send up 12-inch stalks

A mass of foamflower (*Tiarella*) is a froth of mid-spring bloom, and can give a repeat show if deadheaded.

topped with little grape clusters of buds that open into creamy-white or pale-pink flowers lasting many weeks. If deadheaded, they'll continue to produce new flowers through June.

Although most foamflowers are excellent neighbors and never become invasive, there are spreading selections that can usually be identified from the rather unsubtle (fortunately!) hints contained in their names. 'Running Tapestry,' for instance, has a moniker very descriptive of its behavior. Beware the runners!

Of the clumping cultivars suitable for use in the shady border, 'Spring Symphony' is a favorite of mine. Its apple-green leaves are variably wine splashed and have long, finger-like lobes. Pink flowers trending toward coral crown their display in spring. 'Tiger Stripe,' 'Iron Butterfly,' 'Cygnet,' and 'Mint Chocolate' are all popular and worthwhile selections whose names dare you to resist them.

Foamflowers can be used in the border in groups of six to twelve plants spaced fairly closely. They are also ideal massed as a groundcover under crab apples because they bloom simultaneously with that tree, and their flower colors are harmonious. Further south, foamflowers can be evergreen, but in the Northeast (or at least most of it) they will be deciduous. Clip off all leaves in late winter to make a clean backdrop for emerging foliage, or . . . don't bother. The spent leaves will vanish under the new ones.

You can occasionally purchase species foamflowers such as *T. cordifolia* (Zone 3) or *T. wherryi* (Zone 5), but most of the time you'll encounter named cultivars whose winter hardiness can vary. Make inquiries with local nurseries and arboreta to find out about selections that can perform well in your area.

Accent Plants

These accent plants for light shade should be used in borders to complement backbone plants, or as filler for fullness at the back of garden spaces, or to help make the transition from cultivated to uncultivated landscapes. Each entry specifies the use(s) for which each plant is best suited.

USDA ZONE ZONE *Varies*

Aquilegia spp. and cvs.

Columbine

"Sweet" and "charming" are the words that spring to everyone's mind when they see a columbine in bloom. Above a full clump of dainty foliage, bare stalks arise to support dangling flowers whose shape practically defies verbal description. Each one looks like a group of tiny cornucopia horns suspended upside down, sometimes terminating in sweeping spurs topped with a tiny ball finial.

Columbines come in a wide range of sizes and all flower colors except orange. In bloom, they can be as tiny as 6 inches or as tall as 3 feet. Most often, they're offered in color-coordinated groups with names such as 'McKana Hybrids' (Zone 3). If you select a number of these at random in the nursery, you have no way of knowing what colors you're getting, so purchase them in flower if that's important to you.

The bright red and yellow of our native columbine (*Aquilegia canadensis*) jumps out from a sea of forget-me-nots.

Alternatively, to get a particular color, buy a species or a named cultivar. Be aware, however, that some species can be fickle. *A. chrysantha* (Zone 3), for example, is a Rocky Mountain native with yellow flowers that has not performed well for me in the East. It probably isn't adapted to our abundant rain. Other columbines, such as our East Coast native species *A. canadensis* (Zone 3), are just not substantial enough for border use but can be a nice component of a naturalized shady rock garden.

Two or more different columbines in a garden will hybridize to produce a mixed bag of seedlings. (A botanist or horticulturist would call columbines "promiscuous" for their tendency to hybridize readily.) Extras pull out easily and also transplant well when small. If you want lots of columbines and aren't particular about flower color, plant a few you like, then collect their seeds in midsummer and broadcast them throughout your garden. Germination is generally very high from fresh seed, and there's a certain thrill in not knowing what colors you'll have until bloom time.

Columbines flower in late May and June. Afterward, cut back tired or discolored leaves or any that show white "veins" caused by leafminers. Even if you cut off all the leaves, a new flush of growth will soon emerge.

Use medium-sized and tall columbines in mid-border so they will be somewhat concealed if their foliage goes into temporary decline after flowering. Very small columbines can be appreciated only up close, and are most suitable for rock gardens.

Columbines tolerate only light to moderate shade and can also be grown in anything up to full sun in the North without requiring supplemental water or any other special treatment.

Carex cvs.

Sedge

Varies · USDA ZONE · ZONE

I already mentioned *Carex* in the section on plants for deeper shade, where I gave general guidelines for care. There are also other sedges whose light needs seem to be a little higher. *C. elata* 'Bowles Golden' (Zone 5) is unique, like a fountain of slender, lemon-lime blades. It grows to a height of 24 inches and has an airy, semi-transparent appearance because of the thinness of its leaves. Despite its height, place it at the front of your border as a complement to plants with broad or feathery leaves and more ordinary coloration. Blue hostas

Gold leaves, such as those of the striking sedge *Carex elata* 'Bowles Golden,' shine like a lamp in the shade garden all season long.

and green ferns are excellent companions. It also makes a spectacular specimen in a pot. 'Bowles Golden' is not common, but is available via mail order or as a special order through a good nursery.

Two more variegated sedges to try are *C. hakijoensis* 'Evergold' (12 inches tall and 18 inches wide, having narrow green leaves with a broad gold stripe down the center, Zone 5) and *C. morrowii* 'Variegata' (ditto, but with a white stripe, Zone 5). Both are very sun tolerant, too, and are generally evergreen or semi-evergreen depending on local conditions; cut back their leaves by two-thirds in late winter if they look poorly. Otherwise, do nothing.

There are many other beautiful sedges, but not all are winter hardy above Zone 6, so experiment cautiously. Gardeners along the coast will find a significantly broader palette of sedges to work with. A marginally hardy sedge may need only a light winter mulch of straw and/or a protected location in order to thrive.

Dicentra eximia and cvs.

Native Bleeding Heart

Native bleeding heart (*Dicentra eximia* 'Alba' is shown here) will bloom on and off all summer long, a rare trait among perennials.

Our eastern native bleeding heart has one distinct advantage over its exotic relative, old-fashioned bleeding heart (*D. spectabilis*): it does not go dormant early. It is smaller than its cousin (18 inches tall and wide), has finely divided foliage, and blooms continuously in waves from late spring through summer. 'Alba,' the white-flowered form, is identical to the pink form in all other respects. (Another species, *D. formosa*, is native to the West Coast, and its cultivars are common in the nursery trade, but they don't offer any advantage over our East Coast species.)

Use native bleeding heart at the front of the border or in shady rock gardens. It looks particularly good near blue hostas. It also grows supremely well in sun, even in the hottest and driest conditions, making it one of those plants good for use throughout properties with both shade and sun.

To keep the plant neat looking, cut back dying foliage around the perimeter at the base. New leaves will arise in the center of the plant. Flowers are self-cleaning, but deadheading will keep the plant looking more "groomed."

If conditions are right, native bleeding heart may self-sow moderately. Use this to your advantage by planting it in or near a dry-stone wall with soil pockets or a dry-laid terrace, as recommended for *Corydalis lutea*. It will probably sow itself into the tiny rooting spaces available in a charming, random fashion. Any extra seedlings pull out easily when young. Use a dandelion weeder to remove them if you didn't get them out early on.

Heuchera spp. and cvs.

Alumroot · Coralbells

USDA ZONE · Varies

Although you often find members of the genus *Heuchera* listed as shade plants, in my experience that's not true in the North. Here, I find they perform best in full sun. However, there are two alumroots that seem slightly better adapted to shade (as long as it's light shade) than most *Heuchera* and are worth a mention.

All alumroots produce a dense, 12- to 15-inch mound of maple-shaped leaves, many with strikingly colored patterns and variegation. *H. americana* 'Dale's Strain' (Zone 4) has both extensive silvering on its leaf surfaces and subtle pink shades to its darker veins. Small clumps can be used at the front of a border, or large quantities can be planted among all the specimens in a hosta garden. It also pairs well with Christmas fern, and the two together can be massed. Once you try it, you'll probably find yourself using it more and more, as it's a surprisingly good-looking sidekick to a lot of plants.

Heuchera villosa 'Autumn Bride' is an alumroot with great foliage and showy late-season flowers.

The flowers of 'Dale's Strain,' borne in June, are typical of alumroot—wiry, 24-inch wands with a froth of tiny flowers along the top 8 inches or so—but they're an understated green, and I think the plant could do just as well without them. This is a plant to grow for its foliage.

H. villosa 'Autumn Bride' (Zone 5), on the other hand, has both strong foliage and flowers. Its leaf is bright green and sharply toothed. Atypically (for alumroot), it flowers in late summer and early fall, when it produces quantities of large, fat panicles of creamy-white blossoms that may flop a bit under their own weight. A mass of 'Autumn Bride' in flower can be impressive, and it will look equally good in a border or the foreground of a woodland garden.

Primula spp. and cvs.

Primrose

Every woodland garden path should have some primroses (the classic English cowslip *Primula veris* is shown here) scattered informally along its edges.

Although often thought of as houseplants to brighten winter windowsills, primroses are highly variable plants that include both tender dainties and dozens of cold-hardy species that can be grown as perennials in the North. Entire books have been written about the genus *Primula*, so I will just generalize here.

Primroses are small plants having a basal rosette of coarse leaves and flowers held on leafless stalks anywhere from 2 inches to 24 inches tall. Flower color range is remarkable, touching on every hue in the spectrum and including many bicolors. Bloom time is anywhere from April to July. Growing needs vary widely. Nearly all primroses appreciate rich soil, but some require considerable soil moisture and others want sharp drainage. Some may even go dormant after flowering, but others are semi-evergreen.

Because of the widely differing habits and needs of primroses, choose garden varieties carefully. Research them before buying! The best rule I can offer is this: very small primroses can't hold their own in a conventional border. They are most suitable for a shady rock garden or a lightly shaded woodland where the planting is not too dense. For border use, plant taller varieties and position them carefully where they will not be crowded out by more vigorous neighbors. Or, if you have lots of square footage at your disposal, try planting large drifts of tall primroses in areas where they can grow as a monoculture and be admired from a distance at their peak. Foamflower, Siberian bugloss, small ferns, and many other low-growing perennials look good arranged in drifts in front of primroses planted this way.

First, let's look at some of the smaller primroses. *P. veris* (Zone 3), the English cowslip famous in poetry, is one of the easiest to grow and one of the earliest to bloom. Only 8 inches tall in flower, it has clusters of bright, sulphur-yellow blossoms that appear in April. The numerous cultivars of similarly petite *P. vulgaris* and *P. elatior* (both Zone 4) will look familiar to anyone who has bought a primrose in a supermarket. Even shorter than *P. veris*, their flowers are often almost stalkless, tending to sit down among their leaves and really needing to be seen from overhead at very close quarters. *P. denticulata* (Zone 2), the so-called drumstick primrose, is so named because of its fat globe of flowers on 8-inch stems. Finally, there's *P. sieboldii* (Zone 3), a Japanese woodlander that goes dormant after flowering in May and early June, making it essentially a late-spring ephemeral.

For taller, later-blooming primroses, look to *P. japonica* (Zone 3), *P. x bullesiana* (Zone 4), *P. bulleyana* (Zone 5), and *P. beesiana* (Zone 5). They flower from late spring through midsummer in hues of pink, red, orange, and yellow. For that spot in your garden where the soil is always damp yet it's not dismally dark, try *P. florindae*, whose yellow spires (red and orange forms are also available) adorn a waterside setting admirably.

There are many other primrose species and hybrids, but this overview of some of the more useful and easy-to-obtain types contains choices for most shade garden settings.

Tellima grandiflora and cvs.

Fringe Cups

At first (and even second or third) sight, fringe cups will have you saying, "Ah, I know that plant—alumroot." The leaves have the same subtle maple shape. The flower stalks are the same tall wands. The blossoms themselves are the same little pearly drops. Fringe cups and alumroot are, in fact, closely related—kissing cousins in the world of plant genealogy—and you'll find yourself using them the same way.

The species *T. grandiflora* has medium-green leaves, but one variegated cultivar is available that expands the palette of silvery foliage plants for the shade.

The neat, mounding foliage and slender but sturdy flower spikes of fringe cups (*Tellima grandiflora*) make it an ideal plant for narrow beds and borders.

T. 'Forest Frost' looks nearly identical to *H. americana* 'Dale's Strain' as well as any number of other alumroots with sterling and wine leaf markings.

In a border, *Tellima* makes the best impression in a clump about 24 inches wide. In flower, it's about 21 inches high, but the foliage never grows taller than about 8 inches, so it's strictly a front-of-the-border plant. Depending on the light level in your garden, you'll probably have to mass anywhere from four to eight plants together to get a good display. As with alumroot, brighter light will yield thicker growth and stockier, stronger flower stalks better able to support themselves. These shoot up quickly in May to bear alternating, outward-facing, cup-shaped flowers, each one with a long greenish-white or pale-pink fringe around the mouth like a ring of eyelashes, giving rise to the plant's quirky common name.

Tellima is also a good choice for naturalized settings where various wildflowers and low ferns are allowed to intermix informally. It can be invasive in its native Pacific Northwest, but I have never seen it become aggressive in the harsher clime of the Northeast.

Globeflower is a pretty little clumping perennial about 10 inches tall in leaf and 15 inches tall in flower. It produces dense mounds of attractive, deep-green, highly divided leaves. In May, wiry stems elongate, terminating in solitary buttercup flowers ranging from a yellow so pale it's almost ivory to a strong orange-yellow. 'Lemon Queen' is a common and particularly pleasing selection whose medium-yellow flowers go with most companions.

Globeflower is a very well-behaved perennial with few needs once it's established. Its only real demand is to have regular moisture; globeflower does not like to dry out, and a period of drought may force it into early dormancy for the year.

Because globeflower is on the small side, use it in groups of a half dozen or more. Its cheerful flowers will be a welcome spot of sunshine in the shade, where yellow always pops right out of the shadows.

The buttercup chalices of globeflower (*Trollius* x *cultorum*) are among the brightest you'll find for shade.

Spring Ephemerals

These are plants that go dormant during late spring or summer, making them one-or two-season plants. Remember to position them so the gap they leave in the garden will be filled in by a neighboring plant or won't be noticed.

Delphinium tricorne

Dwarf Larkspur

When grown in bright indirect light, this May-blooming wildflower is surprisingly showy. It genuinely resembles a delphinium or larkspur shrunk down to about a quarter of the "normal" size for those plants, having vividly blue-purple flowers on sturdy stalks and finely divided basal leaves.

It goes dormant very quickly after flowering, and its tiny tuberous roots are so easy to disturb that you may want to mark its place in the garden as a reminder not to dig there accidentally. In the border, place it next to plants that flower either earlier or later and have enough foliage to fill the gap it will leave after going dormant without overshadowing it when it's actively growing. I like twinleaf as a companion.

Dwarf larkspur is native to a large swath of states from the Central Plains to the Eastern Seaboard and is highly suitable for naturalizing in woodland environments.

Compact, vivid-blue flower spikes make native dwarf larkspur (*Delphinium tricorne*) a head turner.

Old-fashioned bleeding heart is a large plant (30 to 36 inches tall and at least as wide) and, true to its Latin name, spectacular. In May, and in some years until as late as mid-June, it produces abundant arching stalks of vivid pink-and-white flowers with a complex, "bleeding" heart-like shape. Look carefully at them, and you may see other shapes that have given rise to a host of imaginative common (but now largely disused) names for this old garden standby: lady-in-the-bath, Chinaman's breeches, lady's locket, and lyre flower, among others.

Old-fashioned bleeding heart blooms simultaneously with Siberian bugloss, and the two make a natural combination in the garden. Try cutting a few stalks for early garden bouquets along with hosta leaves, fern fronds, columbines, violets, and (if you have the sun in which to grow them) late daffodils.

After flowering, old-fashioned bleeding heart sports a mound of pretty, divided, blue-green foliage reminiscent of peony leaves without the glossy surface. The one detraction of this glorious plant is that its lovely foliage will not last the season. It's not, strictly speaking, a "spring" ephemeral because it may actually last half the summer or more, but it certainly isn't a long-season plant. Its leaves will begin to yellow in August, and it quickly dies back, leaving a large gap in the garden, so it requires careful siting. Do not place it in the foreground of any garden you intend for season-long beauty. Instead, place it in spring-only gardens, semi-naturalized areas, or at the rear of gardens where there is sufficient depth for other plants in the foreground to mask the "missing" bleeding hearts in late summer.

There is a white-flowered form of old-fashioned bleeding heart called 'Alba' and a pink-flowered, gold-leaved form called 'Gold Heart.' 'Alba' seems to be a little less vigorous and may never need division. The pink form, on the other hand, can double in size from year to year, but may also decline in size some years for no apparent reason.

Old-fashioned bleeding heart is a moderate self-sower, usually giving rise to a dozen or so offspring each year near the parent plant. For easiest removal, dig seedlings early before their taproots have formed.

Shade gardeners cherish the picturesque flowers of old-fashioned bleeding heart (*Dicentra spectabilis*) despite the plant's tendency toward early dormancy.

Bulbs

As I explained earlier, I recommend that bulbs be added to a garden only after the garden has gone through one or two growing seasons and its design has been finalized. That way, the bulbs won't interfere or get lost if the garden is rearranged.

Also recall that the bulbs that do well in shade are minor bulbs. With the possible exception of bluebells, plant minor bulbs in larger groups than you would major bulbs, but not as deeply, and put them where they can be appreciated despite their small size.

USDA ZONE 4

Anemone blanda cvs.

Grecian Windflower

As cheerful as the daisies and asters they resemble, Grecian windflowers always make me smile. You, too, will get a lift from seeing clumps of them raise their simple faces to the sun on clement days in late April and early May.

Growing just 3 to 4 inches tall, each individual plant produces only one or two stems with a pretty, divided leaf somewhat like that of *Corydalis*, and one solitary flower. Because of the sparseness of their foliage, my general advice for using minor bulbs—plant them in generous clumps—goes double for Grecian windflowers. Clumps of thirty or more make a good impression.

Grecian windflowers can be white, blue, or rosy, with the rose shades being highly variable from pale powder-pink to fairly fluorescent. You can usually purchase them as single-color selections, such as 'Blue Star' or 'White Splendor,' or in a mixed-bag medley of colors. All are pleasing. Try interplanting them with spotted geranium (*Geranium maculatum*), whose foliage will completely conceal the windflower's decline into dormancy after flowering.

Unlike most of the other plants in this section, Grecian windflowers are actually corms, not true bulbs. The dormant corms (they will be dormant when shipped to you in autumn) have an odd shape that often stymies gardeners

Grecian windflower (*Anemone blanda*) is a sweet, unassuming spring bulb to appreciate close up.

planting them for the first time, because it's very difficult to determine which end is up! The wiry remnants of dried roots on one side indicate the bottom; a ring of papery tissue marks the top. The truth is that you don't really have to worry too much about how they go in the ground—even if planted upside down, they will still grow and probably eventually right themselves—but do plant them the right way if you can figure it out. Standard advice is to soak them in water overnight before planting, but don't forget about them and leave them submerged for days, or they will begin to rot.

Grecian windflowers will usually supply a fine splash of color for a couple of weeks, which is a long display time for a spring bulb. They do spread, but less aggressively than many other bulbs in most conditions, making them less likely to become a problem plant.

Hyacinthoides spp. and cvs.

Bluebell

USDA ZONE **4**

Both English (*H. non-scripta*) and Spanish (*H. hispanica*, also often called *Scilla hispanica* or *Endymion hispanicus*) bluebells are showy plants. They produce attractive, glossy, dark-green, strap-like leaves, and flowers shaped like long bells whose rims flare back in delightful curlicues. If ever there was a flower whose portrait deserves to grace the surface of fine china, it's this one.

Bluebells (*Hyacinthoides hispanica*) aren't always blue: mauve, pink, and white (shown here) are just as common and just as beautiful.

Spanish bluebells are about 16 inches tall, and English bluebells are a little shorter. English bluebells are typically blue and sometimes white, though it's common to find blue, white, and pink forms of Spanish bluebell. Their size, late bloom time (May), and need for a fair amount of light in order to store energy for the following year make it difficult to find a spot in the border where bluebells look right yet won't be crowded out by perennials, many of which will have emerged fully by the time the bluebells get around to doing their thing. Ferns might make the best companions, because they emerge late and tend to admit some light to the soil surface after they do. Plant bluebells in conservative numbers and make a point of deadheading because they can be aggressive spreaders in some situations.

If you've ever thought that you'd like to have bulbs blooming *with* your spring perennials instead of preceding them, try grape hyacinths. Their foliage comes up early in spring, followed in May by flowers that usually resemble tiny bunches of grapes and have a faint but wonderful sugary fragrance. After blooming, their leaves die back quickly but typically reappear in autumn (an odd trait, but normal for this plant).

There is a lot of variability among the different grape hyacinth species commonly available. Although virtually all of them are about the same size—8 inches tall—nearly everything else can vary. The classic grape hyacinth is *M. armeniacum* (Zone 4). A white-flowered and slightly more slender alternative is *M. botryoides* forma *album* (Zone 3). A number of other grape hyacinths have the same basic outline but flower colors ranging from sky blue to inky purple. *M. latifolium* (Zone 4) apparently couldn't

Grape hyacinth comes in many forms, including bicolor *Muscari latifolium*.

decide which color it wanted to be and has two-tone flowers, azure on top and grape on the bottom. It's also different in that each bulb produces one broad solitary leaf instead of the usual cluster of chive-like foliage.

In addition, some grape hyacinths dispense with the neat cluster-of-fruit look and appear to have been caught in the act of exploding. *M. plumosum* (sometimes called *M. comosum* 'Plumosum,' Zone 4) is a firework in action, with a pinkish-purple haze of flowers. With all these possibilities, I recommend taking a look through a good bulb catalog to familiarize yourself with your options before making a selection.

Grape hyacinths can spread aggressively, so deadhead them to keep clumps distinct and to prevent invasion of your garden. Because they flower late, after many perennials have emerged, position them at the front of your border and avoid putting them near neighboring plants that get large early in the season.

Plants for
Light Shade

PLANTS FOR SPECIAL SITUATIONS

There are many perfectly good shade perennials that, for one reason or another, are really only appropriate for special situations such as shady rock gardens, naturalizing, or some very specific and challenging set of conditions. In addition, many of the plants covered in other sections are also good for these purposes. See the Resources section of this book for lists that should help you find a wide selection of plants suited to a variety of special garden situations. Visit my website at www.amyziffer.com to see photographs of most of the plants mentioned here.

Many, if not all, of the plants in this chapter will not be readily available at retail nurseries, although a nursery with a good native plant section might be able to order them for you if it doesn't grow them. Otherwise, try mail-order suppliers.

4

Actaea spp.

Baneberry · Doll's Eyes

Baneberry is a common woodland plant in the eastern half of the United States. There are two species, *A. pachypoda* and *A. rubra*, virtually identical from an ornamental standpoint. In early May, they both produce delightful fluffy white inflorescences (flowering structures) worthy of close inspection. Each of the tiny component flowers resembles a miniature exploding firework. On the whole, the flower clusters resemble those of the shrub *Fothergilla*.

In both species of baneberry, the flowers can develop into either white or red berries (although only one or the other on any individual plant). The common name, doll's eyes, comes from the fact that the berries have a prominent pupil-like black spot at the blossom end, making it look for all the world as if the white-berried plants had produced a bumper crop of doll-sized eyes on stalks! (It looks better than it sounds.) Many books report that the berries persist until autumn, but I have never found that to be true. Expect a brief display in midsummer.

Baneberry is pretty in flower but not spectacular. Its real strength is as a background plant, because of its medium height (30 inches); and its bushy, good-looking foliage stays reasonably attractive until the plant loses its berries, at which point it may decline. Alternate groups of baneberry with groups of ferns at the rear of your garden for a full, leafy, green effect.

Although many garden plants have poisonous parts, baneberry fruits are more toxic than most, so it's worth a special warning that you may not want to grow this plant if you have young children in your household or pets given to eating garden plants. Wild birds are able to consume the berries with no ill side effects.

In contrast to the tall Japanese anemone profiled earlier, meadow anemone grows as a woodland groundcover. It is extremely aggressive, difficult to control, and nearly impossible to eradicate. Despite the fact that it's native, many gardeners have regretted ever planting it, so consider carefully before deciding to try it.

Meadow anemone forms a 15- to 18-inch mound of pretty, deep-green, deeply divided foliage, and begins blooming in May, when numerous slender stalks rising to about 24 inches appear, each one capped by a large, solitary, single white flower. Peak flowering is in June and may continue for many weeks.

It spreads both vegetatively and by self-sowing, which accounts for its rapid rate of spread. It's so supremely difficult to contain or eliminate because its roots are brittle and break easily when disturbed; any little piece left in the ground will resprout. Although it will grow in significant shade, it doesn't necessarily bloom well there. In light shade, however, meadow anemone is quite floriferous.

Meadow anemone has a wide range across eastern North America. In the wild, it's most commonly found in areas with consistently moist but not waterlogged soils, such as lake embankments or alongside streams. At the same time, though, it's tolerant of salt and general roadside conditions, so it might be an alternative to the exotic orange daylily (*Hemerocallis fulva*) that has been so widely planted for that purpose. One advantage it has over the daylily (aside from being native) is that it isn't browsed by deer, so it doesn't attract them to a dangerous location.

Because meadow anemone is capable of overwhelming most companions, it has no place in a border or even an informal woodland garden in which you hope to maintain much diversity. Use it for naturalizing areas where conditions are too difficult for other, more tractable plants.

Don't confuse meadow anemone with *A. sylvestris* (snowdrop anemone), a European look-alike. Although snowdrop anemone is more tolerant of dry soils and reblooms lightly in fall, there is otherwise little reason to consider growing it instead of the native species, especially because it's noted for having sap that is a strong skin irritant.

3

Caulophyllum thalictroides

Blue Cohosh

Although I don't find it particularly useful in cultivated settings, blue cohosh is a fascinating little collector's plant for those interested in native woodlanders. As its specific name (*thalictroides*) suggests, it has delicate leaves reminiscent of meadow rue atop slender, bare, 24-inch stems. Very early in the year, it produces a crop of small, brown flowers that pass so quickly you'll probably miss them. In summer, these develop into blueberry-like fruits before speedily dropping or being eaten. Much like *Actaea*, it doesn't so much go dormant as just get a bit tattered by late summer. The whole plant is rather slight (although not short) and must be planted in quantity to make an impression. I've never known it to spread more than sparingly.

3

Erythronium americanum

Trout Lily

Here's a story about trout lily. Several years ago, I attended a tour of a woodland garden in a neighboring town. Walking through one secluded portion, I noticed trout lilies poking through the heavy layer of wood chips that had been put down for a walking surface. One was in flower, and I cleared the space around it in the hope that other people who walked by might see it and admire it. As I was finishing up, a woman approached and asked me what I was doing. When I told her about trout lilies, she said, "And to think I've been ripping those out by the hundreds! I'll stop doing that."

Lest you think I'm being snooty, I'll admit that I did something similar once. Before I learned to appreciate jack-in-the-pulpits, a fair number of them met their demise at my hands. I'd love to have them all back now! So you can understand why, every time I see a trout lily (or a jack-in-the-pulpit), it's a reminder to me that I should really take time to understand new things before I pass judgment on them.

Funny that such a tiny, tiny plant should inspire such philosophical musings! Trout lily is definitely for specialized situations. Where it is happy in the wild, you'll see it establish large, loose colonies of hundreds or thousands of plants.

Each one consists of just one or two orchid-like, mottled leaves (the name trout lily comes from the apparent similarity of these markings to those of some kind of trout) and sometimes one dangling yellow flower shaped more or less like a pagoda roof on a 4-inch stem. A spring ephemeral, trout lily goes dormant by late spring or early summer.

This trout lily is quite different from the *Erythronium* 'Pagoda' mentioned earlier, which is a considerably larger and showier hybrid. Our native trout lily's tendency to colonize and its incredibly diminutive size are the qualities that make it strictly for naturalizing. It wants a cool, moist, shady spot. It's particularly nice to see hundreds of trout lilies push their exquisite leaves up through a blanket of moss and *Mitchella repens*.

Podophyllum peltatum

Mayapple

4   USDA ZONE

Mayapple is one of the most difficult plants to pigeonhole, and also one of the most difficult plants to place in the garden; that's why it's in this category. Although mayapple is actually a fairly large plant and even moderately common, I think most people will have some difficulty finding the right spot for it.

Mayapple is a native plant with large, glossy, umbrella-like leaves that are its main ornamental strong point. It forms colonies in spots where it remains undisturbed, in moist or average soil, in anything from deep shade to half sun. In May, each plant produces one pendant flower hidden underneath the leaves, which makes flowering easy to miss. The flower becomes a crab apple–like fruit that's also quite invisible unless you go looking for it.

Mayapple is hard to place because it forms such a dense canopy of foliage when it's actively growing, but at some point during the summer it will go dormant, leaving a gap if it's planted en masse (and it will eventually be a mass because it colonizes). Because it shades companions so thoroughly, mayapple is hard to combine with any late-season plant that might complement it. Additionally, hail or hard downpours can make its stems collapse even before they go dormant, which leaves it looking somewhat drunken.

My best suggestion is to interplant mayapple with large, upright ferns. Alternatively, plant it at the margin of the garden where you won't really notice its absence when it departs. For naturalizing moist-soil areas, it's great.

Rubus odoratus

Purple-flowering Raspberry

Purple-flowering raspberry is a plant that many people get to know only when they rip it out of the ground, thinking it's a bramble that will take over everything. True to its Latin and common names, it looks like a raspberry, albeit a particularly handsome raspberry that's also thorn free. Despite its broad, lobed leaves (they look like the leaves of the goosefoot maple, *Acer pensylvanicum*) and long canes (up to 8 feet), it's a fairly inconspicuous plant until it flowers in June or July. Then you can't help but notice it, because its 2-inch-wide, purplish-pink blooms resembling those of *Rosa rugosa* are among the showiest of any woodland plant. They aren't numerous, but they are pretty and an unexpected thing to find at the edge of the woods. The fruits that form are small and inedible to people but palatable to birds, making this a beneficial wildlife plant.

Flowering raspberry will grow into a conventional thicket when grown in sun, yet in shade it's much more subdued. It rambles loosely, sometimes propping itself up on trees or rocks as if it were a short climbing plant. On a slope, it will sometimes form a pretty little curtain of foliage. This plant is very easy to grow, needing no special care or conditions other than average woodland soil. Once you get it established, it will spread slowly over time into neighboring areas, cropping up here and there, sometimes by rooting and sometimes by seed. Because it's a native plant, you can feel free to just let it go where it will.

Flowering raspberry will never be the centerpiece of any garden, but it is just one more little thing to add interest to highly naturalistic shade plantings. I think it could also be useful for helping to stabilize soil on erosion-prone slopes where the simple act of planting is disruptive.

Senecio aureus

Golden Ragwort · Golden Groundsel

I admit that the inclusion of golden ragwort in this book is based on the success other people have had with it rather than my own. I tried it once, many years ago, and wasn't impressed, but I know now that I was using it all wrong.

It's not a plant for border use. It's an aggressive but native spreader for use in moist, shaded meadows, to help stabilize streambanks, and in other similar situations. In addition, it's not a plant that makes an impression when you see 6 plants growing together. It's a plant that makes an impression when you see 600 growing together. Then, and only then, it will make you say, "Wow!"

Golden ragwort produces a rather meager basal clump of roundish to kidney-shaped leaves. In May, leafless 24-inch stalks elongate and branch into a flat-topped cluster of ten to twelve small, bright-yellow, daisy-like flowers. By planting it in large quantities, you can possibly achieve the effect of a river of sunny yellow coursing through space. It spreads so rapidly from even a small initial planting that it can be an economical approach to naturalizing.

S. aureus has been reclassified as *Packera aurea* and may be seen in the nursery trade and in references under either name.

Tradescantia virginiana

Spiderwort

USDA ZONE 4

People tend to either love or hate spiderwort. When in bloom, which is principally in June, it's beautiful in every way. Its fleshy, grass-like leaves stand erect and make a tropical impression. Small blue, pink, or white flowers present their little faces to the world in a cheerful way, each one lasting just one day. But after flowering, the whole plant simply collapses on itself and its neighbors, becoming a lax, ungainly mess. The good thing is that it can be cut back nearly to the ground at that point, after which it will regrow a moderate amount of foliage, and it will be none the worse for the shearing.

Because it's a native plant, spiderwort is perfectly suitable for naturalizing, but you'll want to place it in a spot with good enough access to allow you to cut it back after flowering. It's also got an incredible light-tolerance range, growing and flowering well in anything from deep shade to full sun, so its use isn't limited to shade gardens. When it's happy, spiderwort will spread both underground and by seed, sometimes to the point of becoming invasive. It's hard to eliminate if you decide you no longer want it, so try it cautiously in a small area before committing to more. Those who like spiderwort are crazy about it, so the strong feelings about this plant are largely a matter of taste.

Zizia aurea

Golden Alexanders

Golden Alexanders shines most brightly in regularly moist, lightly shaded spots such as streambanks and moist meadows. It's a somewhat untidy but still pretty plant in the carrot family, reminding me of a slender, ungroomed celery. In May and June, it produces large umbels of lemon-yellow flowers above slightly glossy, deep-green, divided leaves. It reaches a height of about 24 inches in flower and spreads by seed in a location that makes it happy.

If you find a caterpillar munching on the leaves, it may be a future black swallowtail butterfly, for which golden Alexanders is an important food source. An extremely similar species, *Z. aptera*, is also native to eastern North America but not the Northeast per se.

SHADY ROCK GARDENS

Anemonella thalictroides

Rue anemone

Rue anemone is one of the few herbaceous plants that can be found growing in the raw weather of March. Its leaves are at first bronzy when they push up through the leaf litter, but quickly turn to a bright green as they unfold. Small white to very pale pink or violet flowers are borne in small numbers over several weeks in April and May. Even named cultivars that are reputed to have more vivid flower coloration tend to be pale, so don't be disappointed if you find that to be true. Some double-flowered forms are available.

Rue anemone is a delicate, none-too-robust little plant for spots where it won't experience much competition. It can do well in the very shallow soil at the base of trees where little else will grow, but in my experience it is so easily smothered that it's best reserved for rock garden use, especially because it appreciates good drainage. With luck, time, and a lack of disturbance, rue anemone will form irregular clumps and may self-sow sparingly. As an ephemeral, it will go dormant after flowering. *Anemonella thalictroides* may be listed in some places under the name *Thalictrum thalictroides*.

Wintergreen is another one of those odd little plants, like bunchberry (see next section), that bridge the shrub and the perennial worlds. Although it is a woody plant—my horticultural dictionary calls it a "rhizomatous shrublet"—you'll use it like a ground-hugging perennial in lightly shaded rock gardens and other relatively uncrowded spaces.

Wintergreen forms a low mat about 4 inches tall and slowly spreads to a width of 2 to 3 feet. Its leaves are small, dark green, glossy, and evergreen. Tiny pinkish, pendant flowers like those of blueberries in late spring give rise to brilliant scarlet berries by autumn. Although wintergreen's foliage is usually somewhat marred by leaf spots late in the year, that's less of a shortcoming than you'd imagine. With some sun, the foliage can take on a bit of fall color, usually burgundy.

Wintergreen roots in hardly any soil at all, which makes it a good choice for scrabbling around boulders and ledge outcroppings in rock garden settings. Natural companions include polypody fern, partridgeberry, dwarf crested iris, native columbine, and native bleeding heart.

Wintergreen is very hardy, growing well up into Canada. Its shade tolerance is limited, however, so be sure to plant it in nothing deeper than light shade, or it will languish.

As a rule, irises are not shade plants. One exception for light shade is our native dwarf crested iris, *I. cristata*. It grows about 6 inches tall, sprouting a little forest of typical blade-shaped iris leaves very early in the season. As the leaves mature, instead of remaining stiff and upright, they arch over in a graceful way. Pale-violet or white flowers, usually with a tiny yellow "beard" and looking like two tricornered hats layered one atop the other, lie scattered above the foliage in late spring. Something ineffable about this arrangement of leaf and flower makes a truly charming juxtaposition that invites close examination and appreciation.

Because of its diminutive size and the lovely gentle drape of its leaves, dwarf crested iris is best grown in a raised bed where it can be viewed close to eye level. If you have rock retaining walls supporting narrow garden beds, try positioning clumps of dwarf crested iris right at the front interspersed with lungwort, foamflower, dwarf lady's mantle, bigroot geranium, and the like. Shady rock gardens are also ideal for this delightful little plant, and because it increases at a fast pace, it's great for naturalizing in that environment. For variety in a rock garden, alternate patches of this iris with polypody fern, and encourage the growth of mosses. Dwarf crested iris is easily overwhelmed by larger plants, however, so keep a close eye on invading neighbors.

Although dwarf crested iris, like larger irises, is said to suffer from a susceptibility to various rots and borers, I have never seen it have these problems unless grown in spots that are too dark or too damp. Minor skeletonization of the leaves due to slug and snail feeding at night is the problem you're most likely to encounter.

USDA ZONE ZONE **Varies**

Polypodium virginianum, P. vulgare

Polypody Fern

I will leave it up to the experts to decide whether these two species are synonymous. Some sources say yes, some say no, and I certainly don't know. John Mickel, the noted fern expert, says they are distinct, and I defer to him. Among other differences, he specifies that *P. virginianum* is winter hardy to Zone 2 and *P. vulgare* is winter hardy only to Zone 5.

What I do know is that the polypody of my local woodlands is one of my favorite plants to seek out, despite being as common as dirt. What is it that I find so adorable about this diminutive fern with minimal needs? It does the seemingly impossible: it grows in nothing more than shallow pockets of leaf litter on top of boulders. If large rocks (several feet high and wide) or outcrops of ledge are a feature of your property, you may have a suitable spot for polypody. Look for rocks with concave bowls on their upper surfaces. If you see a spot where small twigs and leaves tend to collect naturally and stay moist, that's perfect. Combine some handfuls of native soil with a liberal amount of leaf mold (half-composted leaves), sprinkle it with water until it's pleasantly damp, and press the mixture into the bowl. Nestle your tiny polypodies into the soil and water them in.

The key to establishing polypody is to water it very, very regularly for its first year or even two. Separated from the ground proper, it has no way to draw water up from beneath and has to survive on whatever moisture pools are in its little lithic world. Of course, you can also plant polypody on any suitable rock that forms a major feature of any kind of garden on your property, so it doesn't have to be relegated to naturalized areas. On its own, however, it can't really be a garden plant; a rock home is essential to its happiness.

Saxifraga stolonifera
Strawberry Begonia

Strawberry begonia, the common name of this charming little garden gem, is rather misleading because *S. stolonifera* doesn't particularly resemble either strawberries or begonias, although it does spread via stolons (runners) like the former and has thick, rounded leaves like the latter. Overall, it looks more like alumroot (*Heuchera*) than anything else, which isn't terribly surprising because these two plants belong to the same plant family. Strawberry begonia is a very eye-catching plant almost certain to make visitors to your garden ask about it.

Strawberry begonia's broad, rounded leaves sport intense white veining against a green ground. It forms a mat of foliage about 3 inches thick, covering soil well and increasing moderately fast. In midsummer, profuse slender stalks shoot up 12 inches, topped by delicate flowers that remind me of white origami cranes. Finally, the flower stalks and the undersides of the leaves are a delightful plum color.

Strawberry begonia is often billed as marginally hardy in our area, but I've grown it for over a decade in Zone 5 with no problem. It looks best when allowed to arrange itself among tumbling rocks, so imagine the effect a strawberry pot is designed to achieve, and try for that look.

This sweet little plant has no particular cultural or maintenance requirements, but you do need to exercise some care when cleaning fallen tree leaves off it in autumn. It roots so shallowly that a rake passing over it can easily dislodge it, so remove leaves by hand or with a low-powered leaf blower instead. Of course, this quality is one thing that makes strawberry begonia so valuable in the rock garden, where it can establish itself in the thinnest soil covering and even grow on heavy clay. Because it will root wherever a piece of it falls, be careful with trimmings or you may find it cropping up all over.

2

Cornus canadensis

Bunchberry

Bunchberry is not for just any property or just any gardener. It's hard to find, and it's a bit particular. But patient property owners with acidic soil, a cool, north-facing slope that doesn't dry out, and a taste for little woodland gems may treasure it.

Bunchberry is a subshrub—an ultra-dwarf woody plant—that can be grown as a groundcover. It can best be described as looking like a branch tip of our spectacular flowering dogwood, *Cornus florida*, taken down to earth. Only 6 inches tall, it bears showy, white, four-part flowers (the parts that look like petals are really bracts, an unimportant distinction from an aesthetic standpoint) displayed in May and June against a very attractive mass of broad green leaves with the characteristic "parallel" veining of all dogwoods. The flowers develop into brilliant red berries and are a late-summer food source for birds. Deer (and far enough north, moose) may browse bunchberry.

The difficulty with growing bunchberry is that the plant likes it *cool*. It wants a location with that unusual combination of well-drained soil and constant yet not excessive moisture. In the wild, you'll find it growing in those weird spots where, say, water seeps out of a rock ledge even in August when it hasn't rained for three weeks, or where the spray from a waterfall mists its surroundings. Upslope of a hemlock ravine, where cool air flows down and collects, is another favorite locale.

Bunchberry also needs mild to moderate soil acidity, which makes it a natural groundcover choice under native rhododendrons, azaleas, and laurels, as long as its other requirements are met. In a spot where it's happy, bunchberry will increase slowly—very slowly—but steadily.

The further north you are, or the higher your elevation in the region covered by this book, the more likely are your chances of success with bunchberry. If you decide to try it, note that you might find it for sale under the synonymous name *Chamaepericlymenum canadense*.

Partridgeberry is a very diminutive native plant for use in the smallest-scale situations. Looking more like a small-leaved euonymus than anything else, it will form a naturalistic 1-inch mat of creeping stems and tiny evergreen leaves. It can be grown successfully with mosses, the two together contrasting pleasingly and forming one cohesive layer of vegetation to help control water runoff and soften the look of rocky areas. In autumn, it will be sprinkled sparsely with small scarlet berries.

This is one of the few plants you can expect to establish in densely shaded areas, although its rate of spread will be painfully slow. It's not showy, but its resilience is admirable, making this a classic example of a plant that gardeners should learn to appreciate for its ability to live where few other plants will flourish.

RESOURCES

PLANTS NATIVE TO EASTERN NORTH AMERICA

Any plant on this list, as well as cultivars and other selections of plants on this list, can be used for naturalizing areas that offer the conditions in which they want to grow, as long as you feel you can contain the plant to your own property. Please see the individual Plant Gallery entries for details about each one.

Actaea pachypoda, A. rubra
Adiantum pedatum
Amsonia tabernaemontana
Anemone canadensis
Anemonella thalictroides
Aquilegia canadensis
Arisaema dracontium, A. triphyllum
Aruncus dioicus
Asarum canadense
Aster cordifolius, A. divaricatus
Carex appalachica, C. pensylvanica
Caulophyllum thalictroides
Chasmanthium latifolium
Cimicifuga racemosa
Cornus canadensis
Delphinium tricorne
Dennstaedtia punctilobula
Dicentra canadensis, D. cucullaria,
    D. eximia
Disporum maculatum
Dodecatheon meadia
Dryopteria australis, D. marginalis, others
Erythronium americanum
Eupatorium rugosum
Gaultheria procumbens
Geranium maculatum
Hepatica acutiloba, H. americana
Heuchera americana, H. villosa
Hydrastis canadensis

Iris cristata
Jeffersonia diphylla
Matteuccia struthiopteris
Mertensia virginica
Mitchella repens
Onoclea sensibilis
Osmunda cinnamomea, O. claytoniana,
    O. regalis
Pachysandra procumbens
Phlox divaricata, P. stolonifera
Podophyllum peltatum
Polemonium reptans
Polygonatum biflorum
Polypodium virginianum, P. vulgare
Polystichum acrostichoides
Rubus odoratus
Sanguinaria canadensis
Senecio aureus
Smilacina racemosa, S. stellata
Stylophorum diphyllum
Tiarella cordifolia, T. wherryi
Tradescantia virginiana
Trillium cuneatum, T. erectum,
    T. grandiflorum, T. luteum, T. sessile
Uvularia grandiflora
Viola biflora, V. canadensis,
    V. labradorica, V. pedata, others
Waldsteinia fragarioides
Zizia aptera, Z. aurea

PLANTS BY USDA ZONE

This list should help gardeners in colder zones find plants with the potential to perform well for them. Cultivars and other selections of plants on this list generally have the same cold hardiness as the species from which they're derived, but hybrids may not. Seek more detailed cold hardiness information if necessary.

ZONE 2

Anemone canadensis
Asarum canadense
Cornus canadensis
Crocus (some)
Matteuccia struthiopteris
Onoclea sensibilis
Osmunda cinnamomea, O. claytoniana,
    O. regalis
Polypodium virginianum
Primula denticulata
Viola labradorica

ZONE 3

Adiantum pedatum
Ajuga reptans
Alchemilla erythropoda
Amsonia tabernaemontana
Aquilegia canadensis, A. 'McKana Hybrids'
Aruncus dioicus
Brunnera macrophylla
Caulophyllum thalictroides
Cimicifuga racemosa
Crocus (some)
Dennstaedtia punctilobula
Dicentra spectabilis
Digitalis grandiflora
Dryopteris marginalis

Erythronium americanum
Galanthus nivalis
Gaultheria procumbens
Hepatica americana
Hosta
Hydrastis canadensis
Mertensia virginiana
Muscari botryoides
Myrrhis odorata
Polygonatum biflorum
Polystichum acrostichoides, P. braunii
Primula japonica, P. sieboldii, P. veris
Rubus odoratus
Sanguinaria canadensis
Scilla bifolia
Senecio aureus
Tiarella cordifolia
Uvularia grandiflora
Viola canadensis
Waldsteinia ternata
Zizia aptera, Z. aurea

ZONE 4

Actaea
Alchemilla mollis
Anemone blanda
Anemonella thalictroides
Aquilegia alpina

Arisaema dracontium, A. triphyllum

Aruncus aesthusifolius

Asarum europeum

Aster divaricatus

Astilbe

Athyrium filix-femina

Cimicifuga simplex

Crocus (some)

Delphinium tricorne

Dicentra cucullaria, D. eximia

Dodecatheon meadia

Dryopteris filix-mas

Epimedium x *rubrum*

Eranthis hyemalis

Erythronium 'Pagoda'

Eupatorium rugosum

Geranium macrorrhizum, G. maculatum,
    G. phaeum

Helleborus niger

Hepatica acutiloba

Heuchera americana 'Dale's Strain'

Hyacinthoides hispanica, H. non-scripta

Iris cristata

Lamiastrum galeobdolon

Lamium maculatum

Ligularia

Lysimachia nummularia 'Aurea'

Mitchella repens

Muscari armeniacum, M. comosum, M.
    latifolium

Phlox divaricata, P. stolonifera

Podophyllum peltatum

Polemonium reptans (possibly colder)

Polygonatum odoratum 'Variegatum'

Primula x *bullesiana, P. elatior* cvs.,
    P. vulgaris cvs.

Pulmonaria (some cvs.)

Smilacina racemosa

Tellima grandiflora

Tricyrtis

Trillium erectum, T. sessile

Vinca minor

Viola biflora, V. pedata

Anemone, Japanese

Aster cordifolius

Athyrium niponicum 'Pictum'

Carex siderostica 'Variegata,' *C. elata*
    'Bowles Golden,' *C. hakijoensis*
    'Evergold,' *C. morrowii* 'Variegata'

Chasmanthium latifolium

Corydalis solida

Crocus (some)

Cyrtomium falcatum

Disporum maculatum

Dryopteris australis, D. cycadina,
    D. erythrosora, D. purpurella

Epimedium (most)

Galium odoratum

Hakonechloa macra

Helleborus x *hybridus*

Heuchera villosa 'Autumn Bride'

Jeffersonia diphylla

Kirengeshoma

Lathyrus vernus

Liriope

Pachysandra procumbens (possibly colder)

Polygonatum humile

Polypodium vulgare

Polystichum setiferum, P. polyblepharum

Primula beesiana, P. bulleyana

Pulmonaria (some cvs.), *P. rubra,*
    P. longifolia

Rodgersia

Sarcococca hookeriana var. *humilis*

Saxifraga stolonifera

Scilla siberica

Smilacina stellata

Stylophorum diphyllum

Tiarella wherryi

Tradescantia virginiana

Trillium grandiflorum, T. luteum
Trollius x *cultorum*
Vancouveria hexandra
Waldsteinia fragarioides

ZONE 6
Crocus (some)
Helleborus argutifolius, H. foetidus
Scilla mischtschenkoana, S. pratensis
Trillium cuneatum

PLANTS THAT GROW WELL
IN BOTH SHADE AND SUN

If you are lucky enough to have both shade gardens and sun gardens on your property, you can bridge the two and give them a unified look by employing certain plants that grow well in both shade and sun. You should check other, more general reference books to discover the exact degree of sun tolerance of these plants. Some may tolerate full sun; others may require midday shade. Some may tolerate sun only with adequate moisture. Please see the individual Plant Gallery entries for details about each one. Cultivars, hybrids and other selections of the plants on this list generally have the same light tolerance as the species from which they are derived.

Ajuga reptans
Alchemilla erythropoda, A. mollis
Amsonia tabernaemontana
Anemone canadensis
Anemone vitifolia 'Robustissima' and other Japanese anemones
Aquilegia
Arisaema triphyllum
Aruncus aesthusifolius, A. dioicus
Aster cordifolius, A. divaricatus
Astilbe
Carex hakijoensis, C. morrowii (half sun)
Chasmanthium latifolium
Cimicifuga racemosa, C. simplex
Crocus
Delphinium tricorne
Dicentra eximia, D. spectabilis
Digitalis grandiflora
Epimedium
Eranthis hyemalis
Eupatorium rugosum
Galanthus
Gaultheria procumbens
Geranium macrorrhizum, G. phaeum

Hakonechloa macra (up to full sun for species; half sun for variegated cvs.)
Heuchera villosa 'Autumn Bride' (half sun)
Hosta (some)
Hyacinthoides hispanica, H. non-scripta
Iris cristata
Liriope muscari, L. spicata (half sun)
Mertensia virginica
Muscari
Myrrhis odorata
Podophyllum peltatum (half sun)
Primula (half sun)
Pulmonaria
Rubus odoratus
Sanguinaria canadensis
Scilla
Senecio aureus
Stylophorum diphyllum
Tellima grandiflora
Tiarella (half sun)
Tradescantia virginiana
Tricyrtis (half sun)
Vinca minor (half sun)
Viola
Zizia aptera, Z. aurea

PLANTS FOR MOIST AREAS

Plants on this list, as well as cultivars or other selections of plants on this list, tolerate or prefer consistently moist soils. Please see the individual Plant Gallery entries for details about each one. Note that a high percentage of moisture-loving plants are or can become invasive when they are planted in moist soil.

Anemone canadensis

Aruncus dioicus

Astilbe

Carex (some; research each one specifically)

Dicentra cucullaria

Hydrastis canadensis

Ligularia

Lysimachia nummularia 'Aurea'

Matteuccia struthiopteris

Onoclea sensibilis

Osmunda cinnamomea, O. regalis

Podophyllum peltatum

Primula (some; research each one specifically)

Rodgersia

Senecio aureus

Tradescantia virginica

Viola (some; research each one specifically)

Zizia aptera, Z. aurea

PLANTS FOR ROCK GARDENS

Plants on this list, as well as cultivars or other selections of plants on this list, are small in stature, or prefer good drainage, or are easily overwhelmed by neighbors. Note that a high percentage of these plants are either bulbs or spring ephemerals. In addition, some will colonize and should be used only where that will not become a problem. It's important to choose plants for rock gardens whose size matches the scale of the garden and the size of neighboring plants; not all of these plants will necessarily look "right" together. Please see the individual Plant Gallery entries for details about each one.

Ajuga reptans
Alchemilla erythropoda (if not too dry)
Amsonia 'Blue Ice' (if not too dry)
Anemone blanda
Anemonella thalictroides
Aquilegia canadensis, dwarf columbines in general
Aruncus aesthusifolius
Astilbe 'Sprite' (if not too dry)
Carex (some, if not too dry)
Cornus canadensis (must have consistent moisture)
Corydalis lutea, C. ochroleuca
Corydalis solida
Crocus
Delphinium tricorne (if not too dry)
Dicentra cucullaria, D. eximia
Digitalis grandiflora (if not too dry)
Dodecatheon meadia
Epimedium, especially *E.* x *youngianum* 'Niveum' (if not too dry)
Eranthis hyemalis

Erythronium americanum, E. 'Pagoda'
Galanthus
Gaultheria procumbens
Geranium macrorrhizum
Iris cristata
Lathyrus vernus (if not too dry)
Liriope muscari, L. spicata
Lysimachia nummularia 'Aurea'
Mertensia virginica
Mitchella repens (if not too dry)
Muscari
Phlox divaricata, P. stolonifera
Polygonatum humile
Polypodium virginianum, P. vulgare
Polystichum acrostichoides
Primula (some, if not too dry)
Rubus odoratus
Sanguinaria canadensis
Saxifraga stolonifera
Scilla
Tiarella (if not too dry)
Viola

PLANTS SUITABLE FOR USE
AS GROUNDCOVERS

All the plants listed here, as well as any cultivars derived from them, have applicability as groundcovers, although some might be better suited than others to certain situations. Please see the individual Plant Gallery entries for details about each one.

Ajuga reptans

Anemone canadensis

Asarum canadense

Carex appalachica, C. pensylvanica

Epimedium

Galium odoratum

Geranium macrorrhizum

Lamiastrum galeobdolon

Liriope muscari, L. spicata

Pachysandra procumbens

Sarcococca hookeriana var. *humilis*

Vancouveria hexandra

Vinca minor

Waldsteinia fragarioides, W. ternata

FOR MORE INFORMATION

Each state has a Cooperative Extension service affiliated with an agricultural college, for the purpose of disseminating information on gardening, horticulture, and agriculture (as well as nutrition, 4-H, and a great deal more). This should be your first stop for questions about soil testing, pest and noxious plant identification, use of home gardening products such as pesticides, and the like.

Each state handles inquiries from home gardeners in its own way. Some states have a Cooperative Extension office in each county; others may have only one central location or regional locations. Some may have a designated home and garden education center, or you may be referred to master gardener volunteers for answers to your questions. There may also be specialists such as plant pathologists who can assist you, but usually during limited hours and often for a small fee. In addition, a wide array of publications may be available online or by mail.

When you contact the Cooperative Extension, it's also worth asking if the staff can direct you to any local ornamental display gardens or arboreta with plantings that might be of particular benefit or interest to you (for example, a native plant garden).

The Cooperative Extension System is a valuable resource for home gardeners, and it's worth taking time to learn to navigate the system in your state to get the help you need. Following is a list of contacts for these services in nine Northeast states, current as of mid-2013. Because Web addresses and other contact information can change, if you find that a Web address or phone number here is no longer valid, do a search in your Web browser for the name of your state and/or county along with the words *Cooperative Extension*.

CONNECTICUT

University of Connecticut Home and
  Garden Education Center
(860) 486-6271
(877) 486-6271 (toll-free in Connecticut)
http://www.extension.uconn.edu

MAINE

University of Maine Cooperative
  Extension
(207) 581-3188
(800) 287-0274 (toll-free in Maine)
http://www.extension.umaine.edu

MASSACHUSETTS

Statewide:

University of Massachusetts–Amherst Center for Agriculture Research and Extension

http://ag.umass.edu/agriculture-and-green-industry (look for a Home Gardening link from the main page)

(617) 933-4929 (Massachusetts Master Gardener Association Helpline)

http://massmastergardeners.org

Western Massachusetts:

(413) 298-5355 (Western Massachusetts Master Gardener Association)

http://www.wmmga.org

Barnstable County:

(508) 375-6700 (Master Gardener Association of Cape Cod)

http://www.capecodextension.org

NEW HAMPSHIRE

University of New Hampshire Cooperative Extension

(877) 398-4769 (toll-free from anywhere)

http://extension.unh.edu

NEW JERSEY

Rutgers New Jersey Agricultural Experiment Station

http://njaes.rutgers.edu (look for a link to find your county Cooperative Extension office)

NEW YORK

Cornell Cooperative Extension

http://www.cce.cornell.edu (look for a link to find your community Cooperative Extension office)

PENNSYLVANIA

Penn State Extension

http://extension.psu.edu (look for a link to find your county Cooperative Extension office)

RHODE ISLAND

University of Rhode Island Cooperative Extension Outreach Center

(401) 874-2900

http://cels.uri.edu/ce (look for a link for the Outreach Center)

(800) 448-1011 (University of Rhode Island Master Gardener Hotline, toll-free in Rhode Island)

http://www.urimastergardeners.org

VERMONT

University of Vermont Cooperative Extension

(802) 656-2990

(866) 622-2990 (toll-free in Vermont)

http://www.uvm.edu/extension (look for a Contact link for information on local offices)

(800) 639-2230 (University of Vermont Master Gardener Helpline, toll-free in Vermont)

http://www.uvm.edu/mastergardener

INDEX

blue cohosh, 192

bluebell, 185–186

bluestar, 162

border, shady, defined, 15

Boston ivy, 43

boxwood, 39–40

Brunnera macrophylla, 164–165; 'Emerald Mist,' 164; 'Hadspen Cream,' 164; 'Jack Frost,' 164; 'Langtrees,' 164; 'Looking Glass,' 164; 'Mrs. Morse,' 164; 'Silver Wings,' 164; 'Variegata,' 164

bugbane, 91–92

bugleweed, 160

bulb, 6–7; avoid adding first year, 28; choices for deeper shade, 143–146; choices for light shade, 184–187; positioning in garden, 24; use judiciously, 29–31

bunchberry, 200

Buxus, 39–40

Caladium, 11

Calycanthus floridus, 42–43

Carex appalachica, 90

Carex elata 'Bowles Golden,' 175–176

Carex hakijoensis 'Evergold,' 176

Carex morrowii 'Variegata,' 176

Carex pensylvanica, 90

Carex siderostica 'Variegata,' 90

Carolina allspice, 42–43

Caulophyllum thalictroides, 192

Ceanothus americanus, 42–43

Celandine poppy, 113–114

Chamaepericlymenum canadense, 200

chameleon plant, 81

Chasmanthium latifolium, 165–166

Christmas fern, 152–153

Cimicifuga: 'Atropurpurea,' 91–92; 'Brunette,' 91–92; 'Hillside Black Beauty,' 91–92

Cimicifuga racemosa, 91

Cimicifuga simplex 'White Pearl,' 91

Clethra alnifolia, 42

coleus, 11

columbine, 174–175

common name, 7–9

compost, 63–66; calculating quantity needed, 64; as mulch, 69–72; tips for handling, 71

Convallaria majalis, 81

coralbells, 177–178

corm, 6–7

Cornus (shrubs), 41–42

Cornus canadensis, 200

Corydalis lutea, 119–120

Corydalis ochroleuca, 119–120

Corydalis solida, 134–135; 'George Baker,' 135

crocus, 143–144

Crocus tommasinianus, 144

cultivar, 8–9

Cyrtomium falcatum, 149

deadnettle, 127–128

deer browsing, deterring, 53–58

Delphinium tricorne, 182

Dennstaedtia punctilobula, 154

design of shade gardens: allocating space to backbone, accent, and other plants, 24; considerations when siting a garden, 17–18; defining garden types, 15–17; guidelines for arranging plants, 27–28; sketching, 26–27

Dicentra canadensis, 136

Dicentra cucullaria, 135–136

Dicentra eximia, 176–177; 'Alba,' 176

Dicentra spectabilis, 183; 'Alba,' 183; as example of summer dormancy, 14; 'Gold Heart,' 183

Digitalis grandiflora, 166

Disporum maculatum, 120–121

Dodecatheon meadia, 137